# jQuery Mobile Cookbook

Over 80 recipes with examples and practical tips to help you quickly learn and develop cross-platform applications with jQuery Mobile

**Chetan K Jain**

BIRMINGHAM - MUMBAI

# jQuery Mobile Cookbook

First published: November 2012

Production Reference: 1011112

Published by Packt Publishing Ltd.
Livery Place
35 Livery Street
Birmingham B3 2PB, UK.

ISBN 978-1-84951-722-5

www.packtpub.com

Cover Image by Abhishek Pandey (abhishek.pandey1210@gmail.com)

# Credits

**Author**

Chetan K Jain

**Reviewers**

Shaun Dunne

Ankit Garg

Yousef Jadallah

**Acquisition Editor**

Usha Iyer

**Lead Technical Editor**

Arun Nadar

**Technical Editors**

Kirti Puajri

Lubna Shaikh

**Project Coordinator**

Vishal Bodwani

**Proofreader**

Aaron Nash

Maria Gould

**Indexer**

Hemangini Bari

**Production Coordinator**

Arvindkumar Gupta

**Cover Work**

Arvindkumar Gupta

# About the Author

**Chetan K Jain** loves to code, and has been writing code for over 16 years now. He is a Senior Architect, and has worked on mobile technologies for over 4 years for Nokia. Since then, he has moved on to work as a freelance consultant.

Chetan has significant experience in writing cross-platform mobile apps using jQuery Mobile, HTML5, CSS3, JavaScript, Nodejs, and has also worked extensively on Qt. Prior to mobile technologies, he has worked with Java technology and was also certified as an MCSD and MCSE in his early days.

Chetan is an active contributor to open source development, and tries to help jQuery Mobile development whenever he can. He regularly participates in developer forums, and was earlier a top-ranked member and a "mad scientist" in the Nokia Qt Developer Forum.

Chetan was born in Bangalore and lives there with his wife Shwetha and son Tanmay.

The only time he ventured to live away from Bangalore was when he worked for over 4 years in the USA. His adventure didn't end there. He did a solo US cross country drive in his two door coupe from the east coast to the west and back, driving alone for over 8000 plus miles in 16 days to experience and live life as he calls it. His travelogue can be found at `http://adventure.chetankjain.net`.

Chetan has contributed and published over 15 books to Gutenberg as a volunteer. He has also published four books on Jaina Literature and History written by his mother Saraswathamma. He is a voracious reader, and his other interests include music, movies, and travelling. Photography is his favorite hobby, and his clicks can be found at `http://www.facebook.com/chetankjainphotos/photos_stream`.

Chetan can be reached at `chetankjain@gmail.com`. He also blogs at `http://dev.chetankjain.net`.

# Acknowledgement

First and foremost, my wife Shwetha and son Tanmay deserve full credit for the completion of this book. This book was possible only because of their understanding, support, and countless sacrifices. For days I would be unavailable, miss many family events, and yet they continued to shower me with all their love and affection.

I thank my parents, Mahendra Kumar Jaini and Saraswathamma, for their love, support, and for everything that I am today. I miss my father, but he is always there with me. My mother is my muse, and I follow her footsteps now as an author.

I have a very supportive sister Suma Jain and nephew Poojith Jain who never fail to pep me up. Ashwin Das, is family, and I enjoy bouncing all my ideas with him.

I thank my very close friend, Chidananda P, for all the help and support that he continues to give me. I thank my childhood friend Anand Rao for always being there as my buddy and for encouraging every project of mine.

My venture into mobile space has been very enjoyable. I thank all my former colleagues in Nokia—Prahalad Rao for being a great manager and for directly supporting me at work when I started this book, Sathish EV for all those initial reviews, Bhuwan Lodha for encouraging me to blog, Ashwin Das, Karthik S, Prasad S, Pavanesh, and Krishna KN for all the suggestions given. A very special thanks to Govind Ashrit, who actually urged me to write this book. Thank you guys!

I also thank Shaun Dunne, Ankit Garg, and Yousef Jadallah for reviewing the technical content of the book, and suggesting valuable changes and corrections.

Finally, I thank Packt Publishers and Usha Iyer for giving me this opportunity. My heartfelt thanks to my editors Vishal Bodwani, Arun Nadar, Kirti Pujari, and Lubna Shaikh for tirelessly reviewing my writing—multiple times, and giving me many valuable suggestions. You guys were just great!

# About the Reviewers

**Shaun Dunne** is a Developer working for SapientNitro in London, UK, and has been coding since 2008 with a passion for JavaScript and all the front-end goodness. Working for a large agency over the past few years, Shaun has had the chance to use various web technologies to build large scale applications, and found a passion for getting other people excited about the web.

Shaun has been hacking the mobile web for a couple of years, trying and testing all the tools available and sharing his discoveries where he can, to ensure that others are aware of what is available to use and in what situation.

When he's not working or spending some family time with his kids, he can usually be found on the web, tinkering, blogging, and building things. He's currently working on his own book, a self-published title about SASS and Friends called **UberCSS**, which is due to be released in the winter of 2012.

**Ankit Garg** is a Front-End Developer at iGate Global Solutions. He likes to call himself a Mobile Web Application Developer, a JavaScript Developer, and a blogger.

He likes reading, practicing, and blogging new things in the Mobile Web and JavaScript space. If you would like to reach him, send him an e-mail to `gargankit90@gmail.com`.

**Yousef J. Jadallah** is a software developer. He has good hands-on experience of web and .NET technologies, such as ASP.NET, SQL Server, AJAX, ASP.NET AJAX, C#,VB.NET, jQuery Mobile, HTML5, Web Services, and REST.

He spends most of his leisure time helping the communities on Microsoft technologies, specifically in the Microsoft official forum. He is honored with the Microsoft Community Contributor Award - 2011 (CCA).

He is from Jordan. You can contact with him through his blog: `http://weblogs.asp.net/yousefjadallah`.

# www.PacktPub.com

## Support files, eBooks, discount offers and more

You might want to visit www.PacktPub.com for support files and downloads related to your book.

Did you know that Packt offers eBook versions of every book published, with PDF and ePub files available? You can upgrade to the eBook version at www.PacktPub.com and as a print book customer, you are entitled to a discount on the eBook copy. Get in touch with us at service@packtpub.com for more details.

At www.PacktPub.com, you can also read a collection of free technical articles, sign up for a range of free newsletters and receive exclusive discounts and offers on Packt books and eBooks.

http://PacktLib.PacktPub.com

Do you need instant solutions to your IT questions? PacktLib is Packt's online digital book library. Here, you can access, read and search across Packt's entire library of books.

## Why Subscribe?

- ▶ Fully searchable across every book published by Packt
- ▶ Copy and paste, print and bookmark content
- ▶ On demand and accessible via web browser

## Free Access for Packt account holders

If you have an account with Packt at www.PacktPub.com, you can use this to access PacktLib today and view nine entirely free books. Simply use your login credentials for immediate access.

*To Shwetha and Tanmay, you fill my life with joy and wonder.*

# Table of Contents

# Preface

jQuery Mobile is an award winning, HTML5/CSS3-based open source, cross-platform UI framework. It offers a very cool and highly customizable UI. It is built on the popular jQuery library and uses declarative coding, making it easy to use and learn. It is the market leader today, considering the numerous browsers and platforms that it supports.

*jQuery Mobile Cookbook* presents over eighty recipes written in a simple and easy manner. You can quickly learn and start writing the code immediately. Advanced topics, such as using scripts to manipulate, customize, and extend the framework, are also covered. These tips address your common everyday problems. The book is very handy for both beginner and experienced jQuery Mobile developers.

You start by developing simple apps using various controls and learn to customize them. Later, you explore using advanced aspects, such as configurations, events, and methods.

Develop single and multi-page applications. Use caching to boost performance. Use custom transitions, icon sprites, styles, and themes. Learn advanced features, such as configurations, events, and methods. Explore the new features and semantics of HTML5 using it with jQuery Mobile.

*jQuery Mobile Cookbook* is an easy read, and is packed with practical tips and screenshots.

## What this book covers

*Chapter 1, Get Rolling,* begins with a brief introduction on what the jQuery Mobile framework is and what it can do for you. You will get to write your first jQuery Mobile cross-platform app here. You will also see how to use the online `JSBin` tool to develop and test your apps.

*Chapter 2, Pages and Dialogs,* here you will learn how to compare and use single page and multi-page template applications. You will learn various performance-enhancing techniques, such as prefetching and using the DOM cache to improve your page loading speed. You will create new custom transitions using JavaScript and CSS, and also learn to use page redirection for a login page. You will also create a custom styled dialog, and use the HTML5 History API to create your own custom pop up.

*Chapter 3, Toolbars*, here you will learn how to use fixed and full screen toolbars and how to persist your navigation links across pages. You will see how you can create and add custom round buttons, images, and a custom back button to the header, and a grid layout to the footer.

*Chapter 4, Buttons and Content Formatting*, here you will use JavaScript to dynamically create a button and assign an action to it. Then, you will learn how to use a custom icon, add a custom icon sprite, and finally replace the existing icon sprite provided by the jQuery Mobile framework. You will learn how to create nested accordions (collapsible sets), how to create a custom layout grid, and finally see how to format and display XML and JSON content in your app.

*Chapter 5, Forms*, shows you how to natively style forms, disable text controls, and group radio buttons into a multi-row grid. You will learn to customize a checkbox group, auto initialize select menus, and create dynamic flip switch and slider controls. You will also see how to validate and submit a form to a server using POST, and also how to fetch data using GET. Finally, you will learn how to create an accessible form.

*Chapter 6, List Views*, here you will learn how to use various list types and also customize them. You will use an inset list, custom number a list, and then create a read-only list. You will see how to format list content, use a split button, and an image icon list. You will also create a custom search filter for your list, and finally see how you can use JavaScript to modify a list.

*Chapter 7, Configurations*, shows you how to tweak, configure, and customize the various options and settings provided by the jQuery mobile framework. Configuring the active classes, enabling Ajax, auto initializing pages, configuring default transitions, customizing error and page loading messages, and using your own custom namespace are all covered along with a few more advanced configuration options.

*Chapter 8, Events*, shows you how to use the various events available in the framework. You will learn to use the orientation, scroll, touch, virtual mouse, and layout events along with the page initialization, page load, page change, and page remove events. You will also see how to use the page transition and animation events.

*Chapter 9, Methods and Utilities*, here you will see how to use the methods and utilities provided in the framework. The chapter runs through the methods provided by the framework and lists working recipes for each of these. You will see how to load a page, change a page, and also how to do silent scrolling.

*Chapter 10, The Theme Framework*, here you will learn how to theme a nested list, style button corners, and use custom backgrounds and fonts. You will explore how to override the global active state and override an existing swatch. Finally, you will use the ThemeRoller web tool to create and use your own swatch.

*Chapter 11, HTML5 and jQuery Mobile,* here you will see how to use various HTML5 features in your jQuery mobile app. You will explore some new HTML5 semantics, use the Application Cache to take your app offline, use Web Workers to see how asynchronous operations are done, and you will use web storage to store data using local and session storage. Then you will see how to draw in 2D using the Canvas, use SVG image and apply a Gaussian blur filter on it, track your device location using the Geolocation API, and finally see how to use audio and video in your app.

# What you need for this book

To work with jQuery Mobile, all you need is just your favorite text editor to write the HTML code. You can then run this code in your favorite browser and launch your app on a wide variety of platforms and devices. The full and detailed list of supported platforms and devices is available at `http://jquerymobile.com/gbs`.

To install and run the recipes in the cookbook, you will have to download and install the `node.js` web server from `http://www.nodejs.org`. The online docs at the nodejs website has the simple steps that are required to install on your specific platform (Windows/ Linux/Mac). The source code bundle accompanying this cookbook just needs to be extracted, and it contains all the required nodejs modules. You can now launch the recipes directly in your browser. Refer to the `Readme.txt` file in the source code bundle for detailed instructions on how to do this.

# Who this book is for

If you are a beginner with jQuery/JavaScript skills, this book offers you numerous examples to get you started.

If you are a seasoned developer, this book lets you explore jQuery Mobile in greater depth.

# Conventions

In this book, you will find a number of styles of text that distinguish between different kinds of information. Here are some examples of these styles, and an explanation of their meaning.

Code words in text are shown as follows: "Now, open the `main.html` file in your favorite browser, and you will see an output similar to the following screenshot:".

A block of code is set as follows:

```
<body>
  <!-- Main Page -->
  <div id="main" data-role="page">
    <div data-role="header">
      <h1>Welcome - JS BIN</h1>
    </div>
    <div id="content" data-role="content">
      <p>The jQuery Mobile Cookbook</p>
    </div>
    <div data-role="footer">
      <h4>Enjoy reading the book ...</h4>
    </div>
  </div>
</body>
</html>
```

When we wish to draw your attention to a particular part of a code block, the relevant lines or items are set in bold:

```
<!DOCTYPE html>
<html>
<head>
<link href="http://code.jquery.com/mobile/latest
  /jquery.mobile.css" rel="stylesheet" type="text/css" />
<script src="http://code.jquery.com
  /jquery-1.7.1.min.js"></script>
<script src="http://code.jquery.com/mobile/latest
  /jquery.mobile.js"></script>
<meta name="viewport" content="width=device-width,
  initial-scale=1">
<title>Welcome using JS Bin</title>
</head>
```

**New terms** and **important words** are shown in bold. Words that you see on the screen, in menus or dialog boxes for example, appear in the text like this: "You can also manually run the script by clicking on the **Run with JS** button."

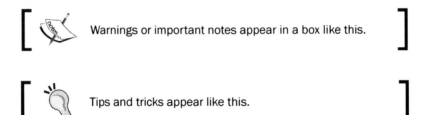

Warnings or important notes appear in a box like this.

Tips and tricks appear like this.

# Reader feedback

Feedback from our readers is always welcome. Let us know what you think about this book—what you liked or may have disliked. Reader feedback is important for us to develop titles that you really get the most out of.

To send us general feedback, simply send an e-mail to `feedback@packtpub.com`, and mention the book title via the subject of your message.

If there is a book that you need and would like to see us publish, please send us a note in the **SUGGEST A TITLE** form on `www.packtpub.com` or e-mail `suggest@packtpub.com`.

If there is a topic that you have expertise in and you are interested in either writing or contributing to a book, see our author guide on `www.packtpub.com/authors`.

# Customer support

Now that you are the proud owner of a Packt book, we have a number of things to help you to get the most from your purchase.

## Downloading the example code

You can download the example code files for all Packt books you have purchased from your account at `http://www.PacktPub.com`. If you purchased this book elsewhere, you can visit `http://www.PacktPub.com/support` and register to have the files e-mailed directly to you.

## Errata

Although we have taken every care to ensure the accuracy of our content, mistakes do happen. If you find a mistake in one of our books—maybe a mistake in the text or the code—we would be grateful if you would report this to us. By doing so, you can save other readers from frustration and help us improve subsequent versions of this book. If you find any errata, please report them by visiting `http://www.packtpub.com/support`, selecting your book, clicking on the **errata submission form** link, and entering the details of your errata. Once your errata are verified, your submission will be accepted and the errata will be uploaded on our website, or added to any list of existing errata, under the Errata section of that title. Any existing errata can be viewed by selecting your title from `http://www.packtpub.com/support`.

# Piracy

Piracy of copyright material on the Internet is an ongoing problem across all media. At Packt, we take the protection of our copyright and licenses very seriously. If you come across any illegal copies of our works, in any form, on the Internet, please provide us with the location address or website name immediately so that we can pursue a remedy.

Please contact us at `copyright@packtpub.com` with a link to the suspected pirated material.

We appreciate your help in protecting our authors, and our ability to bring you valuable content.

# Questions

You can contact us at `questions@packtpub.com` if you are having a problem with any aspect of the book, and we will do our best to address it.

# 1
# Get Rolling

In this chapter, we will cover the following recipes:

▸ Writing your first jQuery Mobile application

▸ Using JS Bin to create a simple application

# Introduction

The **jQuery Mobile Framework** is an open source cross-platform UI framework. It is built using HTML5, CSS3, and the very popular jQuery JavaScript library, and it follows Open Web standards. It provides touch-friendly UI widgets that are specially styled for mobile devices. It has a powerful theming framework to style your applications. It supports AJAX for various tasks, such as page navigation and transitions.

As jQuery Mobile follows the open web standards, you can be sure that your application can get maximum support and compatibility with a wide range of browsers and platforms. You can write your application once and it will work seamlessly on iPhones, iPads, Android phones and tablets, Blackberry, Bada, Windows, Symbian, Meego, and even the upcoming HTML5-based platforms, such as Boot2Gecko and Tizen. The same code will run on Chrome, Firefox, Opera, IE, Safari, and other browsers on your desktop. Further, it will work even on your smart TV or any other gadget that has a compatible browser which is compliant with the open web standards. The market reach potential is phenomenal.

The list of the currently certified supported browsers, platforms, and the grade of support is available on the jQuery Mobile website at `http://www.jquerymobile.com/gbs`. Note that some features, such as CSS 3D animations and AJAX, might not be supported on certain older and legacy platforms. Here, the framework resorts to **Progressive Enhancement**. This means that the basic functionality is supported initially. Later, when a more capable future browser or platform becomes available, your application automatically makes use of its capabilities and offers upgraded functionality. In most scenarios, you will not have to write the code or interfere in any way. This is a big plus when you compare mobile web applications with mobile native applications.

While coding native applications, you will have to write the code in different languages, based on the platform. You will then have to compile the code for each platform, and build binary packages that can run on the device. Upgrading the application to support the next version means you have to go back and redo the whole exercise of checking/fixing your code, rebuilding, and repackaging. This overhead compounds as you add support for more platforms. The whole thing just becomes unmanageable after a point. You are better off by just supporting the top one or two platforms for your application.

Of course, there are advantages of using native applications. The performance of your application could be a very crucial factor. There are certain applications where you have to go native, especially when you expect real-time responses. Also, with native apps, you can access core OS and device features, such as camera, accelerometer, contacts, and calendar. This is not easily done today with HTML5.

**HTML5** is a relatively new entrant for mobile applications. But the gap is closing by the day. There are libraries already available that expose the native features using simple JavaScript API, which is directly available to your HTML5 app. PhoneGap is one such popular library. Firefox's Boot2Gecko and Intel/Samsung's Tizen are totally based on HTML5, and you should be able to access the core device functionality directly from the browser here. Things do look very promising for the future.

The jQuery Mobile framework has a wide array of plugins and tools that help you build your application. It has a very active and vibrant developer community, and new features are continuously being added. It is strongly backed by companies, such as Filament Group, Mozilla, Nokia, Palm, Adobe, Rhomobile, and others. Within its first year (in 2011), the framework has already won awards, such as the Packt Open Source Award and the .NET Innovation Award.

Web-based mobile applications have evolved. They used pure native code for the UI in the early days, then came flash and other plugin-based UI (such as Silverlight). But even Adobe and Microsoft (with its Windows 8 platform) are going full steam ahead on HTML5 development. So, the situation is ripe for the explosive growth of an open source web standards-based cross-platform framework, such as jQuery Mobile.

The jQuery Mobile framework requires you to use declarative syntax (HTML markup) for most of the basic tasks and for building the UI. You have to fall back to scripting with JavaScript only, where declarative syntax does not help, and of course for adding your application logic. This is different from many other UI frameworks that are available in the market today. The other frameworks require you to write much more JavaScript and have a much steeper learning curve.

If you are familiar with HTML, CSS, and jQuery/JavaScript, then you will find it very easy to learn jQuery Mobile. There are many popular IDEs and UI builders that you can use to visually drag-and-drop UI controls and develop in jQuery Mobile. But to get started, all you need is your favorite text editor to write the code. You will also need a browser (running on your desktop or mobile) to test the application. You are now ready to write your first jQuery Mobile cross-platform application.

# Writing your first jQuery Mobile application

A simple jQuery Mobile application consists of a page, which forms the basic building block for your application. The page follows a basic structure with three main parts, the **header**, the **page content**, and the **footer**. You can build feature-rich applications with workflows using multiple pages, each page with its own functionality, logic, and navigational flow. This recipe shows how to create a page and write your first jQuery Mobile application.

## Getting ready

Copy the full code of this recipe from the `code/01/welcome` folder. You can launch this code using the URL: `http://localhost:8080/01/welcome/main.html`.

## How to do it...

Carry out the following steps:

1. Create the following `main.html` file using your favorite text editor:

```
<!DOCTYPE html>
<html>
  <head>
    <title>Welcome</title>
    <meta name='viewport' content='width=device-width,
      initial-scale=1'>
```

2. Include the jQuery and jQuery Mobile JavaScript files:

```
<link rel='stylesheet' href='http://code.jquery.com
  /mobile/1.1.1/jquery.mobile-1.1.1.min.css' />
<script src='http://code.jquery.com/jquery-
  1.7.1.min.js'></script>
<script src='http://code.jquery.com/mobile
  /1.1.1/jquery.mobile-1.1.1.min.js'></script>
</head>
<body>
```

3. Create the jQuery Mobile page:

```
<!-- Main Page -->
<div id='main' data-role='page'>
  <div data-role='header'>
    <h1>Welcome!</h1>
  </div>
  <div id='content' data-role='content'>
    <p>The jQuery Mobile Cookbook</p>
```

```
      </div>
      <div data-role='footer'>
        <h4>Enjoy reading the book ...</h4>
      </div>
    </div>
  </body>
</html>
```

## How it works...

Create `main.html` as an HTML5 document starting with the `<!DOCTYPE html>` declaration. In the `<head>` tag of the file, add a `<meta>` tag and specify that the viewport should occupy the entire device width by using the `content='width=device-width'` attribute. Include the jQuery Mobile stylesheet by using the `<link>` tag pointing to the CSS file location on the jQuery Mobile Content Delivery Network (CDN) site.

Next, include the JavaScript libraries; first the jQuery and then the jQuery Mobile JavaScript files. Use the `<script>` tags and point `src` to the CDN location, as shown in the code. You are now ready to create the page.

The page, its header, footer, and content are all `<div>` containers, which are styled by using the `data-role` attributes. Add a `<div>` tag with `data-role='page'` to the `<body>` tag. Add three `div` tags with `data-role='header'`, `'content'`, and finally the `'footer'` as child elements within the page. This will create the page header, content, and footer respectively. You can add any text, forms, lists, or other HTML controls within these `<div>` tags. The framework will enhance and render the controls in a touch-friendly mobile-enabled style.

Now, open the `main.html` file in your favorite browser, and you will see an output similar to the following screenshot:

Open and compare the output of this file in different browsers, mobile devices, and tablets. You will see that on all-compliant and certified browsers/devices, the page opens up and looks pretty much the same.

Congratulations! You just created your first cross-platform jQuery Mobile web application.

## There's more...

At the time of writing this recipe, jQuery Mobile v1.1.1 was the stable version and is used in all the recipes in this book. The supported jQuery library recommended is jQuery v1.7.1.

You can use the libraries directly from the jQuery Mobile CDN, as shown in this recipe. You could also download the library files (available in a single archive) at `http://www.jquerymobile.com/download`, and host the files locally within your network. When hosted locally, you just have to update the links in your code to point to the correct location of the files on your network (or to the path on your hard disk), as shown in the following code snippet:

```
<link rel="stylesheet" href='[local path]/jquery.mobile-
  1.1.1.min.css' />
<script src='[local path]/jquery-1.7.1.min.js'></script>
<script src='[local path]/mobile/1.1.1/jquery.mobile-
  1.1.1.min.js'></script>
```

### The Page theme

By default, the framework provides five basic color schemes or combinations called **color swatches**. They are named a, b, c, d and e. By default, swatch d is used when you create a page. This gives the page a bright combination of white and black colors, as seen in the previous screenshot. You can change the color swatch of your page and header/footer by using the `data-theme` attribute, as shown in the following code snippet:

```
<div data-role='page' data-theme='a'>
  <div data-role='header' data-theme='b'>
....
  <div data-role='footer' data-theme='b'>
```

The output will now be similar to the following screenshot:

## See also

▶ The *Using JS Bin to create a simple application* recipe

▶ The *Writing a single-page template application* and *Writing a multi-page template application* recipes in *Chapter 2, Pages and Dialogs*

# Using JS Bin to create a simple application

**JS Bin** is an open source web application built by *Remy Sharp*, available at http://www.jsbin.com. JS Bin allows you to directly enter your HTML, CSS, and JavaScript code online, and also allows you to include the required jQuery and jQuery Mobile libraries. You can add and directly run your JavaScript code and preview the output on your browser. You can also share your code and collaborate with others for review or troubleshooting. You can finally download your code once everything works as desired. It is a very popular tool used by many jQuery Mobile developers. This recipe shows you how to create a simple jQuery Mobile application using JS Bin.

## Getting ready

The code in this recipe was created using the JS Bin web application available at http://www.jsbin.com. The code is available in the code/01/jsbin source folder. You can launch the code using the URL http://localhost:8080/01/jsbin/main.html.

## How to do it...

1. Launch the JS Bin web application tool at the URL http://www.jsbin.com, and you will see a basic HTML template.

2. Select the **Add Library** link on the top-left panel, and include the latest jQuery Mobile library files. Next, edit the <head> section, as shown in the following code snippet:

```
<html>
  <head>
    <link href="http://code.jquery.com/mobile/latest
      /jquery.mobile.css" rel="stylesheet" type="text/css" />
    <script src="http://code.jquery.com
      /jquery-1.7.1.min.js"></script>
    <script src="http://code.jquery.com
      /mobile/latest/jquery.mobile.js"></script>
    <meta name="viewport" content="width=device-width,
      initial-scale=1">
    <title>Welcome using JS Bin</title>
  </head>
```

3. Add code to the `<body>` section to create a simple jQuery Mobile page:

```
<body>
  <!-- Main Page -->
  <div id="main" data-role="page">
    <div data-role="header">
      <h1>Welcome - JS BIN</h1>
    </div>
    <div id="content" data-role="content">
      <p>The jQuery Mobile Cookbook</p>
    </div>
    <div data-role="footer">
      <h4>Enjoy reading the book ...</h4>
    </div>
  </div>
</body>
</html>
```

4. The preview or output is now visible in the **Output** pane on the right side of the screen.

5. You can now download the source file (or copy-and-paste into a local file) to have a simple working jQuery Mobile application.

## How it works...

Launch the JS Bin web application in your browser. You will see the following screen in your browser, with a basic HTML template (which you can edit) on the left side. A menu bar is available at the top and an **Output** pane is available on the right, to instantly preview the output of your code:

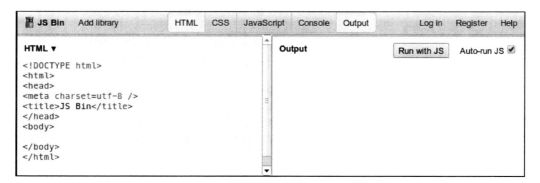

You can click on the various menu options and see how the **CSS** or **JavaScript** panes can be made visible or hidden. Selecting the **Auto-run JS** option will allow you to run your JS code automatically; you can leave it on. You can also manually run the script by clicking on the **Run with JS** button.

Click on the **Add library** menu option and select the **jQuery Mobile Latest** option as shown in the following screenshot:

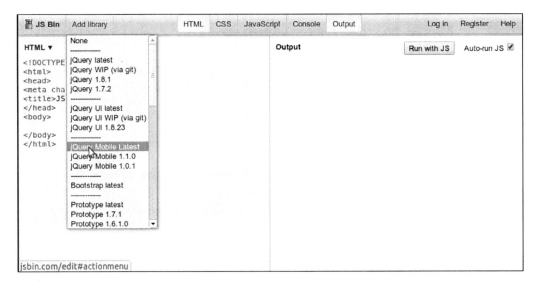

This will include the links and references to the jQuery Mobile and jQuery libraries in the `<head>` section of the HTML.

 When you add the jQuery Mobile library to your code using JS Bin, make sure you edit and set the correct versions for both jQuery Mobile and jQuery libraries that you want to use with your application. When this recipe was written, jQuery v1.6.4 was being used in JS Bin, whereas jQuery v1.7.1 is recommended to be used with jQuery Mobile v1.1.1.

Next, edit the `<meta>` tag to set the correct viewport `width` and `scale`, as shown in the code. Then, add a page to the `<body>` tag using a `div` tag with `data-role="page"`. Create the header (`data-role="header"`), page content (`data-role="content"`), and footer (`data-role="footer"`), as shown. As you add these sections, you will notice that the **Output** pane on the right side of the screen gets updated and shows the output preview of your code.

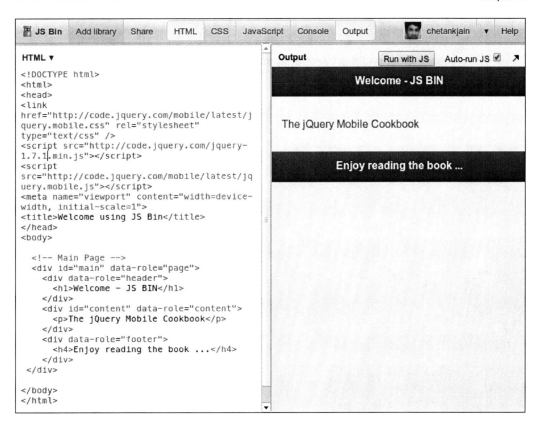

You can also add CSS styles and JavaScript, and check how it works. Finally, your code is ready and you can copy-and-paste it locally into your editor. You can also click on the **JS Bin** menu option at the top-left to download the file. Now, launch the local file in your browser, and you will see that the output matches what was displayed in the **Output** pane of JS Bin.

## There's more...

This recipe shows you the simple steps required to create a basic jQuery Mobile application using JS Bin. JS Bin provides many features that are nice to use, such as creating and using ready templates, saving and forking your code using GitHub, and cloning your code. This tool is best suited for when you want to store your files online and collaborate on your source files. For more information and tutorials on using JS Bin, refer to http://jsbin.tumblr.com/.

> You can register for free and log in to JS Bin with your user account to make use of the save, download, or clone features. Only the basic features are available without user login.

## See also

▸ The *Writing your first jQuery Mobile application* recipe

# 2
# Pages and Dialogs

In this chapter, we will cover:

- ► Writing a single-page template application
- ► Writing a multi-page template application
- ► Prefetching pages for faster navigation
- ► Using the DOM cache to improve performance
- ► Custom styling a dialog
- ► Using CSS to create a bouncing page transition
- ► Using JS to create a slide and fade page transition
- ► Using `data-url` to handle a login page navigation
- ► Using the History API to create a custom error pop up

## Introduction

A **Page** is the basic jQuery Mobile object written within a `<div data-role="page">` container that gets displayed on the screen. It can contain the header, the page content, and the footer. You can embed various HTML5 controls and widgets within a page. The jQuery Mobile framework automatically enhances and displays all these controls, making them tap-friendly (finger-friendly). Your application can have a series of individual HTML files each representing a single page, or it can have one single HTML file containing multiple page `div` containers within it. You can provide links to open other pages within a page, and when the user clicks on a link, the new page opens using Ajax with CSS3 animation. The current page is then hidden from view.

A **Dialog** is a page having the `data-role="dialog"` attribute. You can also load a page as a dialog by adding the `data-rel="dialog"` attribute to the page link. The dialog is styled differently from a page, and it appears in the middle of the screen above the page. The dialog also provides a close button in its header.

# Writing a single-page template application

In a **single-page template** application, each page of the application will have its own HTML file. A page is wrapped within a page container as `<div data-role="page">`. When you launch the app, the jQuery Mobile framework will load the first page of the app (or the main page) into the DOM, whose reference is held all through the app cycle. The main page just gets hidden when the user navigates to another page, which now is marked as an active page. Except for the main page, all other pages get removed from the DOM when the user navigates away from them. Navigation between the pages is specified using anchor links. The anchor links are decorated as buttons using the `data-role="button"` attribute. On clicking any link, navigation occurs with some cool CSS3 transitions, and the new page is pulled in via Ajax.

This recipe shows you how to create a single-page template application and navigate between the pages of the app.

## Getting ready

Copy the full code of this recipe from the `code/02/single-page` sources folder. You can launch this code using the URL `http://localhost:8080/02/single-page/main.html`.

## How to do it...

Carry out the following steps:

1.  Create `main.html`, and add a page container with the header, footer, and page content to it. Add a link to open `page2.html`:

```html
<div id="main" data-role="page">
  <div data-role="header">
    <h1>Header of main.html</h1>
  </div>
  <div data-role="content">
    <a href="page2.html" data-role="button">
      Go to Page 2</a>
  </div>
  <div data-role="footer">
    <h4>Footer of main.html</h4>
  </div>
</div>
```

2. Since this is a single-page template app, add each page to its own HTML file. Next, create `page2.html` and add the second page of the app to it. Add a link to go back to `main.html`:

```
<div id="page2" data-role="page">
  <div data-role="header">
    <h1>Header of page2.html</h1>
  </div>
  <div data-role="content">
    <a href="#" data-role="button" data-rel="back"
      data-theme="b">Go Back</a>
  </div>
  <div data-role="footer">
    <h4>Footer of page2.html</h4>
  </div>
</div>
```

## How it works...

Create `main.html`, and add a page to it using the `<div>` page container with the `data-role="page"` attribute specified. Add the header, footer, and page content, as shown in the code. Now, add an anchor link to the page content to open the second page, `page2.html`. You can style this link as a button by using the `data-role="button"` attribute.

Next, create `page2.html` and add a page to it using the `<div>` page container with the `data-role="page"` attribute specified. Add the header, footer, and page content to it, as shown in the code listing. Here, in the page content, add an anchor link to go back to `main. html`. Also, set the `data-role="button"` attribute to style this link as a button.

Now, when you launch the app, the `main.html` page is first loaded into the DOM. This page stays in the DOM throughout the life cycle of the app. The following screenshot is displayed:

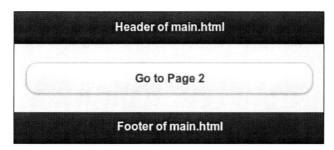

When you click on the button to open `page2.html`, the main page is hidden from view, and `page2.html` is displayed and made active, as shown in the following screenshot:

Now, click on the link to go back to `main.html`. The browser opens the `main.html` page again and hides `page2.html`.

In `page2.html`, the anchor button has a `data-rel="back"` attribute. This indicates that the previous page in the browser history should be loaded. The `href` link is ignored and so you can set it to #.

**Setting the title for a single-page template app**

Use the `<title>` tag to set the page title for each page in a single-page app. This ensures that relevant titles are displayed as you navigate through the various pages in your app.

## There's more...

It is recommended that most applications use single-page templates, for the following reasons:

▶ Pages are lighter, cleaner, and more modular, and thus easier to maintain.

▶ The DOM size is relatively smaller.

▶ Pages work well on multiple platforms and environments. They work even where JavaScript is not supported. You can target more devices this way.

On the flip side:

▶ It consumes more bandwidth as each page visit generates a new request.

▶ Opening a previously loaded page again will generate a fresh request.

▶ First load is faster, but every subsequent page has to be fetched.

To conclude, single-page template apps are more suited for larger applications and in situations where you want to target as many platforms as possible.

## Turning off Ajax navigation

In this recipe, in #page2, the href value is set to #. If you set the href value to the absolute or relative URL of the page, that is href="main.html", then Ajax navigation will still work. To prevent pages being loaded via Ajax, add the data-ajax="false" attribute to the link. The framework will not use the custom CSS3 transitions when Ajax is turned off.

```
<a href="page2.html" data-role="button" data-ajax="false">text</a>
```

**Using URL instead of data-rel="back"**

It is always better to use URLs in href of the anchor link while navigating in single page apps. This way, Ajax navigation would work where Ajax is supported. In C grade browsers, where Ajax is not supported, the app would still continue to work, since it uses href for navigation. In such browsers, if your app relies only on the data-rel="back" attribute, and does not use href, then page navigation would break down.

## Using data-rel and data-direction

When you add both the href and data-rel="back" attributes to an anchor link, the href attribute is ignored by the framework. The page will only consider the data-rel attribute and navigate "back"; that is, it will navigate to the page present as the previous entry in the browser history stack. If you specify the data-direction="reverse" attribute, the framework will reverse the direction of the most recent page transition used. The data-direction attribute does not depend on the data-rel attribute, and can be used independently in any transition.

```
<a href="page2.html" data-role="button"
    data-direction="reverse">text</a>
```

## Page container is optional

Specifying the <div data-role="page"> page container is optional in a single-page template application. The page contents are automatically wrapped with a page container by the jQuery Mobile framework.

Always use a div page container to wrap your page. It is easier to read and maintain the code. It also allows you to add page-specific data attributes such as data-theme to your page.

## See also

▶ The *Writing a multi-page template application*, *Prefetching pages for faster navigation*, and *Using the DOM Cache to improve performance* recipes

▶ The *Writing your first jQuery Mobile application* recipe in *Chapter 1, Introduction*

# Writing a multi-page template application

In a multi-page template application, the HTML file will have multiple pages in it. Each page is wrapped within a page container as `<div data-role="page">`. The page ID is used to identify the pages for linking or invoking any actions on them. The page ID must be unique within your app. When you launch the app, the jQuery Mobile framework loads all the available pages into the DOM and displays the first page it finds in the HTML. Navigation between the pages is specified by using anchor links, and you can decorate these links as buttons by using the `data-role="button"` attribute. On clicking any link, navigation occurs with some cool CSS3 transitions, and the new page is pulled in via Ajax. This recipe shows you how to create a multi-page template application and navigate between the multiple pages it contains.

## Getting ready

Copy the full code of this recipe from the `code/02/multi-page` sources folder. You can launch this code using the URL `http://localhost:8080/02/multi-page/main.html`.

## How to do it...

Carry out the following steps:

1. Create `main.html`, and add the `#main` page to it. Define the header, page content, and footer, as shown in the following code snippet. Add a link to open the `#page2` page in the page content:

```
<div id="main" data-role="page">
  <div data-role="header">
    <h1>Header of #main</h1>
  </div>
  <div data-role="content">
    <a href="#page2" data-role="button">Go to Page 2</a>
  </div>
  <div data-role="footer">
    <h4>Footer of #main Page</h4>
  </div>
</div>
```

2. Next, in `main.html`, add the second `#page2` page in its own page `div` container, as shown in the following code snippet. Add the header, page content, and footer to this page. Finally, add a link to go back to the `#main` page in its page content:

```
<div id="page2" data-role="page" data-title="Multi-Page Template">
  <div data-role="header">
    <h1>Header of #page2</h1>
  </div>
```

```
<div data-role="content">
    <a href="#" data-role="button" data-rel="back" data-
theme="b">Go Back</a>
</div>
<div data-role="footer">
    <h4>Footer of #page2</h4>
</div>
</div>
```

## How it works...

Create main.html, and add two pages, #main and #page2, to it. First, add the #main page using the <div> page container with the data-role="page" attribute specified. Add the header, footer, and page content, as shown in the code. Now, add an anchor link to the page content to open the second page, #page2. You can style this link as a button by using the data-role="button" attribute.

Next, add the #page2 page using the <div> page container, with the data-role="page" attribute specified. Add the header, footer, and page content to it as shown in the code listing. Here, in the page content, add the anchor link to go back to the #main page. Set the data-role="button" attribute to style it as a button. Also, add the data-rel="back" attribute to it. This indicates to the jQuery Mobile framework that this link should open the previous page available in the browser history.

Now, when you launch the app, all the pages are loaded into the DOM and they stay in the DOM throughout the life cycle of the app. The framework opens the first page it finds. So, #main is displayed with a button to open #page2, as follows:

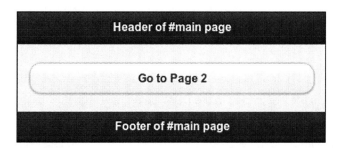

When you click on the button to open the second page, the #main page is hidden from view, and the #page2 page is displayed and made active, as follows:

Finally, click on the link to go back to the #main page. Since data-rel="back" was used, the browser opens the #main page again and hides #page2.

**Setting the title for a multi-page template app**

Use the <title> tag to set the page title for the first or the main page of the multi-page template app. Use the data-title attribute to set the title of all the other pages. This will ensure that the correct titles are shown for each page.

## There's more...

It is recommended that the following factors be considered before using a multi-page template to build your app:

▶ A multi-page template application is heavier due to the large DOM size.

▶ The DOM size is relatively larger and heavier because all the pages are loaded into it upfront.

▶ The application needs JavaScript support. This limits your choice of target platforms, and you might have to ignore many popular legacy platforms. But this exclusion list is getting thinner by the day as the older phones/platforms get phased out.

On the plus side:

▶ Only the first page load is slower, but subsequent page navigations are fast.

▶ All the pages are pre-loaded in the DOM, so no new requests (to the server) are required for subsequent page navigations. This means lesser bandwidth.

To conclude, multi-page template apps are more suited for relatively smaller applications and situations where you know the capabilities of your target platforms, including JavaScript support.

The updated list of browsers and platforms supported by jQuery Mobile is available at `http://www.jquerymobile.com/gbs`. It also details the grade of support provided on these platforms.

## Using transitions

The `data-transition` attribute can be used to specify various transitions that are available by default with jQuery Mobile. The following code opens `#page2` using a flip transition:

```
<a href="#page2" data-transition="flip" data-role="button">text</a>
```

## Turning off Ajax navigation

If you pass the `data-ajax="false"` attribute while loading a page in a multi-template app, it does not completely stop Ajax navigation. The default fade transition will then be used to load the pages regardless of the transition specified in the `data-transition` attribute.

```
<a href="#page2" data-ajax="false" data-role="button">text</a>
```

## Page container is mandatory

Specifying the `<div data-role="page">` page container is mandatory for all the pages within a multi-page template application. Use the page container for all your apps and all your pages regardless of whether they use the single-page or multi-page templates.

## See also

▸ The *Writing a single-page template application, Prefetching pages for faster navigation*, and *Using the DOM Cache to improve performance* recipes

▸ The *Writing your first jQuery Mobile application* recipe in *Chapter 1, Introduction*

# Prefetching pages for faster navigation

Using a single-page template for your mobile app makes your mobile app faster and lighter. But you have to fetch each page during navigation. You can see the `ui-loader` spinning icon every time a page loads. This problem does not happen with a multi-page template application, as all the pages are already preloaded into the DOM. By using the **prefetch** feature, a single-page template application can be made to mimic the multi-page template application.

A page marked for prefetch is loaded in the background and is immediately available when the user tries to open it. You can prefetch pages in two ways. The first is by just adding the `data-prefetch` attribute to the anchor link. The second way is by using JavaScript to call the `loadPage()` method. This recipe shows you how to improve page loading speed by prefetching pages in your jQuery Mobile app.

## Getting ready

Copy the full code of this recipe from the `code/02/prefetch` sources folder. You can launch this code using the URL `http://localhost:8080/02/prefetch/main.html`.

## How to do it...

The steps to be followed are:

1.  Create `main.html` and add two links to it. The first link points to `prefetch.html` and the second link to `prefetch-JS.html`. After the `main.html` file is loaded, the linked pages in it can be prefetched in the background using the `data-prefetch` attribute on the first link, as shown in the following code snippet:

    ```
    <div id="main" data-role="page">
      <div data-role="header">
        <h1>Header of Main Page</h1>
      </div>
      <div data-role="content">
        <a href="prefetch.html" data-role="button"
           data-prefetch>Prefetch Page</a>
        <a href="prefetch-JS.html" data-role="button">
           Prefetch Page using JS</a>
      </div>
      <div data-role="footer">
        <h4>Footer of Main Page</h4>
      </div>
    </div>
    ```

2.  Next, add the JavaScript given in the following code snippet to the `<head>` section of `main.html`. Here, use the `loadPage()` method to load the `prefetch-JS.html` file in the background, into the DOM:

    ```
    $("#main").live("pageshow", function(event, data) {
      $.mobile.loadPage( "prefetch-JS.html",
        { showLoadMsg: false } );
    });
    </script>
    ```

3.  Now, create the `prefetch.html` file as shown in the following code snippet. This is a regular page which is prefetched in the `main.html` page (in step 1), using the `data-prefetch` attribute. Also add a link to navigate back to `main.html`:

    ```
    <div id="prefetch" data-role="page">
      <div data-role="header">
        <h1>Header of Prefetched Page</h1>
      </div>
    ```

```
      <div data-role="content">
        <a href="#" data-role="button" data-rel="back"
            data-theme="b">Go Back</a>
      </div>
      <div data-role="footer">
        <h4>Footer of Prefetched Page</h4>
      </div>
    </div>
```

4. You will see that in step 2, the `prefetchJS.html` was prefetched using JavaScript. Now, create `prefetchJS.html`, as shown in the following code snippet, and add a link to navigate back to `main.html`:

```
<div id="jsprefetch" data-role="page">
  <div data-role="header">
    <h1>Header of JS Prefetched Page</h1>
  </div>
  <div data-role="content">
    <a href="#" data-role="button" data-rel="back"
        data-theme="b">Go Back</a>
  </div>
  <div data-role="footer">
    <h4>Footer of JS Prefetched Page</h4>
  </div>
</div>
```

## How it works...

Create `main.html`, and add two links to it. Point the first link to `prefetch.html` and set the `data-prefetch` attribute to this link. This page is now automatically fetched in the background and is immediately available for opening when `main.html` is loaded.

Point the second link to the `prefetch-JS.html` file. To prefetch this page using JavaScript, add an event handler for the `pageshow` event of `#main`. In this callback function, invoke the `loadPage()` method to fetch the `prefetch-JS.html` file. Also set the `showLoadMsg` option as `false`, to prevent the spinning `page ui-loader` message from being shown. Next, create the two HTML files as shown in the code. Add the link to navigate back to `main.html` in both the pages.

Now, when you launch the app, both the HTML files are prefetched. You can observe this prefetch behavior using your browser's code inspector, as shown in the following screenshot:

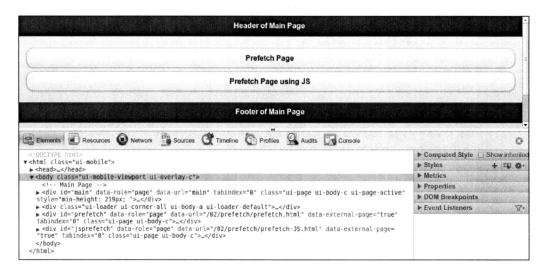

This screenshot shows the code inspector in the Google Chrome browser right after loading the `main.html` page. We can see that both the `#prefetch` and `#jsprefetch` pages are already prefetched and available in the DOM. Now, navigating to these prefetched pages is almost immediate, and the spinning `ui-loader` icon animation does not show up. This makes your app much faster and gives a better user experience to the user. If prefetch was not used, the page would have loaded only when you navigated to it.

Using the `data-prefetch` attribute is the easier way to prefetch pages, as you don't have to write any further code with it. But prefetching a page with JavaScript using `loadPage()` allows you to provide more options to the `loadPage()` method and have a better control over the behavior of your page load. You can also build in conditional prefetch with this approach.

## There's more...

Avoid using prefetch on too many pages, as all the pages have to be fetched and stored in the DOM. This means more memory utilization, and memory is a scarce resource on mobile devices. This will slow down your app. More pages prefetched also means more bandwidth utilized. So use it judiciously.

### When prefetch is not completed

If a page hasn't been fully prefetched and you try to navigate to that page, then the `ui-loader` spinner comes up and the page is shown only after the page is completely fetched. This could occur on slower connections.

## Prefetched pages are not permanently cached

When a page is prefetched, it is available in the DOM. If you navigate to this page and then navigate away, the page is automatically removed from the DOM. So if it is a frequently visited page, you have to add it to the DOM cache instead.

### See also

▸  The *Using the DOM cache to improve performance* recipe

▸  The *Using loadPage() to load a page* recipe in *Chapter 9, Methods and Utilities*

# Using the DOM cache to improve performance

During page navigation in a single-page template application, each new page is fetched and stored in the DOM. The page remains in the DOM and is removed once you navigate away from the page. Only the main or the first page of the app always remains in the DOM. As seen in the previous recipe, prefetching commonly-used pages could help in improving performance to some extent. But when you visit a prefetched page and navigate away from it, the page gets removed from the cache. So the problem of multiple fetching of frequently visited pages is not fully solved.

With DOM caching, specific pages are marked to be cached in the DOM. These pages, once loaded, remain in the DOM all through the life cycle of the app. You can use the DOM cache in two ways. The first is by adding the `data-dom-cache` attribute to the page container of the page that is to be cached. The second way is by using JavaScript. This recipe shows you how to improve the performance of your app by using the DOM cache.

### Getting ready

Copy the full code of this recipe from the `code/02/dom-cache` sources folder. You can launch this code using the URL `http://localhost:8080/02/dom-cache/main.html`.

### How to do it...

The steps to be followed are:

1.  Create the `main.html` file with links to navigate to the the two pages, `cached.html` and `cachedJS.html`. Both these pages, in turn, specify that they should be cached in the DOM:

```
<div id="main" data-role="page">
  <div data-role="header">
    <h1>Header of Main Page</h1>
```

```
      </div>
      <div data-role="content">
        <a href="cached.html" data-role="button">
          Cached Page
        </a>
        <a href="cached-JS.html" data-role="button">
          JS Cached Page
        </a>
      </div>
      <div data-role="footer">
        <h4>Footer of Main Page</h4>
      </div>
    </div>
```

2. Create the `cached.html` page and set the `data-dom-cache` attribute of its page container. Also add a button to go back to the `main.html` page:

```
<div id="cached" data-role="page" data-dom-cache="true">
      <div data-role="header">
        <h1>Header of Cached Page</h1>
      </div>
      <div data-role="content">
        <a href="#" data-role="button" data-rel="back">
          Go Back
        </a>
      </div>
      <div data-role="footer">
        <h4>Footer of Cached Page</h4>
      </div>
    </div>
```

3. Finally, create the `cached-JS.html` file, and cache it by using JavaScript added to the page `div` container, as shown in the following code snippet. Add a button to navigate back to `main.html`:

```
<div id="jscached" data-role="page">
      <script>
        $("#jscached").page({ domCache: true });
      </script>

      <div data-role="header">
        <h1>Header of JS Cached Page</h1>
      </div>
      <div data-role="content">
        <a href="#" data-role="button" data-rel="back">
          Go Back
```

```
        </a>
      </div>
      <div data-role="footer">
        <h4>Footer of JS Cached Page</h4>
      </div
    </div>
```

## How it works...

Create `main.html` and add two links to open the `cached.html` and `cached-JS.html` files. Next, create the `cached.html` file with a link to go back to `main.html`. Here, set the `data-dom-cache="true"` attribute to the page container. This indicates that the page must be cached in the DOM once it is loaded.

Now create the `cached-JS.html` file with a link to return to `main.html`. Here, add the given script to the page `div` container. In the script, set the `domCache` option on the page to `true`. Now, when this page is loaded, it gets cached in the DOM.

Launch the app and navigate between the pages. During page navigation, each new page is fetched and stored in the DOM. You can observe the DOM cache behavior using your browser's code inspector. The following image shows the Chrome code inspector snapshot after both the pages were visited and cached in the DOM. The current active page is shown as `#main`; this is indicated by the `ui-page-active` class added to its page's `div` container. The other two pages are cached and are also seen available in the DOM.

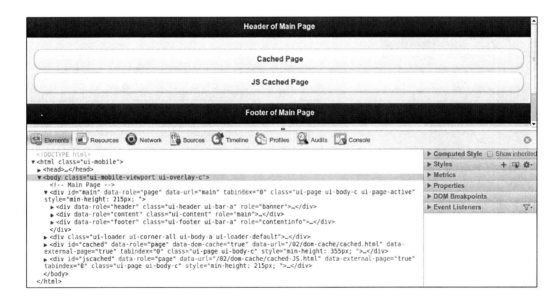

**Adding scripts to the page div and not the <head> element**

When using Ajax navigation, the `<head>` section is processed only on the first page or the main page of your app. The `<head>` element of each of the remaining pages is ignored and only their page's `div` containers are processed. Thus, to ensure that your script is executed in these pages, you have to include the `<script>` tag within the page's `div` container.

## There's more...

If you want to cache all pages ever visited in your app, it becomes cumbersome to add the caching option in each of these pages. There is a way to do this globally using JavaScript. Add the following script to the `<head>` section of your main page. Now, every page visited automatically gets cached in the DOM.

```
<script>
    $.mobile.page.prototype.options.domCache = true;
</script>
```

### DOM caching can slow down your app

Having a large number of pages cached in the DOM could make your app very heavy and slow it down. In such situations, you will have to write extra code to manage the cached pages in the DOM, and perform any clean ups that are required. So, use DOM caching on selected frequently accessed pages only.

## See also

> ▸ The *Prefetching pages for faster navigation* recipe

# Custom styling a dialog

You can style a page as a dialog by using the `data-role="dialog"` attribute on the page container. You can also specify the `data-rel="dialog"` attribute in the anchor link used to open the page. The page now gets styled as a dialog, and opens with a pop transition. When you add a header to the dialog, a close icon is created on the header, by default, in the left side of the header. In some applications/platforms, you might want to position this close button on the right side of the header. There is no ready option available to change this icon's position. This recipe shows you how to build a dialog with a custom styled header to position the close button at the right side of the header.

## Getting ready

Copy the full code of this recipe from the `code/02/custom-dialog` sources folder. You can launch this code using the URL `http://localhost:8080/02/custom-dialog/main.html`.

## How to do it...

The steps to be followed are:

1. Create `main.html` with the `#main` page. Add a link here to open the `#customdialog` page as a dialog using the `data-rel="dialog"` attribute:

```
<div id="main" data-role="page">
  <div data-role="header">
    <h1>Header of Main Page</h1>
  </div>
  <div data-role="content">
    <a href="#customdialog" data-role="button"
       data-rel="dialog">Open Custom Dialog</a>
  </div>
  <div data-role="footer">
    <h4>Footer of Main Page</h4>
  </div>
</div>
```

2. Create the `#customdialog` page in `main.html`, and add the custom header to the dialog that positions the close button on the right side of the header. The default header enhancement is prevented in this code:

```
<div id="customdialog" data-role="page">
  <div class="ui-corner-top ui-overlay-shadow ui-header ui-bar-a"
    role="banner">
    <a href="#main" data-icon="delete" data-iconpos="notext"
       class="ui-btn-right ui-btn ui-btn-icon-notext ui-btn-corner-
       all ui-shadow ui-btn-up-a" title="Close" data-theme="a"
    data-
       transition="pop" data-direction="reverse">
       <span class="ui-btn-inner ui-btn-corner-all">
         <span class="ui-btn-text">Close</span>
         <span class="ui-icon ui-icon-delete ui-icon-shadow"></
    span>
       </span>
    </a>
    <h1 class="ui-title" tabindex="0" role="heading"
        aria-level="1">Custom Dialog</h1>
  </div>
```

3. Finally, add the page content with a link to go back to the #main page:

```
<div data-role="content">
  <a href="#" data-role="button" data-rel="back"
     data-theme="b">Go Back</a>
</div>
<div data-role="footer">
  <h4>Footer of Dialog</h4>
</div>
</div>
```

## How it works...

Create `main.html` with two pages, #main and #customdialog, in it. Add a link in the #main page to open the #customdialog page as a dialog, by setting the `data-rel="dialog"` attribute. Next, create the #customdialog page and add a button to go back to the #main page. Now, in the header of #customdialog, do not use the `data-role="header"` attribute. This will prevent the dialog header from being enhanced with the default style. The close icon will not be placed at the left side of the header now. You can now add your custom header and set custom styles to it, as given in the code listing earlier. Launch the app and open the dialog, you will see the dialog pop up. This dialog now has a custom styled header with the close icon on the right side of the header, as shown in the following screenshot:

To understand how the custom style was arrived at, first create a page that opens a regular dialog. Using the code inspector of your browser and observe the code enhancements done by the jQuery Mobile framework to the header of the dialog. Copy this generated code "as is" into your custom dialog code. Then you have to make the changes mentioned in the following sections.

The first change is to fix the close icon's position. You will see that the close action is performed with the help of an anchor link that has been added into the header code. Here, replace the `ui-btn-left` class with the `ui-btn-right` class. This will position the icon to the right in the header. The `jquery.mobile.css` file already has these class definitions in it.

With this change, the close icon now appears at both the left and the right positions in the header. This is because the header still has the `data-role="header"` attribute. This makes the framework enhance the entire header and automatically add the close icon on the left side. But, since you have already added all these generated classes manually, you can now safely remove the `data-role="header"` attribute from your code. Retain all the other code and classes that you have added. Now, when you launch the code, you will only see a single close icon positioned at the right side of your header.

## There's more...

This technique is a very important one. It can be used to customize how your jQuery Mobile apps should look and feel. The framework provides many basic options, elements, and attributes that you can add to your apps. The framework then enhances these by adding more markup code and styles internally, making it look good in your browser. This enhanced code is not visible in the **View Source** option of your browser. But, with a code inspector or debugging tool, you can view the enhanced code, copy it to your HTML files, tweak it, and get the result you want. The following screenshot shows the code inspector view for the custom dialog header created using this recipe:

### Customizing CSS

The dialog page can further be enhanced by introducing your own styles in a custom CSS file. Check for all classes that have `ui-dialog` in the `jquery.mobile.css` file. Copy the styles that you want to tweak into your custom CSS and set appropriate new values. The following line of code shows a sample change where the top margin of the dialog is set to `-12px` instead of the default `-15px`:

```
.ui-dialog { margin-top: -12px; };
```

## See also

▶ The *Adding a customized round button to the header* recipe in *Chapter 3, Toolbars*

# Using CSS to create a bouncing page transition

As you navigate between the pages of your app, the jQuery Mobile framework uses CSS3 animations to show some cool transition effects. The **fade** transition is used by default for pages, and the **pop** transition is used for dialogs. You can navigate into a page with a particular transition, and when you navigate out of the page, you can reverse the direction of the transition. jQuery Mobile comes with a default set of 10 transitions as of v1.1.1. The jQuery Mobile online docs has a nice online demo showing all the available transitions. But that's not all; you can use CSS to create your own custom transitions and use them in your app. This recipe shows you how to use CSS and create a bouncing page effect during page transitions.

## Getting ready

Copy the full code of this recipe from the `code/02/custom-css-transition` sources folder. You can launch this code using the URL `http://localhost:8080/02/custom-css-transition/main.html`.

## How to do it...

The steps to be followed are:

1.  Create the `customtransition.css` file, and define the `bounceup` custom transition as shown in the following code snippet. Animate the `Y` position property of the page in the CSS:

    ```
    .bounceup.in, .bounceup.in.reverse {
      -webkit-transform: translateY(0) ;
      -webkit-animation-name: bounceupin;
      -webkit-animation-duration: 1s;
      -webkit-animation-timing: cubic-bezier(0.1, 0.2, 0.8, 0.9);
    }
    @-webkit-keyframes bounceupin {
      0% { -webkit-transform: translateY(100%); }
      90% { -webkit-transform: translateY(-10%); }
      100% {-webkit-transform: translateY(0); }
    }
    ```

2.  Define the reverse animation next:

    ```
    .bounceup.out, .bounceup.out.reverse {
      -webkit-transform: translateY(100%);
      -webkit-animation-name: bounceupout;
      -webkit-animation-duration: 1s;
      -webkit-animation-timing: cubic-bezier(0.1, 0.2, 0.8, 0.9);
    ```

```
}
@-webkit-keyframes bounceupout {
  0% { -webkit-transform: translateY(0); }
  90% { -webkit-transform: translateY(110%); }
  100% {-webkit-transform: translateY(100%); }
}
```

3. Create `main.html` and include the reference to the `customtransition.css` stylesheet in its `<head>` section, as follows:

```
<meta name="viewport" content="width=device-width,
  initial-scale=1">
<link rel="stylesheet" href="http://code.jquery.com
  /mobile/1.1.1/jquery.mobile-1.1.1.min.css" />
<link rel="stylesheet" href="customtransition.css" />
<script src="http://code.jquery.com/jquery-1.7.1.min.js">
</script>
<script src="http://code.jquery.com/mobile
  /1.1.1/jquery.mobile-1.1.1.min.js"></script>
```

4. Create the `#main` page with a link to open `#page2`. Set the `bounceup` custom transition defined earlier to the `data-transition` attribute:

```
<div id="main" data-role="page">
  <div data-role="header">
    <h1>Header of Main Page</h1>
  </div>
  <div data-role="content">
    <a href="#page2" data-role="button"
      data-transition="bounceup">Go to Page 2</a>
  </div>
  <div data-role="footer">
    <h4>Footer of Main Page</h4>
  </div>
</div>
```

5. Finally, create the `#page2` page with a link to go back to the `#main` page:

```
<div id="page2" data-role="page" data-title="Custom
  Transition using CSS">
  <div data-role="header">
    <h1>Header of Page 2</h1>
  </div>
  <div data-role="content">
    <a href="#" data-role="button" data-rel="back"
      data-theme="b">Go Back</a>
  </div>
```

```
<div data-role="footer">
  <h4>Footer of Page 2</h4>
</div>
</div>
```

## How it works...

Create the `customtransition.css` file and define the custom `bounceup` transition. First, define the `.bounceup.in` and `.bounceup.in.reverse` classes, with both having the same values. This will make both the transitioning into a new page and out of it (reverse) look similar. In the class, set the `Y` co-ordinate or the vertical position of the new page on the screen using the `translateY` property. Animate this property over the given duration of 1 second, using a Cubic Bezier animation curve. Next, define the keyframes for the animation of the `Y` co-ordinate (this is specified using the `bounceupin` animation name). The keyframes define the values of `Y` at various times within the animation.

You can use a simple trick to get the bounce effect that is used in this animation. Set the value of `Y` to beyond the screen at 90 percent duration, and then set it to the edge of the screen at 100 percent duration, or at the completion of the animation. This gives it a neat bouncing effect as the new page animates into the screen, extends out of the screen for a short duration, and comes back to the correct position. Similarly, define the `.bounceup.out` and `.bounceup.out.reverse` animations for the current page while it navigates out of the screen, as shown in the code.

Now, create `main.html` and include the CSS file in its `<head>` section after including the `jquery.mobile.css` file. Create the #main page, and add a link to open the #page2 page with the custom transition using the `data-transition="bounceup"` attribute. Finally, create the #page2 page with a link to go back to the #main page. Now when you launch the app and click on the buttons, the page navigation will occur, using a nice custom bouncing animation.

During a page transition, there is a **from** and a **to** page. jQuery Mobile applies the `out` class style on the from page (current page) and the `in` class style on the **to** page (new page). If the reverse transition is to be supported, the word `reverse` is suffixed to the `in` and `out` classes, as shown in the CSS file. Using these styles, jQuery Mobile will apply the right transition effects on the pages. You can further tweak the code in this recipe, and explore further with CSS animations to create more page animations. You can get as creative as you want!

# There's more...

The CSS styles are listed in this recipe to support only the web kit browsers (Chrome and Safari). You can explore this further and try to make it work on other browsers, such as IE, Firefox, or Opera. You will have to add vendor-specific prefixes to the CSS properties. Also, the browser should be capable of supporting the CSS property used. The vendor prefixes required for the popular browsers are as follows:

- **Chrome and Safari**: -webkit
- **Opera**: -o
- **Firefox**: -moz
- **IE**: -ms

## Adding vendor prefixes to the customtransition.css file

To incorporate support for other browsers, you will have to extend the customtransition.css file provided in this recipe. You can do this by adding vendor prefixes for the properties, as follows:

```
.bounceup.in, .bounceup.in.reverse {
  -webkit-transform: translateY(0);
  -moz-transform: translateY(0);
  -ms-transform: translate(0)
  -o-transform: translate(0)
  transform: translate(0)

  -webkit-animation-name: bounceupin;
  -moz-animation-name: bounceupin;
  -ms-animation-name: bounceupin;
  -o-animation-name: bounceupin;
  animation-name: bounceupin;
}
```

This has to be done for all the specified CSS properties that have the -webkit prefix in the code listed in this recipe.

**CSS3 animation support in various browsers**

The minimum browser versions required to support CSS3 animations are Chrome, Firefox 5.0, IE 10, Safari 4.0 on the desktop and Android browser 4, Firefox Mobile 5.0, and Safari Mobile (iOS 2) on the mobile.

### When the CSS3 property becomes a standard

The last line for each property shown in the preceding CSS is the name of the property after it becomes the standard. At this point, the browsers will drop support for that specific property's vendor prefixes. But you will not have to modify a single line of code in your CSS, as the standard property is already available in your file. The browser will skip all the properties it does not understand and pick up the standard property. So things will work just fine.

### Progressive enhancement

You will notice that the transition animation in this recipe will not work properly on all the browsers. But the basic functionality of page navigation works fine everywhere. The best support for CSS3 animation, as of writing this recipe, is offered by the web kit browsers. But the beauty of CSS3 is that as browsers continue to improve and as users upgrade their devices, the user will automatically get a better experience with your app. You will not have to modify any code or make any upgrade releases. This is called **Progressive Enhancement**. Using jQuery Mobile means that your code is already using progressive enhancement. This would not be so easy if your app was natively written.

## See also

▸ The *Using JS to create a slide and fade page transition* recipe

▸ The *Configuring your default transitions* recipe in *Chapter 7, Configurations*

# Using JS to create a slide and fade page transition

In the previous recipe, you learned to add a custom transition to your jQuery Mobile app using CSS. You can also create custom transitions using JavaScript. This recipe shows you how to create a "slidefade" (slide and fade) effect during page transition in your app by using JavaScript.

## Getting ready

Copy the full code of this recipe from the `code/02/custom-js-transition` sources folder. You can launch this code using the URL `http://localhost:8080/02/custom-js-transition/main.html`.

## How to do it...

Carry out the following steps:

1. Create the `customtransition.js` JavaScript file and define your custom transition by adding a `mycustomTransition()` method, as shown in the following code snippet. Here, define how the `from` and `to` pages should animate during the transition:

```
function mycustomTransition( name, reverse, $to, $from ) {
    var deferred = new $.Deferred();
    // Define your custom animation here
    $to.width("0");
    $to.height("0");
    $to.show();
    $from.animate(
        { width: "0", height: "0", opacity: "0" },
        { duration: 750 },
        { easing: 'easein' }
    );
    $to.animate(
        { width: "100%", height: "100%", opacity: "1" },
        { duration: 750 },
        { easing: 'easein' }
    );
```

2. Next, use the standard template copied directly from `the jquery.mobile.js` file to complete the transition function definition:

```
// Standard template from jQuery Mobile JS file
reverseClass = reverse ? " reverse" : "";
viewportClass
    = "ui-mobile-viewport-transitioning viewport-" + name;
$to.add( $from ).removeClass( "out in reverse " + name );
if ( $from && $from[ 0 ] !== $to[ 0 ] ) {
    $from.removeClass( $.mobile.activePageClass );
}
$to.parent().removeClass( viewportClass );
deferred.resolve( name, reverse, $to, $from );
$to.parent().addClass( viewportClass );
if ( $from ) {
    $from.addClass( name + " out" + reverseClass );
}
$to.addClass( $.mobile.activePageClass + " " + name
    + " in" + reverseClass );

return deferred.promise();
}
```

3. Finally, register the custom transition with the name `slidefade` with the jQuery Mobile framework:

```
// Register the custom transition
$.mobile.transitionHandlers["slidefade"] = mycustomTransition;
```

4. Next, create the `main.html` file, and include the `customtransition.js` file in the `<head>` section:

```
<meta name="viewport" content="width=device-width,
  initial-scale=1">
<link rel="stylesheet" href="http://code.jquery.com
  /mobile/1.1.1/jquery.mobile-1.1.1.min.css" />
<script src="http://code.jquery.com/jquery-1.7.1.min.js">
</script>
<script src="http://code.jquery.com/mobile/1.1.1
  /jquery.mobile-1.1.1.min.js"></script>
<script src="customtransition.js"></script>
```

5. Define the `#main` page, and include a link to open `#page2`. Use the custom `slidefade` transition with the `data-transition` attribute:

```
<div id="main" data-role="page">
  <div data-role="header">
    <h1>Header of Main Page</h1>
  </div>
  <div data-role="content">
    <a href="#page2" data-role="button"
      data-transition="slidefade" data-theme="b">Go to Page 2</a>
  </div>
  <div data-role="footer">
    <h4>Footer of Main Page</h4>
  </div>
</div>
```

6. Finally, define the `#page2` page with a link to go back to the `#main` page:

```
<div id="page2" data-role="page" data-title="Custom Transition
using JS">
  <div data-role="header">
    <h1>Header of Page 2</h1>
  </div>
  <div data-role="content">
    <a href="#" data-role="button" data-rel="back"
        data-theme="b">Go Back</a>
  </div>
  <div data-role="footer">
```

```
        <h4>Footer of Page 2</h4>
    </div>
</div>
```

## How it works...

Create the `customtransition.js` file and define the `mycustomTransition` function. Here, first create a jQuery `$.Deferred` object. Then, write your custom transition code. Set the initial width and height of the `to` page (or the target page) to zero. Make it visible by calling the `show()` function. Next, define the animation for the `to` and `from` pages (the from page is the current page).

 The jQuery `$.Deferred` object can be used to register and invoke multiple synchronous or asynchronous callbacks, and then return their results. You can read more about this feature and the methods it provides at `http://api.jquery.com/category/deferred-object/`.

Call the `animate()` function and set options such as the width, height, opacity, duration of the animation, and animation curve, as shown in the code listing. Set the values, so that the from page is animated in such a way that its width and opacity become zero over the duration specified. This will slowly hide the page while sliding it to the left. Similarly, animate the to page such that in the given duration, width, height, and opacity reach 100 percent from 0. The to page fades in from the left to occupy the full screen. Now, both these animations happen together, giving a nice end result to the transition.

Once the transition is complete, the code must ensure that the right page is set as the active page. You can copy this code snippet and the other default actions that are required by the framework directly from the standard template, which is already defined in the `jquery.mobile.js` file. Now, once the transition is completed, invoke the `deferred.resolve()` function. Also return the promise of the deferred object from the transition handler.

Finally, you should register the custom transition handler with the framework using the `slidefade` name. This will ensure that when you specify the `slidefade` transition name in the `data-transition` attribute, the correct transition is picked and used from the `$.mobile.transitionHandlers` directory.

Create `main.html` and include the `customtransition.js` file in the `<head>` section. Define the `#main` page with a link to open #page2 using the `data-transition="slidefade"` attribute, as shown in the code. Also define #page2 with a link to go back to the #main page. You don't have to set the transition in #page2 as JavaScript already takes care of the reverse animation. Launch your app and when you navigate between the pages, you will see the new page slide in while the current page fades out, giving you the custom slide and fade transition. On second thoughts, probably "slide and shrink" would be a better name for this transition.

## There's more...

If you have defined a custom transition in your app and used it for most of your page navigations, then you can directly set this custom transition as the default transition to be used for all your pages. This way, the `data-transition` attribute need not be specified with every link. This is specified in the `customtransition.js` file. Add the line after registering your custom transition handler (at the end of the file), as follows:

```
$.mobile.defaultTransitionHandler = myCustomTransition;
```

In the preceding code snippet, `myCustomTransition` is the newly-defined transition handler. Now, all the pages would use the `slidefade` transition. But this does not affect the `Dialog` transitions, which use the pop transition by default.

### JavaScript transitions compared to CSS3 transitions

Use CSS3 transitions over JS transitions in spite of the fact that you might run into vendor prefixes and incompatible browsers. With CSS3 transitions, the code required is lesser and it is much easier to develop and maintain it. Also you will not have to program the entire logic of the animation from scratch. With future versions of jQuery Mobile, the page transition framework or the logic might change, and this will break your custom JS transition.

Whereas, with CSS3, the beauty lies in the fact that your apps are progressively enhanced and fall back to basic functionality on lack of CSS3 support. As browsers improve and get upgraded, the vendor prefixes will ensure that your code works better without you modifying a single line of code. When the vendor prefixes go away, the standard attribute will get picked and everything will continue to work just fine. So use JS transitions only when you want to do more complex stuff and when CSS3 transitions would not fully support your requirement.

## See also

 ▸   The *Using CSS to create a bouncing page transition* recipe

 ▸   The *Configuring your default transitions* recipe in *Chapter 7, Configurations*

# Using data-url to handle the login page navigation

When you write a login page in your app, once the user enters valid credentials, you will want to redirect the user to a different page or to a different folder on success. This recipe shows you how to redirect the user to a different page during a login page navigation scenario, by using the `data-url` attribute.

## Getting ready

Copy the full code of this recipe from the `code/02/data-url` sources folder. You can launch this code using the URL `http://localhost:8080/02/data-url/login/main.html`.

## How to do it...

The steps to be followed are:

1. Create two folders called `login` and `records`. The `login` folder will contain `main.html`, and the `records` folder will contain the `index.html` and `data.html` files.

2. In the `login` folder, create `main.html` as a multi-page document. Here, first add the `#main` page as shown in the following code snippet. Also add a link to open the `#login` page.

```
<div data-role="page" id="main">
  <div data-role="header">
    <h1>Header of Main Page</h1>
  </div>
  <div data-role="content">
    <p>Page: login/main.html #main</p>
    <p><a href="#login" data-role="button">
      Login to Records folder</a></p>
  </div>
</div>
```

3. Next, create the `#login` page in `main.html` with a link to open the `index.html` file. Specify the `data-url` attribute pointing to the `records` folder (for page redirection), as shown in the following code snippet:

```
<div data-role="page" id="login"
    data-url="http://localhost:8080/02/data-url/records/"
    data-title="data-url main# Login Page">
  <div data-role="header">
    <h1>Header of Login Page</h1>
  </div>
  <div data-role="content">
    <p>Page: login/main.html #login</p>
    <p><a href="index.html" data-role="button">
      Go to Index Page</a></p>
  </div>
</div>
```

4. Now, create the `index.html` file in the `records` folder, as shown in the following code snippet. Add a link to open the `data.html` file here. Also set `data-url` for the page, as given in following the code:

```
<div data-role="page"
    data-url="http://localhost:8080/02/data-url/records/"
  <div data-role="header">
    <h1>Header of Index Page</h1>
  </div>
  <div data-role="content">
    <p>Page: records/index.html</p>
    <p><a href="data.html" data-role="button">
        Go to Data Page</a></p>
  </div>
</div>
```

5. Finally, create the `data.html` file in the `records` folder. Add a link to the `index.html` file here. The `data-url` attribute is not set here, and the navigation will still work since the page redirect done earlier was successful:

```
<div data-role="page">
  <div data-role="header">
    <h1>Header of Data Page</h1>
  </div>
  <div data-role="content">
    <p>Page: records/data.html</p>
    <p><a href="index.html" data-role="button"
        data-theme="b">Go to Index Page</a></p>
  </div>
</div>
```

## How it works...

Each of the pages in the previous code listed also displays the page URL of the current page just below the page header. Keep an eye on this text, and compare it with the address shown in the browser address bar as you navigate through the pages in this recipe.

First, create the `login` and `records` folders. In the `login` folder, create the `main.html` file, which is a multi-page document. Add the `#main` and `#login` pages to it. In the `#main` page, add a **Login to Records folder** button to open the `#login` page. Next, create the `#login` page, and specify its `data-url` attribute as `http://localhost:8080/02/data-url/records`. Add an **Open the Index Page** button to this page, to open the `index.html` file located in the `records` folder. Now, when you launch the app and click on the `login` button, the `#login` page is shown. But the browser address bar will show the URL as `http://localhost:8080/02/data-url/records/`, as shown in the following screenshot. Whereas the text above the **Go to Index Page** button still says that the current page location is `login/main.html #login`.

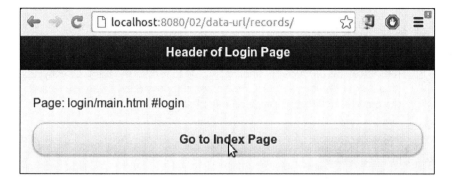

This redirect occurred because the `data-url` attribute was used in the `#login` page `div` container. The jQuery Mobile framework updates the address bar with the value of this attribute instead of the actual URL used to fetch the page.

This is a very handy feature that allows you to perform redirects in your app. This recipe does not show the username or password being validated by the server. But in real life, the user would enter the username/password credentials in the `#main` page and on a successful response from the server, you can redirect the user to restricted folders and webpages. Do not redirect any unauthenticated users, and they will not be able to access any pages in the `records` folder.

Next, add the `index.html` and `records.html` files as given in the code. Add links to these pages to enable navigation between them. Now, in the `#login` page, when you click on the **Open the Index Page** button, the `href` attribute only specifies `index.html` in the code. But since the redirect has already occurred at this point, the `index.html` file from the `records` folder is opened. The `index.html` file is now the landing page here and allows you to access other pages, such as `data.html`, which are all located in the `records` folder. An alternate approach to using `data-url` is that you could also use the `changePage()` method to redirect the user to the `index.html` page on a successful login.

In `index.html`, set the `data-url="http://localhost:8080/02/data-url/records"` attribute to support proper navigation when the user clicks on the back or forward buttons of the browser, If this is not done, navigation will break if you click on the back button in `index.html`. `data-url` helps you set the correct value on the history stack.

You can play with the back and forward buttons of your browser to see how the address bar is updated when compared to the text shown below the header as you navigate through the app.

**Using proper values for data-url**

You can specify any value for the `data-url` attribute, and the same will be shown in the address bar. But you should take care to see that it is a valid reference and the browser should be able to render the page. Specifying incorrect or non-existent URLs will break the navigation when you refresh the browser or when you click on the back/forward buttons.

## There's more...

jQuery Mobile sets and maintains the `data-url` attribute for all the pages in your app. Only the first page of your app does not require `data-url`, as it is always available in the DOM and can be referenced by its ID or URL. For all other pages, if the `data-url` attribute is not specified, it gets added with the value of the page ID by default. For external pages in the same domain, the relative path of the page is used as the value for `data-url`. For pages from different domains, the absolute path is used.

### Using data-url as the href link

If a page `div` tag contains both the page ID and `data-url`, you can either use `data-url` or the page ID in the value of the `href` attribute value and navigate to that page.

### Working with sub-hash urls

Some plugins dynamically break a page into separate pages. These pages have to be reached via deep links. These pages should have their `data-url` attribute specified in the following manner:

```
data-url="page.html&ui-page=subpage"
```

## See also

▸ The *Submitting a form using POST* recipe in *Chapter 6, Forms*

# Using History API to create a custom error pop up

The jQuery Mobile framework does not track dialogs in history. A dialog will thus not reappear when you click on the back button of your browser. Using a dialog for some features, for example to show an error pop up or an alert, has a minor issue that is very visible. When the dialog is opened from a page, the address bar will show the page URL suffixed with the `#&ui-state=dialog` text. This might not be desirable to all. This recipe shows you how to use the **History API** and customize a regular dialog to appear, such as a pop up without any changes to the URL, making use of the History API.

## Getting ready

Copy the full code of this recipe from the `code/02/history` sources folder. You can launch this code using the URL `http://localhost:8080/02/history/main.html`.

## How to do it...

The steps to be followed are:

1. Create `main.html`, and add a link to open the `errordialog.html` file as a dialog. Also add an `input` button, as shown in the following code snippet:

```
<div id="main" data-role="page">
  <div data-role="header">
    <h1>Header of Main</h1>
  </div>
  <div data-role="content">
    <a href="errordialog.html" data-theme="b"
      data-role="button" data-rel="dialog">
      Dialog
    </a>
    <input type="submit" value="Popup" id="linkButton"
      data-theme="b"/>
  </div>
  <div data-role="footer">
    <h4>Footer of Main</h4>
  </div>
</div>
```

2. Add the following script to the `<head>` section of `main.html` to open `errorpopup.html` as a dialog on the `click` event of the `input` button:

```
$("#main").live("pageinit", function(event) {
    $("#linkButton").bind( "click", function(event, ui) {
        $.mobile.changePage( "errorpopup.html", {
            changeHash: false,
            role: "dialog"
        });
    });
});
```

3. Create the `errordialog.html` file to show a custom error message. Also add a button to go back to `main.html`, as shown in the following code snippet:

```
<div id="errordialog" data-role="page">
  <div data-role="header">
    <h1>Error !</h1>
```

```
      </div>
      <div data-role="content">
        <p>Please correct and resubmit<p>
        <a href="main.html" data-role="button"
            data-theme="b">Close</a>
      </div>
    </div>
```

4. Create `errorpopup.html`, and add the following script inside the page container. This is a regular dialog but it has a custom styled header. Remove its entry from the history stack when you click on the anchor link:

```
<div id="errorpopup" data-role="page">
  <script>
    $("#errorpopup").live("pageinit", function(event) {
      $("a").click(function(event) {
        history.back();
      });
    });
  </script>
```

5. Then, add a custom header to the page and also add the link to go back to `main.html`:

```
<div class="ui-corner-top ui-overlay-shadow ui-header ui-bar-a"
  role="banner">
  <h1 class="ui-title" tabindex="0" role="heading"
    aria-level="1">
    Error !
  </h1>
</div>
<div data-role="content">
  <p>Please correct and resubmit<p>
  <a href="main.html" data-role="button" data-
    theme="b">
    Close
  </a>
</div>
</div>
```

## How it works...

Create `main.html` with the `#main` page having a link to open the `errordialog.html` page. Add an input submit button (`id="linkButton"`) as shown. Next, create the `errordialog.html` page with a button to go back to `main.html` as given in the code. When you launch the app and click on the first button (**Dialog**), the `errordialog.html` page is opened as a regular dialog with the pop transition. You will see the address bar change and show the `#&ui-state=dialog` text at the end of the URL, as shown in the following screenshot. Close and open this dialog a couple of times, and then if you press and hold the back button, the browser's history is displayed and you will see entries for the **Error Dialog** made in the history stack list:

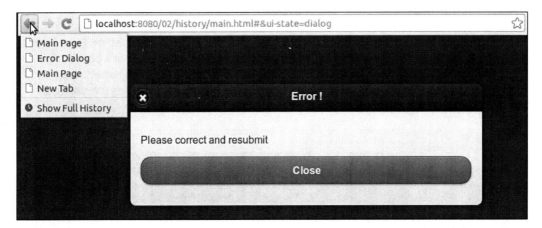

Now, in `main.html`, add the given script to the `pageinit` event handler that gets invoked when the app starts. Here, handle the `click` event of the `#linkButton` input button, and invoke the `changePage()` method in the callback with the options described in the following section, to open the `errorpopup.html` page. Set the `role` option as `dialog` to open the page as a dialog. Also, set the `changeHash` option to `false`, to indicate that the URL hash must not be changed in the address bar when the page is opened.

Next, create `errorpopup.html` and add the given script inside the page container. In this script, bind the `pageinit` event that gets invoked when the page is initialized. Here, add an event handler for the `click` event of the anchor button. In this callback, invoke the `history.back()` method to remove the history entry made on the history stack. You should add this script in the page container, so that it gets invoked every time the page gets loaded and initialized in the DOM.

Next, add a custom header to the error pop-up page container. This custom header is the same as the one used in the *Custom styling a dialog* recipe, earlier in this chapter. This dialog header is customized to make it look more like a pop up and to avoid the close button, which is present by default in the dialog header. Finally, in the page content, add a button to go back to `main.html`.

Now, launch the app again and click on the second button (**Popup**). The custom dialog created is shown as a pop up, as shown in the following screenshot:

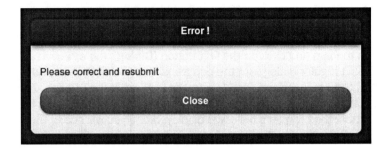

This pop up behaves differently from the default dialog. The **Close** icon is not present. You will note that the browser's address bar is not changed. You will also see that the **Error Popup** page title is not shown in the history list when you click and hold the browser's back button. Close the pop up and go back to main.html. You can click and hold the browser's back or front button to see that the pop up is never shown in the history list, whereas the dialog is listed, as shown in the following screenshot:

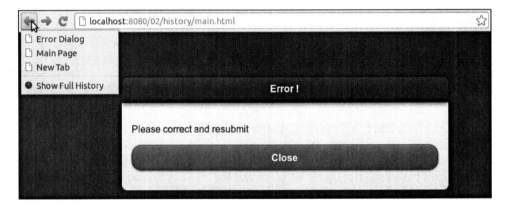

<h2>There's more...</h2>

The History API is very easy to use, and provides additional methods with which you can handle and manipulate the history stack in the browser. You can use the pushState() method to add a new entry into the history. With replaceState(), you can replace the history entry and the URL of an existing entry in the stack. This is a very handy method and lets you manipulate the history to suit your app's needs. As shown in the code listed in this recipe, history.back() takes you back one step in the history, whereas history. forward() takes you one step forward. To go to a specific entry in the history stack, you can also use the history.go() method, passing it a numerical value on how many entries you want to jump. So, history.go(-3) will take you three entries back, and a plus value will take you three entries forward.

## The popstate event on a dialog

Whenever you click on the back or forward buttons, a `popstate` event is thrown. This event is handled by the framework using the `onpopstate` handler, and the framework navigates to the next or previous page as desired. If `popstate` results in the target page being a dialog, the framework handles the event and does not navigate back to the dialog. Thus the dialog is not shown again when you click on the forward or back buttons in your browser.

## The Popup widget

At the time of writing this recipe, jQuery Mobile v1.1.1 was used. So the error pop-up dialog created in this recipe is not a true pop up, as it still displayed in a separate page and does not hover over the original page. The **Popup** widget will be available with jQuery Mobile v1.2.0. Then you can add a simple, true pop up using the `data-rel="popup"` attribute, as shown in the following code snippet:

```
<a href="#myPopup" data-rel="popup">Open Popup</a>
<div data-role="popup" id="myPopup">
  <p>A simple true popup!<p>
</div>
```

You can optionally set the pop up not to be tracked in history using the `data-history="false"` attribute. You can read more about using pop ups at http://jquerymobile.com/demos/1.2.0/docs/pages/popup/index.html.

## See also

▶ The *Custom styling a dialog* recipe

▶ The *Using page initialization events* recipe in *Chapter 8, Events*

▶ The *Using changePage() to change a page* recipe *Chapter 9, Methods and Utilities*

# 3
# Toolbars

In this chapter we will cover:

- ▶ Using fullscreen fixed toolbars
- ▶ Using persistent navbars in toolbars
- ▶ Customizing the header with multiple buttons
- ▶ Adding a customized round button to the header
- ▶ Adding an image to the header
- ▶ Adding a customized back button
- ▶ Adding a layout grid to the footer

## Introduction

The jQuery Mobile framework provides two toolbars, the **Header** and the **Footer**. The header is the first container in the page and the footer is the last. Header is used to specify the title of the application or the page, and can include the standard **navbar** for navigation. The footer is used for a variety of purposes. It can include standard buttons and form controls and can be customized to suit your needs. It can also contain a navbar for page navigation. The footer is also usually used to display the copyrights and license information.

## Using fullscreen fixed toolbars

**Fixed toolbars** remain in the same position on the screen when the page is scrolled. When the page content of your application occupies the entire viewport, the fixed toolbars will overlap the page content. You cannot toggle the visibility of the fixed toolbars here. To toggle the toolbar visibility, you can use the fixed toolbars in the **Fullscreen mode**. This recipe shows you how to create a simple **Photo Viewer** application that uses fullscreen toolbars.

## Getting ready

Copy the full code of this recipe from the `code/03/fullscreen-toolbars` sources folder. This code can be launched using the URL `http://localhost:8080/03/fullscreen-toolbars/main.html`.

## How to do it...

1. In `main.html` create the `#main` page and a `<img>` tag to display a scaled down image of the **Niagara Falls**, as shown in the following code:

```
<div id="main" data-role="page">
  <div data-role="header">
    <h1>Photo Gallery</h1>
  </div>
  <div data-role="content">
    <img src="../../resources/images/niagara.png" width="150"
height="100" />
    <br>The Niagara Falls, NY, US, 24/12/2011
    <br><a href="#photo" data-role="button" data-
inline="true">View full screen</a>
  </div>
  <div data-role="footer" data-position="fixed">
    Footer of Photo Gallery
  </div>
</div>
```

2. Create the `#photo` page to display the image in fullscreen mode:

```
<div id="photo" data-role="page" data-fullscreen="true" data-add-
back-btn="true">
  <div data-role="header" data-position="fixed" >
    <h1>The Niagara Falls, NY, US</h1>
  </div>
  <div data-role="content">
    <img src="../../resources/images/niagara.png" width="100%"
height="100%" />
  </div>
  <div data-role="footer" data-position="fixed">
    Date taken: 24/12/2011
  </div>
</div>
```

# How it works...

In `main.html`, create the `#main` page to display the thumbnail image of the **Niagara Falls** using the `<img>` tag with a small `width` and `height`. Add a link to open the `#photo` page. When you first launch the application, the following screen is displayed with a smaller sized image of the snap:

Next create the `#photo` page, with fixed toolbars using the `data-fixed="true"` attribute. Set the page container to occupy the full screen using the `data-fullscreen="true"` attribute. Add the image using the `<img>` tag with `100%` width and `height`.

Now when you click on the **View full screen** button in #main, the #photo page is opened with the fullscreen image of the **Niagara Falls**. The fixed toolbars can also be seen. When you tap the screen now, the visibility of the toolbars is toggled. The fullscreen display looks like the following screenshot:

## There's more...

The fullscreen toolbars will overlap over the page content by default. You will not be able to access any content that is shown below the toolbar. You will have to tap the screen, toggle the toolbar visibility, and then access the page content. This could become a usability issue for the users of your application. So use this feature judiciously.

 Fullscreen toolbars are ideal in pages where you have to display full screen content such as photos, previews, slideshows, or videos.

## The position—fixed CSS property

Browsers have to support the `position:fixed` CSS property for the proper dynamic positioning of the fixed toolbars. Most modern browsers support this property. For older browsers, this support might not be there and the framework gracefully degrades and falls back to using regular static toolbars. In these older platforms, you can use **Polyfills** to support fixed toolbars and a detailed note on this is available at `http://jquerymobile.com//test/docs/toolbars/bars-fixed.html`.

## Toggling the fixed toolbar visibility

As already mentioned in this recipe, you can tap the screen to toggle the visibility of the fixed toolbars. This change on tap behavior can be controlled by using the `tapToggle` property (by default `true`) of the **fixedtoolbar plugin**. To enable or disable tapping, use the following code snippet, that uses a jQuery selector to find the toolbar:

```
// to disable tap to toggle toolbars use
$("[data-position='fixed']").fixedtoolbar({ tapToggle: false });

// to enable tap to toggle toolbars use
$("[data-position='fixed']").fixedtoolbar({ tapToggle: true });
```

## Toggling the fixed toolbar visibility using JavaScript

You can also use JavaScript to toggle the fixed toolbars' visibility by calling the `show` or `hide` methods on the `fixedtoolbar` plugin as shown in the following code. The code snippet uses the jQuery selector to find the toolbar.

```
$("[data-position='fixed']").fixedtoolbar('show');
// or
$("[data-position='fixed']").fixedtoolbar('hide');
```

## See also

▸  The *Using persistent navbars in toolbars* recipe

# Using persistent navbars in toolbars

The **Navbar widget** can be used to provide navigation links in your application. A **Persistent Navbar** stays fixed in the same position in your application, like a fixed tab bar, as you navigate between pages. This recipe shows you how to use persistent navbars in the toolbars to create a simple **TV Menu UI**.

## Getting ready

Copy the full code of this recipe from the `code/03/persistent-navbar` sources folder. This code can be launched using the URL `http://localhost:8080/03/persistent-navbar/main.html`.

## How to do it...

1. In `main.html` create a simple **TV Menu UI** with three pages in it, "#movies", "#songs", and "#serials". Add the #movies page with its header and footer having navbars as shown in the following code:

```
<div id="movies" data-role="page" >
  <div data-role="header" data-id="persistheader"
    data-position="fixed">
    <h1>Movies</h1>
    <div data-role="navbar">
      <ul>
        <li><a href="#" data-role="button"
            class="ui-btn-active ui-state-persist">
            Movies</a></li>
        <li><a href="#songs" data-role="button">Songs</a></li>
        <li><a href="#serials" data-role="button">Serials</a></li>
      </ul>
    </div>
  </div>
  <div data-role="content">
    <h3>This is the Movies Page</h3>
  </div>
  <div data-role="footer" data-id="persistfooter"
    data-position="fixed" >
    <div data-role="navbar">
      <ul>
        <li><a href="#" data-role="button">New</a></li>
        <li><a href="#" data-role="button">Popular</a></li>
        <li><a href="#" data-role="button">Classics</a></li>
      </ul>
    </div>
  </div>
</div>
```

2. Next add the `#songs` page with similar content, as shown in the following code:

```
<div id="songs" data-role="page" >
  <div data-role="header" data-id="persistheader" data-
position="fixed">
    <h1>Songs</h1>
    <div data-role="navbar">
      <ul>
        <li><a href="#movies" data-role="button">Movies</a></li>
        <li><a href="#" data-role="button"
            class="ui-btn-active ui-state-persist">
            Songs</a></li>
        <li><a href="#serials" data-role="button">Serials</a></li>
      </ul>
    </div>
  </div>
  <div data-role="content">
    <h3>This is the Songs Page</h3>
  </div>
  <div data-role="header" data-id="persistheader"
    data-position="fixed">
    <div data-role="navbar">
      <ul>
        <li><a href="#" data-role="button">New</a></li>
        <li><a href="#" data-role="button">Popular</a></li>
        <li><a href="#" data-role="button">Classics</a></li>
      </ul>
    </div>
  </div>
</div>
```

3. Finally, add the `#serials` page as in the following code:

```
<div id="serials" data-role="page" >
  <div data-role="header" data-id="persistheader"
    data-position="fixed">
    <h1>Serials</h1>
    <div data-role="navbar">
      <ul>
        <li><a href="#movies" data-role="button">Movies</a></li>
        <li><a href="#songs" data-role="button">Songs</a></li>
        <li><a href="# " data-role="button"
            class="ui-btn-active ui-state-persist">
            Serials</a></li>
      </ul>
    </div>
  </div>
</div>
```

```
<div data-role="content">
  <h3>This is the Serials Page</h3>
</div>
<div data-role="header" data-id="persistheader"
  data-position="fixed">
  <div data-role="navbar">
    <ul>
      <li><a href="#" data-role="button">New</a></li>
      <li><a href="#" data-role="button">Popular</a></li>
      <li><a href="#" data-role="button">Classics</a></li>
    </ul>
  </div>
</div>
</div>
```

## How it works...

Create `main.html` and add three pages to it: `#movies`, `#songs`, and `#serials`. In `#main` page, add a fixed header by specifying `data-position="fixed"`. To persist this header across all the pages, set the attribute `data-id="persistheader"`. Now add a navbar with three links as shown in the previous code. The first link points to the same page and so use `#` for the `href` tag. Also add the attribute `class="ui-btn-active ui-state-persist` to indicate that this button should be in active state when you navigate into this page. Next add a footer to the page with a navbar having three links, **New**, **Popular**, and **Classics**, as shown in the previous code. Add the attributes `data-id="persistfooter"` and `data-position="fixed"` to indicate that this is a fixed footer and it is to be persisted across all the pages. You should use the same `data-id` value for the headers of all three pages. Similarly the same `data-id` should be used for the footers of the three pages. Using the same value will create a sticky `navbar`, which will stay put and not transition when the page transition occurs.

Next add the `#songs` page with similar content as the **Movies** page. Set the same `data-id` values to the header and footer as mentioned earlier. Now set the second button to active state in the header `navbar` by setting the attribute `class="ui-btn-active ui-state-persist"` to it. Finally, add the "`#serials`" page with fixed persistent header and footer as in the earlier pages. Here set the third button in the header `navbar` as active. When you launch the application, you can navigate to the three pages using the header navbar. All the three pages have the same header and footer.

You can randomly select different buttons in the footer for the three pages. When you navigate back and forth between the pages, you will see that the footer button state is persisted and remembered for the pages. The screen is displayed as shown in the following screenshot:

 The persistent navbar is very handy in menu driven applications, where it is often used to provide navigation between the pages.

## There's more...

You can set icons to the navbar buttons by adding the `data-icon` attribute. The icon position can be set to `top`, `bottom`, `right`, or `left` using the `data-iconpos` attribute as shown in the following code:

```
<a href="#" data-role="button" data-icon="home" data-
iconpos="right">Home</a>
```

### 3D page transitions with persistent fixed toolbars

If you use persistent fixed toolbars with pages that have 3D page transitions, you could run into positioning issues. The performance could also be slow. So it is better that you convert these pages to use 2D animations, such as `slide`, `slidup`, `slidedown`, `fade`, or `none`.

## See also

▸ The *Using fullscreen fixed toolbars* recipe

# Customizing the header with multiple buttons

When you add buttons to the page header, they line up to the left side of the header and only one button can be positioned to the right side by default. This recipe shows you how to add four buttons to the header, with two of them positioned to the right-hand side.

## Getting ready

Copy the full code of this recipe from the `code/03/multiple-header-buttons` sources folder. This code can be launched using the URL `http://localhost:8080/03/multiple-header-buttons/main.html`.

## How to do it...

1. Create a new stylesheet called `jqm.css` and define two new custom styles as given in the following code:

```css
.ui-btn-nexttoleft {
  position: absolute;
  left: 80px;
  top: .4em;
}
.ui-btn-nexttoright {
  position: absolute;
  right: 80px;
  top: .4em;
}
```

2. Include the previous stylesheet in the `<head>` tag of `main.html` as shown in the following code:

```html
<link rel="stylesheet" href="http://code.jquery.com/mobile/1.1.1/jquery.mobile-1.1.1.min.css" />
<link rel="stylesheet" href="jqm.css" />
<script src="http://code.jquery.com/jquery-1.7.1.min.js"></script>
<script src="http://code.jquery.com/mobile/1.1.1/jquery.mobile-1.1.1.min.js"></script>
```

3. Now add four buttons to the page header using the default styles provided by the jQuery Mobile framework and also use your custom styles, as shown in the following code:

```html
<div id="main" data-role="page">
  <div data-role="header">
```

```
    <a href="#" data-role="button" data-theme="c"
        class="ui-btn-left">
        Button1</a>
    <a href="#" data-role="button" data-theme="c"
        class="ui-btn-nexttoleft">
        Button2</a>
    <h1>Custom Header</h1>
    <a href="#" data-role="button" data-theme="c"
        class="ui-btn-nexttoright">
        Button3</a>
    <a href="#" data-role="button" data-theme="c"
        class="ui-btn-right">
        Button4</a>
</div>
<div data-role="content">
    This page has a custom styled Header with multiple buttons
</div>
</div>
```

## How it works...

Create the `jqm.css` stylesheet and define two new classes, `.ui-btn-nexttoleft` and `.ui-btn-nexttoright`, to specify the absolute positions that will be used by the buttons. Create `main.html` and include the link to the previous stylesheet after including the link to the `jquery.mobile.css` file as shown in the previous code.

Next add a header with `<h1>` text in the middle of the header and two anchor buttons on both its sides. Add the attribute `class="ui-btn-left"` to the first button to make it appear in the left-hand corner. Add the attribute `class="ui-btn-nexttoleft"` to the second button. Similarly, add the attribute `class="ui-btn-nexttoright"` to the third button and finally add `class="ui-btn-right"` to the fourth button, which will appear in the right-hand corner. The second and third buttons use the custom classes that you have defined. Now when you launch the page, the buttons are positioned in the header as shown in the following screenshot:

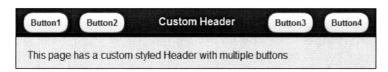

Take care while using absolute values in your stylesheet; you might have to modify the absolute positions if the text size or layout changes.

## There's more...

Using the attribute `data-role="header"` to the header `div` container causes the jQuery Mobile framework to enhance the header in the standard way. You can skip this attribute and customize the header in your own way by using the class `"ui-bar"` in your `div` container. You can also include widgets other than buttons in the header.

```
<div class="ui-bar">
```

## See also

▸ The *Custom styling a dialog* recipe in *Chapter 2, Pages and Dialogs*

▸ The *Adding a customized round button to the header* recipe

▸ The *Adding an image to the header* recipe

# Adding a customized round button to the header

The jQuery Mobile framework allows you to add custom controls to the header of a page. This recipe shows you how to add a custom round button to the header of your application.

## Getting ready

Copy the full code of this recipe from the `code/03/round-button-header` sources folder. This code can be launched using the URL `http://localhost:8080/03/round-button-header/main.html`.

## How to do it...

1. Create a new stylesheet called `jqm.css` and define a custom `roundbtn` class in it:

```
.roundbtn  {
   width: 40px;
   height: 40px;
   margin-top: 20px;
   -webkit-border-radius: 20px;
   -moz-border-radius: 20px;
   -ms-border-radius: 20px;
   -o-border-radius: 20px;
   border-radius: 20px;
}
```

2. Create `main.html` and include the previous stylesheet in the `<head>` tag:

```
<link rel="stylesheet" href="http://code.jquery.com/mobile/1.1.1/
jquery.mobile-1.1.1.min.css" />
<link rel="stylesheet" href="jqm.css" />
<script src="http://code.jquery.com/jquery-1.7.1.min.js"></script>
<script src="http://code.jquery.com/mobile/1.1.1/jquery.mobile-
1.1.1.min.js"></script>
```

3. Add an `About` button to the header of the `#main` page using the newly defined `roundbtn` style, as shown in the following code:

```
<div id="main" data-role="page" >
  <div data-role="header" style="height: 50px" >
    <h1 style="margin: 15px">Custom Round Button</h1>
    <a href="#about" data-rel="dialog" data-role="button"
    class="roundbtn ui-btn ui-shadow ui-btn-up-c ui-btn-left">
      <br>About</a>
  </div>
  <div data-role="content">
    This page has a Round button in the Header
  </div>
</div>
```

4. Add the `#about` dialog as, in the following code:

```
<div id="about" data-role="page" >
  <div data-role="header" >
    <h1>About</h1>
  </div>
  <div data-role="content">
    Round Button Demo
  </div>
</div>
```

## How it works...

Create the `jqm.css` stylesheet and define a new class `roundbtn` with `width`, `height`, and `border-radius` properties as shown in the previous code. To create a round button set the `border-radius` property value to exactly half the value of the `width` property. Finally, add the vendor specific properties for `border-radius` to ensure that the border radius works well on various browsers.

Create `main.html` and include the link to the above stylesheet after including the link to the `jquery.mobile.css` file as shown in the previous code. Next create the `#main` page and add a header with `<h1>` text to it. Set the `height` of the header to `50px` using the style attribute to ensure the round button with `40px height` (as specified in the CSS) fits properly in the header. Next add an anchor link in the header with attributes `data-role="button"` and `data-rel="dialog"` to open the `"#about"` page as a dialog. Add the `roundbtn` style to this button using the `class` attribute. Also add the other classes that are added by the framework while enhancing an anchor link to a button. You can obtain this list of classes by inspecting the anchor element using your browser's developer tools. You have to add these classes manually to ensure that the round button gets the proper style as it has been customized.

Finally, define the `#about` page as given in the previous code. When you launch the application, a round button is now displayed in the header as shown in the following screenshot. Clicking on the round button will open the `#about` dialog.

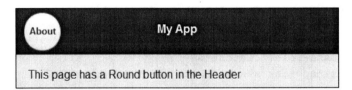

## There's more...

Your browser should support the `border-radius` or the corresponding vendor specific prefix `border-radius` property in the CSS. If it does not, you will see a rectangular button instead of a round button.

## See also

- ▶ The *Using CSS to create a bouncing page transition* recipe in *Chapter 2, Pages and Dialogs*, for a note on vendor prefixes
- ▶ The *Custom styling a dialog* recipe in *Chapter 2, Pages and Dialogs*
- ▶ The *Customizing the header with multiple buttons* recipe
- ▶ The *Adding an image to the header* recipe

# Adding an image to the header

The header of a jQuery Mobile page usually contains the text which is to be used as the page header. You can also add other content and markup to the header. This recipe shows you how to add an image to the header of your application.

## Getting ready

Copy the full code of this recipe from the `code/03/header-image` sources folder. This code can be launched using the URL `http://localhost:8080/03/header-image/main.html`.

## How to do it...

In this recipe, the image `ABC.png` is used as the logo image for a a fictitious company, ABC Inc.

1. Create `main.html` and add the above image to its header. The image is linked to a dialog as shown in the following code:

```
<div id="main" data-role="page" data-theme="a">
  <div data-role="header" data-theme="a">
    <h1>ABC Company</h1>
    <a href="#about" data-rel="dialog" data-theme="a" class="ui-
btn ui-shadow ui-btn-up-a">
      <img src="../../resources/images/ABC.png" width="24"
height="24" alt="About ABC" /></a>
  </div>
  <div data-role="content">
    This page has an Image in the Header
  </div>
</div>
```

2. Add the `#about` dialog as shown in the following code:

```
<div id="about" data-role="page" >
  <div data-role="header" >
    <h1>About ABC</h1>
  </div>
  <div data-role="content">
    <img src="../../resources/images/ABC.png" width="24"
height="24" alt="ABC" style="margin-right:5px" />ABC Company Inc.
  </div>
</div>
```

## How it works...

In `main.html`, create a `#main` page and add a header with `<h1>` text to it. Now add an anchor link in the header to open the `#about` page as a dialog by using the attribute `data-rel="dialog"`. Specify a custom style to the anchor link using the attribute `class="ui-btn ui-shadow ui-btn-up-a"`. Do not add `data-role="button"` as the framework would then enhance this link as a button. Next add an `<img>` element pointing to the `ABC.png` image as shown in the previous code. Scale this image to a suitable size by using the `width` and `height` attributes. Finally, define the `#about` page as given in the code. When you launch the application, the header of the `#main` page displays the `ABC.png` image on the left corner as shown in the following screenshot. Clicking on this image opens the `#about` dialog page.

## There's more...

You can also use native styling for the image and avoid any custom styles being set on the anchor element to display only the image. It is done by using the attribute `data-role="none"` as in the following code:

```
<a href="#about" data-role="none" data-rel="dialog" data-theme="a">
  <img src="../../resources/images/ABC.png" widht="24" height="24"
      alt="About ABC" />
</a>
```

## See also

- ▶ The *Customizing the header with multiple buttons* recipe
- ▶ The *Adding a customized round button to the header* recipe

# Adding a customized back button

When a new page is opened in your application, the jQuery Mobile framework provides an option to add a **Back** button to the header of the page to help you navigate back to the previous page. The **Back** button is not visible by default. This recipe shows you how to dynamically add and customize the **Back** button in your application using JavaScript.

## Getting ready

Copy the full code of this recipe from the `code/03/custom-back-button` sources folder. This code can be launched using the URL `http://localhost:8080/03/custom-back-button/main.html`.

## How to do it...

1. Create `main.html` and add two anchor links in it. The first link opens a page with a **Back** button in its header and the second link opens a page without the **Back** button.

2. Also add a submit button to the page as shown in the following code:

```
<div id="main" data-role="page">
  <div data-role="header">
    <h1>Header of Main Page</h1>
  </div>
  <div data-role="content">
    <a href="page1.html" data-role="button">Page with Header Back
Button</a>
    <a href="page2.html" data-role="button">Page without Header
Back Button</a>
    <input type="submit" id="addbackbtns" value="Click to Add and
Customize the Back Button" data-inline="true" data-role="button">
  </div>
</div>
```

3. Add the following script to the `<head>` section of the page and bind it to the `click` event of the submit button:

```
$("#main").live("pageinit", function(event) {
  $("#addbackbtns").bind("click", function(event, ui) {
    $.mobile.page.prototype.options.addBackBtn = true;
    $.mobile.page.prototype.options.backBtnText = "Prev";
    $.mobile.page.prototype.options.backBtnTheme = "e";
  });});
```

4. Create `page1.html` with a **Back** button in its page header as shown in the following code:

```
<div id="page1" data-role="page" data-add-back-btn="true">
  <div data-role="header">
    <h1>Header with Back Button</h1>
  </div>
  <div data-role="content">
    This page has a Header with the Default Back Button
  </div>
</div>
```

5. Create `page2.html`, which does not have the **Back** button by default:

```
<div id="page2" data-role="page">
  <div data-role="header">
    <h1>Header without Back Button</h1>
  </div>
  <div data-role="content">
    This page has a Header without any buttons
    <a href="main.html" data-rel="back" data-direction="reverse"
data-role="button">Back</a>
  </div>
</div>
```

## How it works...

Create `main.html` and add two anchor links to it, which open `page1.html` and `page2.html` respectively. Create `page1.html` and add the attribute `data-add-back-btn="true"` to the page `div` container as shown in the previous code. Now when you click on the first button in `main.html`, it opens `page1.html` and you can see the **Back** button displayed in the page header. Click on it to go back to `main.html`.

Create `page2.html` and do not add the `data-add-back-btn` attribute to it. Now when you click on the second button in `main.html`, it opens `page2.html` and there is no **Back** button in the header. You can add an anchor link to the page content to navigate back to `main.html`.

Now in `main.html`, add a submit button with `id="addbackbtns"` and text **Click to Add and Customize Back Button**. In the `pageinit` event handler, which gets invoked after the page has initialized at startup, bind the `click` event of the submit button to a callback function. Here set the option `addBackBtn` of the `$.mobile.page.prototype` object to `true` as shown in the previous code. This will automatically enable the **Back** button on all the pages in your application. Also you can customize the **Back** button further by setting its text and theme using the `backBtnText` and `backBtnTheme` options as shown in the previous code.

Now you can visit both the pages from `main.html` and see that the back buttons are now available and have the same style. Both have yellow color and their text is set to **Prev**, as shown in the following screenshot:

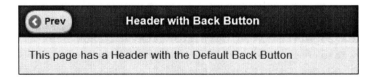

## There's more...

As mentioned in the recipe, you can set the following property and globally enable the **Back** button for all the pages in your application:

```
$.mobile.page.prototype.options.addBackBtn = true;
```

When the **Back** button is enabled by default on all the pages, you can set it off for a particular page by adding the attribute `data-add-back-btn="false"` to its page `div` container:

```
<div id="page3" data-role="page" data-add-back-btn="false">
```

## See also

▶ The *Customizing the header with multiple buttons* recipe

▶ The *Adding a customized round button to the header* recipe

# Adding a layout grid to the footer

A **Layout Grid** allows you to place controls in columns next to each other. This recipe shows you how to add multiple form controls to the page footer using a layout grid.

## Getting ready

Copy the full code of this recipe from the `code/03/footer-layoutgrid` sources folder. This code can be launched using the URL `http://localhost:8080/03/footer-layoutgrid/main.html`.

## How to do it...

1. Create `main.html` and add a footer to its page. Add a layout grid to the page footer and add form controls to this layout grid, as shown in the following code:

```
<div data-role="footer" data-position="fixed" class="ui-bar">
  <fieldset class="ui-grid-a">
    <div class="ui-block-a" data-role="fieldcontain">
      <label for="syncslider">Sync (mins):</label>
      <input type="range" name="syncslider" id="syncslider"
value="5" min="1" max="60"/>
    </div>
    <div class="ui-block-b">
      <div data-role="fieldcontain">
        <fieldset data-role="controlgroup" data-type="horizontal">
          <legend>Share :</legend>
```

```
            <input type="radio" name="sharefile" id="shareFileNone"
    value="sharefile-1" checked="checked" data-theme="c"/>
            <label for="shareFileNone">None</label>
            <input type="radio" name="sharefile"
    id="shareFileFriends" value="sharefile-2" data-theme="c"/>
            <label for="shareFileFriends">Friends</label>
            <input type="radio" name="sharefile"
    id="shareFilePublic" value="sharefile-3" data-theme="c"/>
            <label for="shareFilePublic">Public</label>
          </fieldset>
        </div>
      </div>
    </fieldset>
  </div>
```

## How it works...

Create `main.html` and add a footer to it. Style the footer by specifying the attribute `class="ui-bar"`. This creates a horizontal bar in which you can add your custom controls. Now add a two column layout grid to the footer by creating a `fieldset` element with the attribute `class="ui-grid-a"`.

Add a `div` container with the attributes `data-role="fieldcontain"` to the first column of the layout grid. You must add the attribute `class="ui-block-a"`, to indicate that this `div` container is placed in the first column of the grid. Now add a Slider widget to this column by adding an `input` element with `type="range"`.

Similarly add a `div` container with the attributes `data-role="fieldcontain"` and `class="ui-block-b"`, to indicate that this `div` container should be placed in the second column of the layout grid. Add three radio buttons to this column in a single group by adding the attribute `data-role="controlgroup"`. Also add the attribute `data-type="horizontal"` to place the radio controls in a horizontal row (by default they are laid out vertically below each other).

The footer now looks as shown in the following image:

## There's more...

Up to five columns can be specified in a layout grid by styling the grid using the corresponding class, as shown in the following code:

- ▸ Two column grid – use the `ui-grid-a` class
- ▸ Three column grid – use the `ui-grid-b` class
- ▸ Four column grid – use the `ui-grid-c` class
- ▸ Five column grid – use the `ui-grid-d` class

 Given the lack of real estate in mobile devices, use the four or five column layout grids selectively. The UI might look cramped and there may not be enough space to fill in your form controls.

### Size of the controls in a layout grid

Adding a form control or a widget to a layout grid column will cause the control to occupy the entire width of the column. If you do not want this behavior, you will have to modify the style of your control.

 The Button and Select form controls support the `data-inline="true"` attribute. You can set this attribute to the controls and they will retain their actual compact sizes, and they will not resize to occupy the entire width of the column.

### Breaking to the next row in a layout grid

If your layout grid has multiple rows, you have to add the various controls in their own div containers, starting with `class="ui-block-a"` for the first column and moving to `class="ui-block-e"` for the fifth column. Adding a sixth `ui-block` or using a `div` container with `class="ui-block-a"` at any point of time in between will cause the columns to wrap and the newly added `div` container now moves to the next row.

 Start a row with the class `ui-block-a` and move towards `ui-block-e` in a proper sequence.

Do not repeat the same ui-blocks in the same row.

## See also

- ▸ The *Using persistent navbars in toolbars* recipe
- ▸ The *Creating a custom layout grid* recipe in *Chapter 4, Buttons and Content Formatting*

# 4
# Buttons and Content Formatting

In this chapter we will cover:

- ▶ Scripting a dynamically added button
- ▶ Using a custom icon in a button
- ▶ Adding a custom icon sprite
- ▶ Replacing the default icon sprite
- ▶ Using alternate icons in a collapsible
- ▶ Creating a nested accordion
- ▶ Creating a custom layout grid
- ▶ Using XML content
- ▶ Using JSON content

## Introduction

In a jQuery Mobile app, you can add buttons, form controls, and lists as the page content of your app. The page content is a `div` container with the attribute `data-role="content"`. You can display data and format it using the ready styles and layouts that are provided by the framework. You can group and display data in **collapsible blocks** and in **collapsible sets** or **accordions**. You can show data in multiple columns using the **Layout Grid**. You can also use the table and other HTML elements in your app.

# Scripting a dynamically added button

Buttons are standard HTML form elements that are enhanced by the **button plugin** in the jQuery Mobile framework to make them finger friendly and also to look good in a wide variety of mobile devices. You can add buttons to your app by using the `<button>` tag or the `<input>` tag. You can also style the anchor element as a button by adding the `data-role="button"` attribute to it. This recipe shows you how to dynamically add a button to a page using JavaScript and bind an action to this newly added button.

## Getting ready

Copy the full code of this recipe from the `code/04/dynamic-button` sources folder. You can launch this code using the URL `http://localhost:8080/04/dynamic-button/main.html`.

## How to do it...

In `main.html`, create the `#main` page and add a button to it. When you click on this button, use JavaScript and create a second button and also assign an action to it:

1. Create the `#main` page in `main.html` and add the following code content to it:

   ```
   <div data-role="content">
     <input type="submit" id="addContentBtn" data-inline="true"
       value="Click to add new button"><br>
     <div id="newcontent"></div>
   </div>
   ```

2. Add the following script to handle the `click` event of the button. In the callback function, create the new button and also assign an action to it.

   ```
   $("#main").live("pageinit", function(event) {
     $("#addContentBtn").bind("click", function(event, ui) {
       var str="<a href='#page2' data-role='button' data-
   inline='true'>"
             +"Disable 1st button and Go to Page 2</a>";
       $("#newcontent").html(str).trigger("create")
           .bind("click", function(event, ui) {
         $("#addContentBtn").button("disable");
       });
     });
   });
   ```

3. Add `#page2` as given in the following code. This is a multi-page document. This page is opened when you click the dynamically added button.

   ```
   <div id="page2" data-role="page" data-add-back-btn="true">
     <div data-role="header">
   ```

```
        <h1>Page2 Header</h1>
    </div>
    <div data-role="content">
        <h3>This is Page 2</h3>
    </div>
</div>
```

## How it works...

Create `main.html` with a page `#main` and add a button with `id="addContentBtn"` to the page content. Also add an empty `div` container, `id="newcontent"` to the page. When you load this page, you will see only one button with text **Click to add new button** displayed on the screen.

Next add the given script. Add a `pageinit` event handler that gets invoked after the page has been initialized. Here, bind the `click` event of the button to a callback function. In the callback function, add an anchor link with `data-role="button"` to the empty `"#newcontent"` div. Since the page is already initialized, you have to explicitly call the `create` method to trigger the framework to revisit this link and enhance it to a button. Now when you click on the first button, you will see that the second button, **Disable 1st button and Go to Page 2**, is created and displayed. In the script also add code to bind the `click` event of the new button to a callback function. Here, invoke the `disable` method on the first button.

Finally create a new page with `id="page2"` that will get opened when you click on the new button. Add the `data-add-back-btn="true"` to #page2 to provide a **Back** button to help navigate back to the #main page. Now when you click on the second button, the dynamically added script gets invoked and the first button is disabled and the page navigates to open `page2`. You can click on the **Back** button in `page2` and go back to the #main page. You will see that the first button is now disabled by the dynamic script that you had added.

## There's more...

The button plugin also provides methods to `enable`, `disable`, and `refresh` the button:

```
$(buttonselector).button("enable");
$(buttonselector).button("disable");
$(buttonselector).button("refresh");
```

### Button options

Buttons provide numerous markup options using the `data-` attributes. They are **corners** (`data-corners`), **icon** (`data-icon`), **iconpos** (`data-iconpos`), **shadow** (`data-shadow`), **iconshadow** (`data-iconshadow`), **inline** (`data-inline`), and **theme** (`data-theme`).

You can call the `buttonMarkup` method on an anchor link to enhance it as a button. The following line of code takes a native anchor link and adds the button role to it and also sets the `data-icon="alert"` and `data-inline="true"` attributes:

```
$("a").buttonMarkup({ icon: "alert", inline: "true"});
```

# Using a custom icon in a button

Buttons can contain text, icons, or both. The icon can be positioned in one of the four directions within a button. The jQuery Mobile framework provides a set of standard icons that you can use in your app. This recipe shows you how to add a custom icon to a button along with the standard icon provided by the framework.

## Getting ready

Copy the full code of this recipe from the `code/04/custom-icon` sources folder. You can launch this code using the URL `http://localhost:8080/04/custom-icon/main.html`.

## How to do it...

In this recipe, the following image, `square.png` is used for the custom icon image:

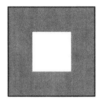

1. Create a new style sheet `jqm-icon.css` and define the custom icon style as in the following code:

```
.ui-icon-square {
  background: #fff;
  background: rgba(0,0,0,.4);
  background-image: url("../../resources/images/square.png");
}
@media only screen and (-webkit-min-device-pixel-ratio: 1.5),
    only screen and (min--moz-device-pixel-ratio: 1.5),
    only screen and (min-resolution: 240dpi) {
```

```
    .ui-icon-square {
      background-image: url("../../resources/images/square-HD.png");
      background-size: 18px 18px;
    }
  }
```

2.  Include the CSS in the `<head>` section of `main.html`, as shown in the following code:

```
<link rel="stylesheet" href="http://code.jquery.com/mobile/1.1.1/
jquery.mobile-1.1.1.min.css" />
<link rel="stylesheet" href="jqm-icon.css" />
```

3.  Use the custom icon with a submit button and with the following different themes.
    Add the default `"home"` icon as well, for comparison.

```
<div data-role="content">
  <h3>Default Icon with text</h3>
  <input type="submit" data-inline="true" value="Home" data-
icon="home" data-theme="a"/>
  <h3>Custom Icon with text</h3>
  <input type="submit" data-inline="true" value="Square" data-
icon="square" data-theme="a"/>
  <h3>Default Icon without text</h3>
  <input type="submit" data-inline="true" data-iconpos="notext"
data-icon="home" data-theme="a"/>
  <h3>Custom Icon without text</h3>
  <input type="submit" data-inline="true" data-iconpos="notext"
data-icon="square" data-theme="a"/>
</div>
```

## How it works...

Create a `jqm-icon.css` stylesheet and add a new icon class in it, `ui-icon-square`.
Specify the `background-image` property and point it to the image file to be used. Specify
the `background` color for the icon and also specify the background color for the **icon
disc** with opacity as shown. Here, the prefix text **ui-icon** indicates to the button plugin that
this is a custom icon and this generates a `square` class. You can now use the `data-
icon="square"` attribute in a button and the framework will fetch and display the `square`
icon on the button.

Create `main.html`, add submit buttons using input tags, and set icons to these buttons using the `data-icon` attribute. First use the default `home` icon and then use the newly added custom `square` icon, with and then without text. For a detailed comparison you can add multiple buttons using the different theme swatches (`data-theme="a"` to `data-theme="e"`). The end result is as shown in the following image. The custom icon looks as good as the default one.

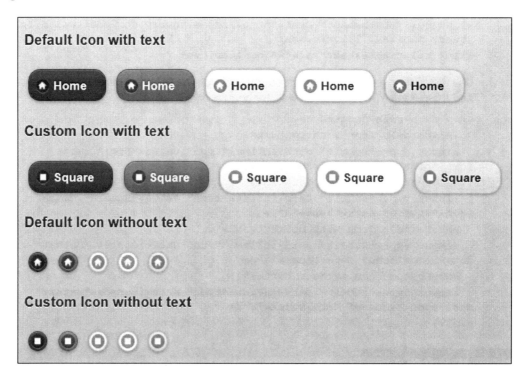

## There's more...

The icon `.ui-icon-square` defined in the CSS is of standard resolution. Most of the new devices support HD resolution today. So to make it work on HD resolutions, you can create a new high resolution image, `square-HD.png` of 36 x 36 pixels size. Use this image in a `@media` query as shown in the CSS and specify the target device resolutions that this high resolution icon should work on. For more details about the `@media` query, see `http://jquerymobile.com/demos/1.1.1/docs/buttons/buttons-icons.html`.

For the standard resolution custom icon, use images of 18 x 18 pixels size saved in a **PNG-8** format with alpha transparency. Set its alpha value to `0.4` and the background color to `#666`. Now your icons will look similar to the default icons provided by the framework.

## Using data-inline

By default, the button is stretched to fit the width of its container. You can specify the attribute `data-inline="true"` to show the button in its compact mode. You can also add multiple inline buttons next to each other in the same row.

## Using data-iconpos

A button can be associated with an icon image by using the `data-icon="home"` attribute. Here, `"home"` is the name of the icon being used. The `data-iconpos` attribute can be used to specify where the icon should be displayed in the button. The possible values are `top`, `bottom`, `left`, and `right`. Using the `data-iconpos="notext"` attribute hides the text completely and resizes the button to show only the icon.

## Using shadows and corners with buttons

Buttons use rounded corners by default and this can be controlled using the Boolean attribute `data-corners`. Shadows are also enabled by default for the button and its icon. This can be controlled by using the attributes `data-shadow` and `data-iconshadow`. The `data-corners`, `data-shadow`, and `data-iconshadow` attributes are all Boolean and take `true` or `false` values.

## See also

► The *Adding a custom icon sprite* recipe
► The *Replacing the default icon sprite* recipe

# Adding a custom icon sprite

The jQuery Mobile framework uses a default **icon sprite** and derives all the icons from it. This recipe shows you how to add a custom icon sprite, with the **divide** and **equals** icons, to the default standard icon set, together forming the keys of a calculator. The standard icon set already has the **plus**, **minus**, and **delete** (**multiply**) icons.

## Getting ready

Copy the full code of this recipe from the `code/04/add-icon-sprite` sources folder. You can launch this code using the URL `http://localhost:8080/04/add-icon-sprite/main.html`.

## How to do it...

In this recipe, the following image, `calc-sprite.png` provides the divide and equals icons:

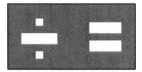

1. Create a new `jqm-sprite.css` stylesheet and define the classes `.ui-icon-divide` and `.ui-icon-equals` for the new icons derived from the custom icon sprite:

```css
.ui-icon-divide, .ui-icon-equals {
  background: #fff;
  background: rgba(0,0,0,.4);
  background-image: url("../../resources/images/calc-sprite.png");
  background-repeat: no-repeat;
  -moz-border-radius: 9px;
  -webkit-border-radius: 9px;
  -o-border-radius: 9px;
  border-radius: 9px;
}
@media only screen and (-webkit-min-device-pixel-ratio: 1.5),
    only screen and (min--moz-device-pixel-ratio: 1.5),
    only screen and (min-resolution: 240dpi) {
  .ui-icon-divide, .ui-icon-equals {
    background-image: url("../../resources/images/calc-sprite-
    HD.png");
    -moz-background-size: 36px 18px;
    -o-background-size: 36px 18px;
    -webkit-background-size: 36px 18px;
    background-size: 36px 18px;
  }
}
.ui-icon-divide { background-position: -0px 50%; }
.ui-icon-equals { background-position: -18px 50%; }
```

2. Include the CSS in the `<head>` section of `main.html`, as shown in the following code:

```html
<link rel="stylesheet" href="http://code.jquery.com/mobile/1.1.1/
jquery.mobile-1.1.1.min.css" />
<link rel="stylesheet" href="jqm-sprite.css" />
```

3. Use the new icons derived from the custom icon sprite along with the default icons as shown in the following code. Display the buttons with text first:

```
<div data-role="content">
  <h3>Default and Custom Icons with Text</h3>
  <input type="submit" data-inline="true" value="plus" data-
icon="plus" />
  <input type="submit" data-inline="true" value="minus" data-
icon="minus" />
  <input type="submit" data-inline="true" value="delete" data-
icon="delete" />
  <input type="submit" data-inline="true" value="divide" data-
icon="divide" />
  <input type="submit" data-inline="true" value="equals" data-
icon="equals" />
```

4. Then display the buttons without text for comparison:

```
  <h3>Default and Custom Icons without Text</h3>
  <input type="submit" data-inline="true" data-iconpos="notext"
data-icon="plus" />
  <input type="submit" data-inline="true" data-iconpos="notext"
data-icon="minus" />
  <input type="submit" data-inline="true" data-iconpos="notext"
data-icon="delete" />
  <input type="submit" data-inline="true" data-iconpos="notext"
data-icon="divide" />
  <input type="submit" data-inline="true" data-iconpos="notext"
data-icon="equals" />
</div>
```

## How it works...

Create a stylesheet `jqm-sprite.css` and add new icon classes `.ui-icon-divide` and `.ui-icon-equals` in it. Specify the `background-image` property and point it to the image file to be used as the icon sprite. Next specify the `background` colors for the icon and for the **icon disc** with opacity as shown. Also specify a `border-radius` of `9px` for the icons. The vendor prefixes are added to ensure this works on various browser platforms. Finally, define the position for each of the new icons within the icon sprite as shown in the last two lines of the CSS file. Add the `@media` query to specify the target device resolutions that the icons should work on; this is explained earlier in this chapter in the *Using a custom icon in a button* recipe.

Here, the prefix text **ui-icon** indicates to the button plugin that these are custom icons and this generates the corresponding classes without the prefix text. You can now use the new icons on buttons using the attributes `data-icon="divide"` or `data-icon="equals"`, and the framework will fetch and display the correct custom icon.

In `main.html`, create the buttons of a simple calculator by adding submit buttons using input tags. Set icons to these buttons using the `data-icon` attribute as shown. Display the buttons with and without text for comparison. Here, the **plus**, **minus**, and **delete** icons are from the default icon sprite. The custom icon sprite contributes the **divide** and **equals** icons. The screen is displayed as shown in the following image:

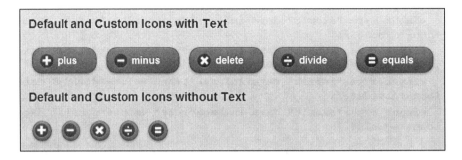

## There's more...

For creating an icon sprite, use a PNG image with a height of `18px`. The total width is a multiple of `18px` multiplied by the number of icons in the sprite. An alpha value of `0.4` and a background color of `#666` are used by the default icon sprite. Use the same in your custom sprite to maintain a consistent look with the default icons. Save the image in a **PNG-8** format with alpha transparency.

### Specifying an invalid icon name

In the code, if you specify an invalid icon name, say `data-icon="random"`, the framework prefixes this with the text `.ui-icon-`and tries to look the class up in the stylesheet. If this is not resolved to a valid icon, the framework now picks up the first icon from the default icon sprite and displays the same instead. The first icon in the default sprite is the `plus` icon and is used in all places where the icon name cannot be resolved.

## See also

▶ The *Replacing the default icon sprite* recipe

▶ The *Using a custom icon in a button* recipe

# Replacing the default icon sprite

This recipe shows you how to replace the default icon sprite provided with jQuery Mobile and use your own instead. The custom icon sprite used here contains icons which form the six faces of a dice.

## Getting ready

Copy the full code of this recipe from the `code/04/replace-icon-sprite` sources folder. You can launch this code using the URL `http://localhost:8080/04/replace-icon-sprite/main.html`.

## How to do it...

In this recipe, the following image, `dice.png` is an icon sprite with six icons for the six faces of a dice. This icon sprite is used to replace the default icon sprite.

1. Create a new stylesheet `jqm-sprite.css` and redefine the default `.ui-icon` class available with jQuery Mobile framework. Replace the default icon classes with new classes for the icons derived from the custom icon sprite as shown in the following code:

```
.ui-icon {
    background: #fff;
    background: rgba(0,0,0,.4);
    background-image: url("../../resources/images/dice.png");
    background-repeat: no-repeat;
    -moz-border-radius: 9px;
    -webkit-border-radius: 9px;
    -o-border-radius: 9px;
    border-radius: 9px;
}
@media only screen and (-webkit-min-device-pixel-ratio: 1.5),
    only screen and (min--moz-device-pixel-ratio: 1.5),
    only screen and (min-resolution: 240dpi) {
    .ui-icon-one, .ui-icon-two, .ui-icon-three, .ui-icon-four, .ui-
icon-five, .ui-icon-six {
        background-image: url("../../resources/images/dice-HD.png");
        -moz-background-size: 108px 18px;
        -o-background-size: 108px 18px;
        -webkit-background-size: 108px 18px;
        background-size: 108px 18px;
    }
}
.ui-icon-one { background-position: -0px 50%; }
.ui-icon-two { background-position: -18px 50%; }
.ui-icon-three { background-position: -36px 50%; }
.ui-icon-four { background-position: -54px 50%; }
.ui-icon-five{ background-position: -72px 50%; }
.ui-icon-six{ background-position: -90px 50%; }
```

2. Include the CSS in the `<head>` section of `main.html`, as shown in the following code:

```
<link rel="stylesheet" href="http://code.jquery.com/mobile/1.1.1/
jquery.mobile-1.1.1.min.css" />
<link rel="stylesheet" href="jqm-sprite.css" />
```

3. Use the new icons derived from the replaced icon sprite to display the six faces of the dice as shown in the following code. Display the buttons with text:

```
<div data-role="content">
    <input type="submit" data-inline="true" value="one" data-
icon="one" />
    <input type="submit" data-inline="true" value="two" data-
icon="two" />
    <input type="submit" data-inline="true" value="three" data-
icon="three" />
    <input type="submit" data-inline="true" value="four" data-
icon="four" />
    <input type="submit" data-inline="true" value="five" data-
icon="five" />
    <input type="submit" data-inline="true" value="six" data-
icon="six" />
```

4. Then display the buttons without text for comparison:

```
<h3>This is how they look without Text</h3>
    <input type="submit" data-inline="true" data-iconpos="notext"
data-icon="one" />
    <input type="submit" data-inline="true" data-iconpos="notext"
data-icon="two" />
    <input type="submit" data-inline="true" data-iconpos="notext"
data-icon="three" />
    <input type="submit" data-inline="true" data-iconpos="notext"
data-icon="four" />
    <input type="submit" data-inline="true" data-iconpos="notext"
data-icon="five" />
    <input type="submit" data-inline="true" data-iconpos="notext"
data-icon="six" />
</div>
```

## How it works...

Create a stylesheet `jqm-sprite.css` and copy the code snippet for the `.ui-icon` class as is from the `jquery.mobile.css` file. Change the `background-image` URL of the icon sprite to point to the custom icon sprite `dice.png` image. Add the individual icon classes with the names `.ui-icon-one` to `.ui-icon-six`. Specify the positions of these icons in the icon sprite. The class `.ui-icon` already specifies the `background` colors for the icons. It also specifies a border radius of 9px for the icons with the required vendor prefixes. Modify the `@media` query and update the names of the new icons instead of the default icons as shown.

Here, the prefix text **ui-icon** indicates to the button plugin that these are custom icons and this generates the corresponding classes without the prefix text. You can now use the replaced icons on buttons using the attributes `data-icon="one"` to `data-icon="six"` and the framework will fetch and display the correct custom icon.

In `main.html`, create the buttons for the six faces of a dice by adding submit buttons using input tags. Set icons to these buttons using the `data-icon` attribute as shown. Display the buttons with and without text for comparison. The buttons for the six faces of a dice are now displayed as shown in the following screenshot, first with text and then without text:

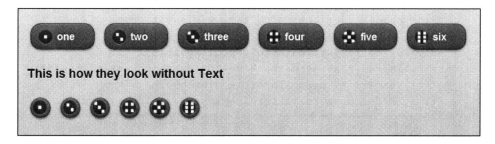

## There's more...

This recipe shows you how to replace the default icon sprite with your own custom icon sprite. You will no longer be able to use the default icons in your application. So replace the default icon set only if you have a valid reason to do it and if your app requires customization of all the icons. A better approach is to add a custom sprite along with the default sprite as shown in the previous recipe.

## See also

- ▶ The *Using a custom icon in a button* recipe
- ▶ The *Adding a custom icon sprite* recipe

# Using alternate icons in a collapsible

A **collapsible** is a container with the `data-role="collapsible"` attribute. You can add a header and other controls inside collapsible content and only the header is displayed when the collapsible block is collapsed. You can click on the **+** icon next to the collapsible to expand it. This recipe shows you how to use alternate icons with a collapsible.

## Getting ready

Copy the full code of this recipe from the `code/04/collapsible` sources folder. You can launch this code using the URL `http://localhost:8080/04/collapsible/main.html`.

## How to do it...

1. In `main.html` add two collapsible blocks using `data-role="collapsible"`, as shown in the following code. By default, the first collapsible uses the standard icons (**plus** and **minus**).

```
<div data-role="content">
  <div data-role="collapsible" data-collapsed="false"
      data-theme="c" data-content-theme="c">
    <h3>Header of the collapsible element</h3>
    The header uses the default plus/minus icons
  </div>
  <div id="collapser" data-role="collapsible"
data-collapsed="false" data-theme="d" data-content-theme="d">
    <h3>Header of the collapsible element</h3>
    The header uses the alternate expand/collapse icons
  </div>
</div>
```

2. Add the following script to the `<head>` section of the page to set alternate arrow icons to the second collapsible:

```
//on initial load
$("#main").live("pagebeforeshow", function(event, data) {
  $("#collapser").find( ".ui-icon-plus" )
    .toggleClass("ui-icon-arrow-r");
  $("#collapser").find( ".ui-icon-minus")
    .toggleClass("ui-icon-arrow-d");
});
// handle expand and collapse events below
$("#main").live("pageshow", function(event, data) {
  $("#collapser").bind("expand collapse", function(event) {
    var isCollapse = (event.type === "collapse");
    $(this).find( ".ui-icon" )
      .toggleClass( "ui-icon-arrow-d", !isCollapse )
      .toggleClass( "ui-icon-arrow-r", isCollapse );
  });
});
```

## How it works...

In `main.html`, add two collapsible blocks; they have the default **plus** and **minus** icons when they are loaded. Add script and create an event handler for the `pagebeforeshow` event to change the icons for the second collapsible (with `id="collapser"`). Use the jQuery `find()` method to find the class `.ui-icon-plus` (**plus** icon) and replace it with the class `.ui-icon-arrow-r` (**right arrow**) using the `toggleClass()` method. Similarly, replace the class `.ui-icon-minus` (**minus** icon) with the class `.ui-icon-arrow-d` (**down arrow)**. Set the `data-collapsed="false"` attribute on the collapsible blocks to show in an expanded mode. The second collapsible now has the arrow icons instead of the default icons when the page is displayed:

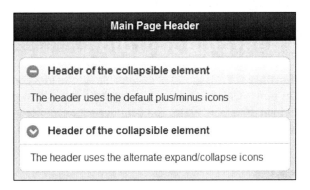

When a collapsible is expanded or collapsed, the framework toggles the icon using standard icons. You can override this behavior by adding an event handler for the `pageshow` event. Based on the event (`expand` or `collapse`) on the collapsible block, find the `.ui-icon` class and replace it with the `.ui-icon-arrow-d` or the `.ui-icon-arrow-r` classes to show the **down** or the **right** arrows. The collapsed blocks now look as shown in the following image:

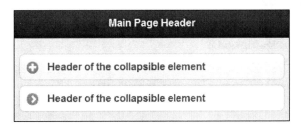

## There's more...

You can theme the collapsible content by using the `data-content-theme` attribute. The header is not affected. The following code themes the collapsible content with swatch `e`:

```
<div data-role="collapsible" data-content-theme="e">
```

### Setting a theme to the collapsible header

Use the `data-theme` attribute and set the theme to the entire collapsible block including the header. Now you can set a different theme to the collapsible content using the `data-content-theme` attribute. It will now look as if you styled the header separately. The following code snippet sets the header theme to swatch `a` and body to swatch `e`:

```
<div data-role="collapsible"
  data-theme="a" data-content-theme="e" >
```

## See also

  ▸  The *Creating a nested accordion* recipe

# Creating a nested accordion

An **accordion** or a **collapsible set** is a group of collapsible blocks in a container with `data-role="collapsible-set"`. Only one collapsible can be expanded at a time and the other collapsibles go back to their collapsed state. You cannot nest accordions directly. This recipe shows you how to create a **nested accordion** in a simple application that displays the various real estate properties available for purchase.

## Getting ready

Copy the full code of this recipe from the `code/04/nested-accordion` sources folder. You can launch this code using the URL `http://localhost:8080/04/nested-accordion/main.html`.

## How to do it...

1.  Add a nested accordion to `main.html` using `data-role="collapsible-set"` as shown in the following code:

```
<div data-role="content">
  <h4>Our current housing projects</h4>
  <div data-role="collapsible-set" data-theme="d" data-content-
    theme="d">
    <div data-role="collapsible" data-collapsed="false">
      <h3>Villas and Row Houses</h3>
      <div data-role="collapsible-set" data-theme="e" data-
        content-theme="e">
        <div data-role="collapsible">
          <h3>ABC Lake View</h3>
          Premium Villas with each villa having its own private
```

```
          beach
        </div>
        <div data-role="collapsible">
          <h3>ABC Nest</h3>
          Serene row houses amidst acres of trees
        </div>
      </div>
    </div>
    <div data-role="collapsible">
      <h3>Apartments</h3>
      <div data-role="collapsible" data-theme="e" data-content-
      theme="e">
        <h3>ABC Sky Rise</h3>
        Luxury 3 bedroom apartments 2 blocks away from ABC Mall
      </div>
    </div>
  </div>
</div>
```

## How it works...

In `main.html`, create a collapsible set with two collapsible blocks in it. The first collapsible shows **Villas and Row Houses** and the second shows **Apartments**. You can now nest another collapsible set under the **Villas and Row Houses** collapsible, as shown in the previous code snippet.

Add two collapsible blocks, nesting them inside the first collapsible block to list two properties. Theme the nested content differently from its parent collapsible using the `data-theme` and `data-content-theme` attributes. The nested collapsible is displayed as shown in the following screenshot:

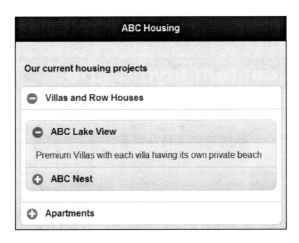

Now to complete the code, add content to the second collapsible **Apartments**. At any point in time, only one collapsible is expanded in this nested accordion, as seen in the following screenshot:

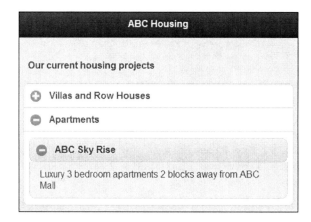

## There's more...

Introducing any other element or content in between two collapsible blocks in a collapsible set breaks the set. The collapsible blocks are no longer synchronized and they become independent of each other when you expand or collapse them.

 As the name indicates, a collapsible set must only contain collapsible blocks.

## See also

▶  The *Using alternate icons in a collapsible* recipe

# Creating a custom layout grid

You can use a **layout grid** to place controls next to each other in your application. By default, the layout grid creates column cells with equal width. This recipe shows you how to customize this and create cells with varying heights and widths.

## Getting ready

Copy the full code of this recipe from the `code/04/layoutgrid` sources folder. You can launch this code using the URL `http://localhost:8080/04/layoutgrid/main.html`.

## How to do it...

1.  Add a layout grid to `main.html` as shown in the following code, using the `ui-grid` and `ui-block` classes:

```html
<div data-role="content">
  <fieldset class="ui-grid-a">
    <div class="ui-block-a" style="width: 25%">
      <div class="ui-bar ui-bar-e">Col A</div>
    </div>
    <div class="ui-block-b" style="width: 50%">
      <div class="ui-bar ui-bar-e">Col B</div>
    </div>
    <div class="ui-block-c" style="width: 25%">
      <div class="ui-bar ui-bar-e">Col C</div>
    </div>
    <div class="ui-grid-solo">
      <div style="height: 40px" class="ui-bar ui-bar-e">A
Single Cell</div>
    </div>
  </fieldset>
</div>
```

## How it works...

Create `main.html` and add a layout grid to its page by adding a `fieldset` element with the attribute `class="ui-grid-a"`. This will create two columns having equal widths by default. But you can add three cells by adding `ui-block-a`, `ui-block-b`, and `ui-block-c` divs as shown in the code. Each div has varying widths, with **Col B** having `50%` width and the other two columns `25%` width each. The total width sums up to 100 percent and the framework automatically lines them up in a single row. If the sum were to exceed 100 percent, then the extra cells would be moved to the next row.

Now in the second row add a single `div` with class `ui-grid-solo` and this will style the cell to have 100 percent width. You can alter the height of this cell as shown in the code using the `style="height:"` attribute. The `ui-bar` and `ui-bar-e` classes style the cells with a border and a gradient color and themes it with swatch `e`. The grid layout now looks as shown in the following screenshot:

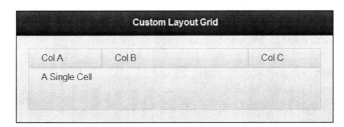

## There's more...

You can theme an individual cell, `ui-block` differently from other cells, by adding the `data-theme` attribute to it. To theme an entire row differently from other rows in the grid, you will have to add the same `data-theme` attribute to all the cells of that row.

### Adding content to a layout grid cell

You can add any sort of element inside the `ui-block` cell of a layout grid. You can even add a layout grid inside this cell. You have to choose wisely how you want your screen to look, keeping in mind the limited screen size of mobile devices.

### Adding a grid layout to any container

You can add a grid to any container by adding the `ui-grid` class to it. The following code snippet styles the entire page as a two column grid:

```
<div id="main" data-role="page" class="ui-grid-a">
```

## See also

▸    The *Adding a layout grid to the footer* recipe in *Chapter 3, Toolbars*

# Using XML content

You can display data obtained from various formats and sources in your application. This recipe shows you how to display a sample set of **Student Records** obtained from an XML file.

## Getting ready

Copy the full code of this recipe from the `code/04/xml-content` sources folder. You can launch this code using the URL `http://localhost:8080/04/xml-content/main.html`.

## How to do it...

1.  Create the `student.xml` file with the student node having attributes `name` and `age`. Each `student` node has multiple `course` child elements. Each `course` element has a `name` attribute and a child `marks` element as shown in the following code:

```
<?xml version="1.0" encoding="utf-8" ?>
<students>
  <student name="Alex" age="22">
    <course name="HTML5">
      <marks>89</marks>
    </course>
```

```
        <course name="CSS3">
          <marks>88</marks>
        </course>
        <course name="JavaScript">
          <marks>80</marks>
        </course>
      </student>
      .  .  .  .
    </students>
```

2. Create the `main.html` file and add one hidden `div` container. You can read the XML data into this `div` and then format and display it:

```
<div id="content" data-role="content" data-theme="b">
  <div id="hiddendiv" hidden="true">hi</div>
</div>
```

3. Include the following JavaScript code in the `<head>` section of `main.html` to load the XML file, format the data, and then display it:

```
$("#main").live("pageinit", function(event) {
  var str="";
  $("#hiddendiv").load("student.xml", function() {
    $("#hiddendiv").find("student").each(function() {
      str += "<div data-role='collapsible' data-theme='d'
        data-content-theme='d'>";
      str += "<h3>" + $(this).attr("name") + ", "
          + $(this).attr("age") +" years</h3>";
      str += "<ul data-role='listview'>";
      var i=0;
      $(this).find("course").each(function() {
        str += "<li>" + $(this).attr("name") + " : "
            + $(this).children("marks").html() + "</li>";
      });
      str += "</ul></div>";
    });
    $("#content").html(str).trigger("create");
  });
});
```

## How it works...

In `main.html`, add a `div` container with `id="hiddendiv"` and hide it by setting the attribute `hidden="true"`. Create an event handler for the `pageinit` event to handle the loading of the XML data as soon as the page is initialized and available in memory. Load the XML data into `hiddendiv` using the jQuery Ajax `load()` method. On successful load, find each `student` node using the jQuery `find()` method. For each `student`, generate HTML code by creating a collapsible (using `data-role="collapsible"`). Set the collapsible header to the student's `name` and `age`. You can obtain these values from the attributes of the `student` node by using the jQuery `attr()` method. Next, find each course within the `student` node and obtain `course name` and `marks`. The `marks` value is read by using the `children()` call, which extracts the first child element of the `course` node. The `course` elements are added to an unordered list (using `data-role="listview"`).

Once the HTML content is built, set it to the `"#content"` page content div and then trigger the `"create"` method to let the jQuery Mobile framework do its magic and generate the enhanced controls, as shown in the following screenshot:

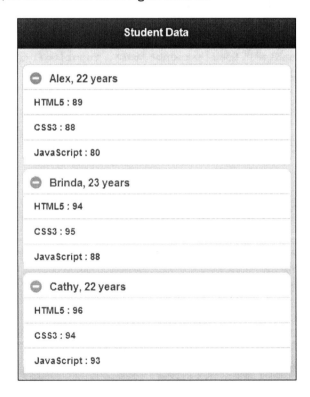

## There's more...

This recipe shows you how to read contents from a XML file located in the same folder using Ajax. You can also send an Ajax request to a server and obtain this XML as the response. The jQuery library has a whole bunch of selectors and manipulators that you can use to read and write XML data. Visit `http://docs.jquery.com` to read more.

 XML structure requires end tags and this makes it bulky. Always try to make your XML as light as possible by using more attributes when possible instead of child nodes. You can also use an algorithm such as *gzip* to compress the XML.

### Using native browser rendering for XML

Almost all browsers know how to render and display XML data directly. The XML content can also be formatted and styled if it has an associated style sheet. In your jQuery Mobile app you can leverage this feature in situations where you can open the content in another page using the `target` attribute on the anchor link, as shown in the following code:

```
<a href="student.xml" target="student" data-role="button">Open Student
details</a>
```

## See also

▸    The *Using JSON content* recipe

# Using JSON content

**JSON** stands for **JavaScript Object Notation**. It is a lightweight data-interchange format and is very easy to use. This recipe shows you how to display the prices of **Precious Metals** from a JSON file.

## Getting ready

Copy the full code of this recipe from the `code/04/json-content` sources folder.
You can launch this code using the URL `http://localhost:8080/04/json-content/main.html`.

## How to do it...

1. Create the `precious.json` file containing an array of the five precious metals. The name, symbol, and the intraday `open`, `close`, `high`, and `low` prices are also available, as shown in the following code:

```json
[
  {
    "name": "Gold",
    "symbol": "Au",
    "price": { "open": 1642.46, "close": 1682.42, "high": 1699.66,
"low": 1638.51 }
  },
  {
    "name": "Silver",
    "symbol": "Ag",
    "price": { "open": 31.24, "close": 33.11, "high": 33.65,
"low": 31.21 }
  },
  {
    "name": "Platinum",
    "symbol": "Pt",
    "price": { "open": 1621.15, "close": 1623.87, "high": 1624.45,
"low": 1620.98 }
  },
  {
    "name": "Paladium",
    "symbol": "Pd",
    "price": { "open": 656.05, "close": 657.35, "high": 657.75,
"low": 655.25 }
  },
  {
    "name": "Rhodium",
    "symbol": "Rh",
    "price": { "open": 1434.38, "close": 1434.68, "high": 1434.98,
"low": 1434.12 }
  }
]
```

2. Create `main.html` and add an empty `div` with `id="preciousdata"` to it. You can read the JSON file, format, and display the data here:

```html
<div id="content" data-role="content" data-theme="b">
  <div id="preciousdata"></div>
</div>
```

3. Include the following JavaScript code in the `<head>` section of `main.html` to fetch and load the JSON file, format the data, and show the price table of the precious metals in a layout grid:

```
$("#main").live("pageinit", function(event) {
  $.getJSON("precious.json", function(metal) {
```

4. Next, store the HTML strings used to create the layout grid in local variables:

```
var blocka = "<div class='ui-block-a' style='width: 40%'>";
var blockb = "<div class='ui-block-b' style='width: 15%'>";
var blockc = "<div class='ui-block-c' style='width: 15%'>";
var blockd = "<div class='ui-block-d' style='width: 15%'>";
var blocke = "<div class='ui-block-e' style='width: 15%'>";
var title = "<div class='ui-bar ui-bar-a' style='text-align:
right'>";
var uibarc = "<div class='ui-bar ui-bar-c' style='text-align:
right'>";
var uibare = "<div class='ui-bar ui-bar-e' style='text-align:
right'>";
```

5. Use the local variables defined above and construct the HTML content for the title of the layout grid:

```
var str="<div class='ui-grid-d'>";
str += blocka + title + "Precious Metal (USD)</div></div>";
str += blockb + title + "Open</div></div>";
str += blockc + title + "High</div></div>";
str += blockd + title + "Low</div></div>";
str += blocke + title + "Close</div></div>";
```

6. Now create the HTML content for each metal, including their price details:

```
for (var i in metal) {
  str += blocka + uibare + metal[i].name
    + " (" + metal[i].symbol + ")</div></div>";
  str += blockb + uibarc + metal[i].price.open
    + "</div></div>";
  str += blockc + uibare + metal[i].price.high
    + "</div></div>";
  str += blockd + uibarc + metal[i].price.low
    + "</div></div>";
  str += blocke + uibare + metal[i].price.close
    + "</div></div>";
}
str += "</div>";
```

7.  Finally, add this data to the #preciousdata div and trigger the "create" method to display the formatted JSON data:

```
$("#preciousdata").html(str).trigger("create");
    });
});
```

## How it works...

In main.html, add an empty div container with id="preciousdata". You can use this to display the formatted JSON data later. Create an event handler for the pageinit event to handle the loading of the JSON data as soon as the page is initialized and available in memory. Use the $.getJSON() jQuery call to fetch the JSON encoded data from the server using a GET request. The JSON data is now available in the metal object.

In the callback function for the getJSON method, create the HTML content for a five column layout grid using the ui-grid-d class. The five columns are titled **Precious Metal (USD)**, **Open**, **High**, **Low**, and **Close**. Create the title row using the ui-block classes for each column cell. Next, loop through the objects in metal and construct the column cells as shown.

Theme the columns alternatively with swatch e and swatch c. You can theme the title differently using swatch a. Finally, set the generated HTML content to the #preciousdata div and trigger the create method to let the jQuery Mobile enhance the layout grid. The JSON with precious metal price data is now displayed as shown in the following screenshot:

| Precious Metals | | | | |
| --- | --- | --- | --- | --- |
| **Precious Metal (USD)** | **Open** | **High** | **Low** | **Close** |
| Gold (Au) | 1642.46 | 1699.66 | 1638.51 | 1682.42 |
| Silver (Ag) | 31.24 | 33.65 | 31.21 | 33.11 |
| Platinum (Pt) | 1621.15 | 1624.45 | 1620.98 | 1623.87 |
| Paladium (Pd) | 656.05 | 657.75 | 655.25 | 657.35 |
| Rhodium (Rh) | 1434.38 | 1434.98 | 1434.12 | 1434.68 |

## There's more...

This recipe shows you how to use the jQuery.getJSON() method to fetch the JSON data from the server. The jQuery library also provides a jQuery.parseJSON() method that you can use to parse a JSON string directly into a JavaScript object, as shown in the following code:

```
var preciousobject= jQuery.parseJSON('{"name":"Gold"}');
```

## JSON for data storage and data transfer

JSON is very popular today for storing and transferring data. JSON is a subset of JavaScript and as seen in this recipe, reading JSON data using JavaScript is very trivial. JSON is lightweight and uses less bandwidth compared to XML (for example, no start and end tags). JSON is also supported out of the box by numerous document oriented databases such as CouchDB and MongoDB.

## JSON parsers

JSON data can also be loaded using the JavaScript `eval()` method. But do this only if you absolutely have to and are very sure about the source of the JSON text file. It is always safer to load the data using a **JSON parser** as this will accept only valid JSON data, and prevent potentially malicious code from running. Refer to `www.json.org` for more details and for accessing a whole range of available JSON parsers. The jQuery JSON methods are usually preferred as they are very handy and also safe to use.

 Always use a properly implemented JSON parser to read and write `.json` files. Avoid using the `eval()` method, which is not secure.

## See also

▶   The *Using XML content* recipe

# 5
# Forms

In this chapter we will cover:

- ▶ Native styling of form controls
- ▶ Disabling text controls
- ▶ Grouping radio buttons in a grid
- ▶ Customizing a checkbox group
- ▶ Creating dynamic flip switch and slider controls
- ▶ Using options to auto-initialize a select menu
- ▶ Validating forms
- ▶ Submitting a form using POST
- ▶ Fetching data using GET
- ▶ Creating an accessible form

## Introduction

The standard HTML form element is enhanced by jQuery Mobile framework to make it touch friendly and also to make it work across multiple devices and platforms. The form can contain multiple controls and you can group these controls using a `fieldset` with `data-role='controlgroup'` attribute set on it. By default, the controls are listed vertically. You can use the `data-type='horizontal'` attribute to line them horizontally. Forms support the **HTTP GET**, **POST**, and other actions. Ajax is used wherever possible for form submissions.

## Native styling of form controls

The jQuery Mobile framework enhances the form and its controls by default. This recipe shows you the different ways you can set native styling for your form controls and also how to auto-initialize these controls.

## Getting ready

Copy the full code of this recipe from the `code/05/native-style` sources folder. This code can be launched using the URL `http://localhost:8080/05/native-style/main.html`.

## How to do it...

1. In `main.html`, add the following script to the `<head>` section to natively style all buttons:

```
$(document).bind('mobileinit', function() {
    $.mobile.page.prototype.options.keepNative = 'button';
});
```

2. Add a form to the page content to set native styles on the controls:

```
<form action='#' method='post'>
  <p><label for='button1'>Button 1</label></p>
  <button name='button1'>Button: keepNative configuration</button>
  <p><label for='button2'>Button 2</label></p>
  <button name='button2' data-role='button'>Button: data-
role='button'</button>
  <p><label for='button3'>Button 3</label></p>
  <button id='button3' name='button3'>Button: buttonMarkup()</
button>
  <script>$('#button3').buttonMarkup(); </script>
  <p><label for='input1'>Input 1</label></p>
  <input type='submit' name='input1' value='Input: default'></
input>
  <p><label for='input2'>Input 2</label></p>
  <input type='submit' name='input1' data-role='none'
value="Input: data-role='none'"></input><p>
  <a href='#'>Default anchor link</a></p>
  <a href='#' data-role='button'>Anchor: data-role='button'></a>
</form>
```

## How it works...

In `main.html`, add an event handler for the `mobileinit` event that gets triggered at the start of the app. Here set the `keepNative` property of the page plugin to `'button'`. Now the framework will not enhance the button controls but will style them natively. Now add `button1` to the form and it will be styled natively. To override this native styling, add `button2` and set the attribute `data-role='button'`. Similarly, add `button3` and call the `buttonMarkup()` method on it using the script as shown in the previous code. Both `button2` and `button3` now get enhanced by overriding the default native styling.

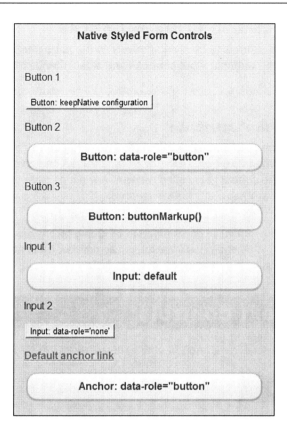

The framework enhances all other controls by default. Add an input button `input1` and you will see that it is enhanced. To natively style controls, you can use the `data-role='none'` attribute as shown in the previous code for the input control `input2`.

For anchor links, the native style is used by default. You can enhance an anchor link by using the `data-role='button'` attribute on it. The form created is shown above.

## There's more...

As already mentioned, form controls are enhanced by the framework to make it finger friendly across all platforms. But these controls may seem to be slightly bigger to be used in other small containers (like toolbars). You can use the **mini version** of the controls by setting the `data-mini = 'true'` attribute on the control. The control is now slightly smaller in size but still finger friendly. You can directly set this attribute on a `controlgroup` and all child elements will automatically be minified. Visit jQuery Mobile online docs to see a comparison of various controls at `http://jquerymobile.com/test/docs/forms/forms-all-compare.html`.

### Setting multiple controls to use native style

You can specify multiple controls to be styled natively by the **page plugin**. The following line of code natively styles all the buttons, input controls, and select menus in the form:

```
$.mobile.page.prototype.options.keepNative = 'button, input, select';
```

### The data-role='none' attribute

Based on the control type, the framework initializes and enhances a control by using its corresponding plugin. When `data-role='none'` is specified, the control is not enhanced by the framework and the control gets styled natively. Any action like setting the theme on the control by using the `data-theme` attribute is ignored.

 The enhanced styles provided by jQuery Mobile are tap and touch friendly and ideal for mobile devices. Avoid native styling in your apps as far as possible.

# Disabling text controls

This recipe shows you the different ways to enable and disable text controls in a form.

## Getting ready

Copy the full code of this recipe from the `code/05/text-controls` sources folder. This code can be launched using the URL `http://localhost:8080/05/text-controls/main.html`.

## How to do it...

1.  In `main.html`, create the following text controls in a form:

```
<form action='#' method='post'>
  <input type='search' id='searchitem' name='searchitem' autofocus
      placeholder='Enter search text' value='' />
  <input type='text' id='textitem' name='textitem'
      placeholder='Enter text item' value='' />
  <textarea id='textarea' name='textarea'
      placeholder='Enter description'></textarea>
  <a href='#' data-role='button' class='ui-disabled'>More
Details</a>
</form>
```

2. Add the following script to the `<head>` section to disable all controls:

```
$('#main').live('pageinit', function(event) {
    $('#textitem').prop('disabled', true);
    $('#textarea').textinput('disable');
```

3. Then handle the `change` event of the search text control to enable all the form controls:

```
$('#searchitem').bind('change', function(event, ui) {
    var str = $(this).attr('value');
    $('#textitem').prop('disabled', true);
    $('#textarea').textinput('enable').append(str
        + ' is absolutely awesome!');
    $('a').removeClass('ui-disabled');
});
});
```

## How it works...

In `main.html`, add a search control with input `type='search'` and add a text with input `type='text'`.Now, add an empty `textarea` as shown in the previous code. Add a link and disable it by setting the attribute `class='ui-disabled'`. In the script, add a `pageinit` event handler that gets invoked after the page has been initialized. Here, disable the text input by calling the `prop('disabled', true)` method to set its `disabled` property. Next, disable the `textarea` by calling the disable method on the **textinput plugin** with the `textinput('disable')` call. Now when the app is loaded, all the controls other than the search input are disabled on the form, as shown in the following screenshot:

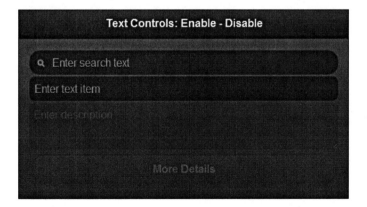

 You cannot use the `disabled` attribute on an anchor link which has been enhanced to a button using `data-role='button'`. This attribute is ignored.

Now to enable the controls, bind the `change` event of the search control to an event handler. Here, enable the `textitem` control by calling the `prop('disabled', false)` method. Next, call the `textinput('enable')` method on the `textarea` to invoke the enable method on its **textinput plugin**. Call the `append()` method on the `textarea` to add text to it. Finally, call the jQuery `removeClass()` method on the anchor link to remove the `'ui-disabled'` class. Now as soon as you type something in the search field, the form controls are all enabled, as seen in the following screenshot:

You can also enable or disable a control by adding the `disabled` attribute to the control using the `attr()` and `removeAttr()` jQuery methods, as shown in the following code:

```
$('#textitem').attr('disabled', 'disabled'); // to disable
$('#textitem').removeAttr('disabled'); // to enable
```

### Auto-initialization of text controls

The textarea and text input controls (input `type='text'`) are automatically enhanced by the framework. You can also theme a text control by using the `data-theme` attribute.

# Grouping radio buttons in a grid

The jQuery Mobile framework allows you to create radio buttons grouped either horizontally or vertically. This recipe shows you how to group radio controls in a 3 x 3 grid in a simple seat reservation form.

Copy the full code of this recipe from the `code/05/radiobutton-grid` sources folder. This code can be launched using the URL `http://localhost:8080/05/radiobutton-grid/main.html`.

## How to do it...

1. In `main.html`, create nine radio controls using a 3 x 3 layout grid. These radio buttons are part of the same control group.

```html
<form action='#' method='post'>
  <fieldset data-role='controlgroup' data-type='horizontal'
      class='ui-grid-a'>
    <div class='ui-block-a' style='width: 30%'>
        <legend>First Row</legend></div>
    <div class='ui-block-b' style='width: 70%'>
        <input type='radio' name='radio-1' id='radio-11'
value='Seat-A1' checked />
        <label for='radio-11'>A-1</label>
        <input type='radio' name='radio-1' id='radio-12'
value='Seat-A2' />
        <label for='radio-12'>A-2</label>
        <input type='radio' name='radio-1' id='radio-13'
value='Seat-A3'/>
        <label id='1-13' for='radio-13' class='ui-corner-
right'>A-3</label>
    </div>
    <div class='ui-block-a' style='width: 30%'>
        <legend>Mid Row</legend></div>
    <div class='ui-block-b' style='width: 70%'>
        <input type='radio' name='radio-1' id='radio-21'
value='Seat-B1' />
        <label id='1-21' for='radio-21' class='ui-corner-left'>B-1</
label>
        <input type='radio' name='radio-1' id='radio-22'
value='Seat-B2' />
        <label for='radio-22'>B-2</label>
        <input type='radio' name='radio-1' id='radio-23'
value='Seat-B3'/>
        <label id='1-23' for='radio-23' class='ui-corner-
right'>B-3</label>
    </div>
    <div class='ui-block-a' style='width: 30%'>
        <legend>Last Row</legend></div>
    <div class='ui-block-b' style='width: 70%'>
        <input type='radio' name='radio-1' id='radio-31'
value='Seat-C1' />
        <label id='1-31' for='radio-31' class='ui-corner-
left'>C-1</label>
```

```
            <input type='radio' name='radio-1' id='radio-32'
        value='Seat-C2' />
            <label for='radio-32'>C-2</label>
            <input type='radio' name='radio-1' id='radio-33'
        value='Seat-C3'/>
            <label for='radio-33'>C-3</label>
        </div>
    </fieldset>
</form>
```

2.  Add the following script to the `<head>` section to fix the styles of the edge radio buttons:

```
$('#main').live('pageshow', function(event) {
    $('#l-13').children('span').addClass('ui-corner-right ui-
controlgroup-last');
    $('#l-23').children('span').addClass('ui-corner-right ui-
controlgroup-last');
    $('#l-21').children('span').addClass('ui-corner-left');
    $('#l-31').children('span').addClass('ui-corner-left');
});
```

## How it works...

In `main.html`, add a horizontal radio control group by specifying `data-role='controlgroup'` and `data-type='horizontal'`. Now add the `ui-grid-a` class to this `fieldset` container to create a two column layout grid. For each row, add the legend in the first column by specifying `class='ui-block-a'` to the `div` container and add the radio buttons in the second column with `class='ui-block-b'`. Add nine radio buttons with appropriate labels as shown in the previous code, with each row containing three radio buttons. This will create a grid of 3 x 3 radio button group.

In the previous code, you will find that the first and last radio buttons in the grid are styled properly but all other edge radio buttons (with labels I-13, I-21, I-23, and I-31) are not styled properly. They have rectangular edges instead of corners. To fix this, copy the style generated by the framework for the label of the very first radio button (`class='ui-corner-left'`) to the inner `span` of the labels I-21 and I-31. Likewise, copy the style generated by the framework for the label of the very last radio button (`class='ui-corner-right ui-controlgroup-last'`) to the inner `span` of the labels I-13 and I-23. The grid of radio buttons is now properly styled, as shown in the following screenshot, and you will be able to select only one radio button in the entire grid at a time:

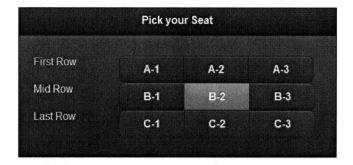

## There's more...

When the framework encounters an `input` control with `type='radio'`, it automatically enhances it to a styled radio button using the **checkboxradio plugin**. You can theme a radio button by using the `data-theme` attribute during initialization. You can turn auto-initialization off and use native styling by using the `data-role='none'` attribute.

## See also

▶ The *Customizing a checkbox group* recipe

# Customizing a checkbox group

The default horizontally grouped checkbox controls do not have an icon and the vertically grouped checkbox controls do not use the active state theme. This recipe shows you how to customize the checkbox and add these styles. It also shows you how to adjust the layout to handle varying screen sizes. You will create a simple **Blog Subscription** form in this recipe.

## Getting ready

Copy the full code of this recipe from the `code/05/custom-checkbox` sources folder. This code can be launched using the URL `http://localhost:8080/05/custom-checkbox/main.html`.

## How to do it...

The form is first created with the horizontal and vertical group of checkbox controls. The horizontal checkbox controls are customized by adding icons to them in the `pageshow` event handler via JavaScript. The `change` event of the checkbox controls indicate whether a checkbox `checked` state was changed. The `change` event handler is used to add and toggle the active state of the checkbox.

1. In `main.html`, create a form with a vertical checkbox control group:

```
<form action='#' method='post'>
  <div data-role='fieldcontain'>
    <fieldset data-role='controlgroup'>
      <legend>Subscribe to:</legend>
      <input type='checkbox' name='posts' id='posts' />
      <label for='posts' id='postslbl'>New Posts</label>
      <input type='checkbox' name='comments' id='comments' />
      <label for='comments' id='commentslbl'>Comments</label>
    </fieldset>
  </div>
```

2. Next add two horizontal toggle sets or checkbox groups:

```
  <div data-role='fieldcontain'>
    <fieldset data-role='controlgroup' data-type='horizontal'>
      <legend>Notify Me:</legend>
      <input type='checkbox' name='notify' id='notify' />
      <label for='notify'>Immediate</label>
      <input type='checkbox' name='digest' id='digest' />
      <label for='digest'>Daily Digest</label>
    </fieldset>
  </div>
  <div data-role='fieldcontain'>
    <fieldset data-role='controlgroup' data-type='horizontal'>
      <legend>Share To:</legend>
      <input type='checkbox' name='twitter' id='twitter' />
      <label for='twitter' id='twitterlbl'>Twitter</label>
      <input type='checkbox' name='facebook' id='facebook' />
      <label for='facebook' id='facebooklbl'>Facebook</label>
    </fieldset>
  </div>
</form>
```

3. Add the following script to the `<head>` section to add icons to the horizontal group:

```
$('#main').live('pageshow', function(event, data) {
  $('#twitterlbl').children('span').append("<span class='ui-icon
ui-icon-shadow ui-icon-checkbox-off'>").trigger('create');
  $('#twitterlbl').addClass('ui-btn-icon-left').
trigger('refresh');
  $('#facebooklbl').children('span').append("<span class='ui-icon
ui-icon-shadow ui-icon-checkbox-off'>").trigger('create');
  $('#facebooklbl').addClass('ui-btn-icon-left').
trigger('refresh');
  updatePosts();
  updateComments();
  $('#posts').bind('change', updatePosts);
  $('#comments').bind('change', updateComments);
});
```

4. Next, bind the `change` event to handle the change in the `checked` state of the controls:

```
function updatePosts(event, ui) {
  if($('#posts').prop('checked')) {
    $('#postslbl').addClass('ui-btn-active').trigger('refresh');
  } else {
    if($('#postslbl').hasClass('ui-btn-active'))
      $('#postslbl').removeClass('ui-btn-active').
trigger('refresh');
  }
}
```

5. Finally, toggle the active state based on the `checked` state of the vertical checkbox:

```
function updateComments(event, ui) {
  if($('#comments').prop('checked')) {
    $('#commentslbl').addClass('ui-btn-active').
trigger('refresh');
  } else {
    if($('#commentslbl').hasClass('ui-btn-active'))
      $('#commentslbl').removeClass('ui-btn-active').
trigger('refresh');
  }
}
```

## How it works...

In `main.html`, add three `fieldset` elements with `data-role='controlgroup'` to the **Blog Subscription** form. Add a vertical checkbox group to the first `fieldset` element with checkboxes for **Posts** and **Comments**. The second control group is a horizontal toggleset for selecting blog notifications (**Immediate** and **As a daily digest**). The third group of checkboxes are also horizontal with options to share in **Twitter** and **Facebook**.

By default, the horizontal togglesets do not have icons. You can customize this and add icons to them. Create an event handler for the `pageshow` event and add the required styles to the labels of the third horizontal toggleset. Add an inner span with `class='ui-icon ui-icon-shadow ui-icon-checkbox-off'` to the labels with `id='twitterlbl'` and `id='facebooklbl'`, and also add the `ui-btn-icon-left` class to the labels. This will add an icon on the left-hand side of the two checkboxes, similar to the icons available with the vertical checkbox controls. Compare this with the other horizontal toggelset.

By default, the vertical checkboxes have icons and when selected these icons show the tick mark. The vertical checkboxes do not get the `btn-active` style (unlike the horizontal checkboxes). To add the active button style, create event handlers for the `change` event on the two vertical checkboxes (with `id='posts'` and `id='comments'`). For each of these checkboxes, use the `prop('checked')` call to find out whether the control is `checked` or not and then add or remove the `ui-btn-active` class to style the vertical checkbox, similar to the horizontal one. The screen is displayed as seen in the following screenshot:

## There's more...

In the previous code, each checkbox group is wrapped in a container with the attribute `data-role='fieldcontain'`. This attribute will cause the framework to dynamically adjust the layout of the controls and the position of their labels based on the screen size. A small horizontal separator line is also added to show the separation. On a wider screen or when landscape orientation is used, the display is as shown in the following screenshot:

### Auto-initialization of checkbox controls

When the framework encounters an `input` control with `type='checkbox'`, it automatically enhances it to a styled checkbox using the **checkboxradio plugin**. You can theme a checkbox by using the `data-theme` attribute during initialization. You can turn auto-initialization off and use native styling by using the `data-role='none'` attribute.

## See also

- ► The *Grouping radio buttons in a grid* recipe

# Creating dynamic flip switch and slider controls

This recipe shows you how to add a **flip switch** and a **slider** control dynamically to a page using JavaScript and also handle their events. Here you will create a simple **Volume Control** form with a volume slider that warns the user when the volume is very high.

Copy the full code of this recipe from the `code/05/dynamic-slider` sources folder. This code can be launched using the URL `http://localhost:8080/05/dynamic-slider/main.html`.

1.  In `main.html`, add the following empty form to the page content:

    ```
    <form id='volumeForm' action='#' method='post'></form>
    ```

2.  Add the following script to the `<head>` section to dynamically add a flip switch and a slider:

    ```
    $('#main').live('pageinit', function(event) {
       var str="<div data-role='fieldcontain' style='width: 50%'><label
    for='flipswitch'>Volume:</label>"
          + "<select name='flipswitch' id='flipswitch' data-
    role='slider' data-track-theme='d'>"
          + "<option value='no'>Off</option><option value='yes'>On</
    option></select></div>"
          + "<div id='volcontainer' data-role='fieldcontain'
    style='width: 100%'>"
          + "<input type='range' name='volume' id='volume' value='8'
    min='0' max='15' data-track-theme='b' disabled /></div>";
       $('#volumeForm').html(str).trigger('create');
    ```

3.  Handle the `change` event of the flip switch to enable the volume slider control:

    ```
    $('#flipswitch').bind('change', function(event, data) {
       if ($(this).slider().val() == 'no') {
          $('#volume').slider('disable');
       } else {
          $('#volume').slider('enable');
       }
    });
    });
    ```

4.  Handle the `change` event on the volume slider to style the slider based on its value:

    ```
    $('#main').live('pageshow', function(event) {
       $('#volume').bind('change', function(event, data) {
          if ($(this).slider().val() > 10) {
             $('#volcontainer').find('.ui-btn-down-b')
             .removeClass('ui-btn-down-b').addClass('ui-btn-down-e');
          } else {
             $('#volcontainer').find('.ui-btn-down-e')
    ```

```
                .removeClass('ui-btn-down-e').addClass('ui-btn-down-b');
        }
    });
});
```

## How it works...

Add an empty form id='volumeForm' to main.html. Create an event handler for the pageinit event, which gets triggered after the page has been initialized. Here, generate the HTML content for the form. Add a flip toggle switch control (id='flipswitch') using a select control with data-role='slider'. This flip switch will toggle the volume **On** and **Off**. Add an input control with type='range' to create a slider control (id='volume'). Add the disabled attribute to the slider so that the control is disabled at startup. Set this HTML content to the empty form and trigger the 'create' method to let the framework initialize and enhance the controls. When the page loads you will see the **Volume Control** form with both the dynamically added flip switch and the disabled slider control, as shown in the following screenshot:

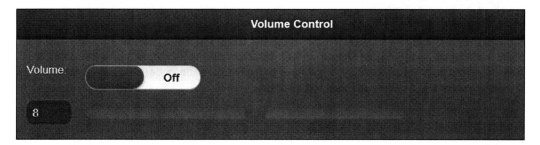

Next add code to handle the change event of #flipswitch and in the event handler, check whether the flip switch is **on** or **off** using the slider().val() call. Based on this value, enable or disable the slider volume control by calling slider('enable') or slider('disable'). Now when you toggle the flip switch value, you will see the slider getting enabled or disabled as seen in the following screenshot:

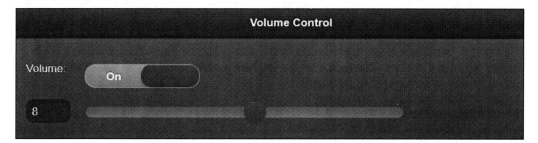

Bind the `change` event of the volume slider control in a `pageshow` event handler and here check for the value of the slider using the `slider().val()` call. If the value is greater than a threshold volume of **10**, set the slider to theme `'e'`, if not already styled so. If the value goes below the threshold of **10**, set the theme back to theme `'b'`. You can use the jQuery `find()` method and replace the `ui-btn-down-b` class with the `ui-btn-down-e` class and vice versa. Now when you set a high volume the slider changes to yellow color, as seen in the following screenshot:

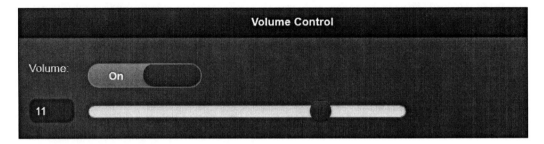

## There's more...

You can theme the flip switch and the slider control using the `data-theme` attribute and the slider track by using the `data-theme-track` attribute during initialization. To manipulate these controls post initialization, you will have to manipulate the underlying native controls and then invoke the `'refresh'` method on them.

## Auto-initialization of sliders

When the framework encounters an `input` control with `type='range'`, it automatically enhances it to a slider control using the **slider plugin**. Likewise the slider plugin enhances the select control with `data-role='slider'` to a flip switch. You can turn auto-initialization off and use native styling by using the `data-role='none'` attribute.

# Using options to auto-initialize a select menu

The native HTML select menu is enhanced by the jQuery Mobile framework to make it finger friendly for mobile devices. This recipe shows you how to auto-initialize the **Select Menu** by setting its control options using JavaScript.

## Getting ready

Copy the full code of this recipe from the `code/05/select-menu` sources folder. This code can be launched using the URL `http://localhost:8080/05/select-menu/main.html`.

## How to do it...

1.  In `main.html`, add the following code to create a select menu:

```
<form action='#' method='post'>
  <div data-role='fieldcontain'>
    <label for='selectid' class='select'>Sample Select Menu</
label>
    <select name='selectid' id='selectid' multiple data-native-
menu='false' data-overlay-theme='e'>
      <option value='Sample Select Menu' data-
placeholder='true'>Sample Select Menu</option>
      <option value='opt1'>Option 1</option>
      <option value='disabledopt' disabled>Disabled Option</
option>
      <option value='opt2'>Option 2</option>
      <optgroup label='Options in Group1'>
        <option value='grp1'>    Group
Option1</option>
        <option value='grp2'>    Group
Option2</option>
      </optgroup>
      <optgroup label='Options in GroupA'>
        <option value='grpA'>    Group
OptionA</option>
        <option value='grpB'>    Group
OptionB</option>
      </optgroup>
    </select>
  </div>
</form>
```

2.  Add the following script to the `<head>` section to set the select menu control options:

```
$('#main').live('pageinit', function(event) {
  $('#selectid').selectmenu({
    theme: 'd',
    inline: false,
    corners: true,
    icon: 'star',
    iconpos: 'left',
    shadow: true,
    iconshadow: true
  });
});
```

## How it works...

In `main.html`, create a form and add a select control to the form with the attribute `multiple` to enable multiple selection. Set the attribute `data-native-menu='false'` to indicate that the select menu should be enhanced by the framework. Also set the `data-overlay-theme='e'` attribute to specify that swatch e (yellow) should be used for the layer on which the select menu is overlaid.

Add the first option element with the `data-placeholder` attribute indicating that this option element text must be used as the header for the select menu. Now add the different option elements as shown in the previous code. The `opt1` and `opt2` elements are regular option items. The element `disableopt` is disabled by adding the attribute `disabled` to the option element. Then add two option groups (**Group1** and **GroupA**) by using the `optgroup` element as shown in the previous code. These can contain sub option elements. The select menu is displayed as shown in the following screenshot:

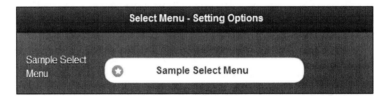

Add a script to the `pageinit` event handler that gets invoked after the page has initialized at startup. Here, set the initial configuration options of the select menu control by passing the option values to the **selectmenu plugin**. In the code, set the values of the attributes `theme`, `inline`, `corners`, `icon`, `iconpos`, `shadow`, and `iconshadow` of the select menu. Now when you click on select menu, the styled menu options are as shown in the following screenshot:

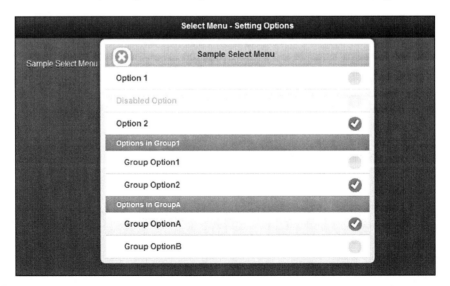

## There's more...

When the framework encounters a `select` element, it automatically enhances it to a select menu by using the **selectmenu plugin**. You can turn auto-initialization off and use native styling by using the `data-role='none'` attribute.

### Opening and closing a select menu

You can call the `open` and `close` methods on the `selectmenu` plugin and programmatically open or close a select menu, as shown in the following screenshot:

```
$('#selectid').selectmenu('open'); // open select menu
$('#selectid').selectmenu('close'); // close select menu
```

# Validating forms

Validating a form before it is submitted to the server saves bandwidth and time as errors can be trapped at the client side itself. A server request can thus be avoided. In a jQuery Mobile application, forms can be validated using JavaScript. This recipe shows you how to validate the entries made in a **Blog Comments Form**.

## Getting ready

Copy the full code of this recipe from the `code/05/validate-form` sources folder. This code can be launched using the URL `http://localhost:8080/05/validate-form/main.html`.

## How to do it...

1. In `main.html`, add the following code to create a form:

```
<form id='commentform' action='#' method='post'>
  <div data-role='fieldcontain'>
    <label for='username'>Name</label>
    <input id='username' name='username' type='text' required
placeholder='Enter Name' />
  </div>
  <div data-role='fieldcontain'>
    <label for='email'>Email ID</label>
    <input id='email' name='email' type='email' required
placeholder='Enter Email' />
  </div>
  <div data-role='fieldcontain'>
    <label for='comments'>Comments</label>
```

```
        <textarea id='comments' name='comments' required
placeholder='Enter Comments <10-100 chars long>'></textarea>
    </div>
    <div id='errmsg' style='color: #f00'></div>
    <input id='submitid' type='submit' data-transition='pop'
value='Submit Comment'/>
</form>
```

2. Add the following script to validate the comments field:

```
$('#main').live('pageinit', function(event) {
  $('#commentform').submit(function() {
    var len = $('#comments').val().length;
    if ( len < 10 || len > 100 ) {
        $('#errmsg').text('Invalid comments. Length must be between
10-100 chars').show().fadeOut(5000);
        return false;
    }
    else
        return true;
  });
});
```

## How it works...

In main.html, add a form (id='commentform') and add the following three fields to the form, **username** (type='text'), **email** (type='email'), and **comments** (textarea). Add the required attribute to all the three fields to specify them as mandatory. Add appropriate hints to the user by using the placeholder attribute as shown in the previous code. Add an empty div (id='errmsg') to the form to display any error messages on form validation.

When you load the form and click on the **Submit Comment** button without entering the **Name** field, the following error message is shown:

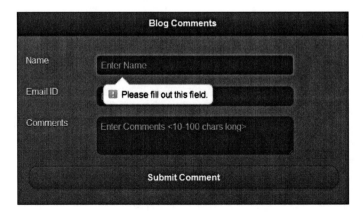

The following error is shown when you click on the submit button without a valid **Email ID**:

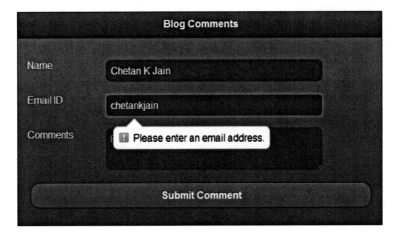

Add the `pageinit` event handler as shown in the previous script. This will get invoked after the page has been initialized at start-up. Here define the `submit()` method of the form to validate the length of the comments. If the comment has an invalid length, display the error message for five seconds after which it fades out. Now since there was an error, return `false` from the `submit` method; the form will not be submitted.

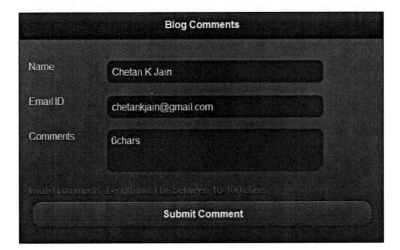

Post successful validation, return `true` from the `submit()` method to successfully submit the form to the server.

## There's more...

In this recipe, the form's `action` is set to # or the same URL as the current HTML page. This form is called a **self-submitting form**. The default response in such cases is the form content itself. If the form was served by a web server, the response to the post can be custom generated. If you are using the nodejs web server that is shipped with the source code of this book, then you will get a custom success response instead of the form contents.

### Unique IDs in a form

In a jQuery Mobile application, since multiple pages can reside in the DOM at the same time, you should ensure that the IDs for the form controls are unique. The IDs should be unique across the entire app and not just in a single page. Lookups and form behavior could fail or behave differently if you do not follow this rule. Some browsers might still support duplicate IDs to a certain extent but this is not guaranteed.

## See also

▸ The *Submitting a form using POST* recipe

▸ The *Fetching data using GET* recipe

# Submitting a form using POST

This recipe shows you how to **POST** and submit a form using Ajax and also how to submit the same forum when not using Ajax. The **Blog Comments** form used in the previous recipe is used here for submission.

## Getting ready

Copy the full code of this recipe from the `code/05/submit-form` sources folder. This code can be launched using the URL `http://localhost:8080/05/submit-form/main.html`. To try out this recipe, you will also need to launch the simple nodejs web server that is shipped along with the source code of this book. Launch the server by using the following command:

```
node jqmserver.js
```

## How to do it...

1. In `main.html`, create the **Blog Comments** form as shown in the following code:

```
<form id='commentform' action='/postComment' data-transition='pop'
method='post'>
  <div data-role='fieldcontain'>
    <label for='username'>Name</label>
    <input id='username' name='username' type='text' required
placeholder='Enter Name' />
  </div>
  <div data-role='fieldcontain'>
    <label for='email'>Email ID</label>
    <input id='email' name='email' type='email' required
placeholder='Enter Email' />
  </div>
  <div data-role='fieldcontain'>
    <label for='comments'>Comments</label>
    <textarea id='comments' name='comments' required
placeholder='Enter Comments <10-100 chars long>'></textarea>
  </div>
  <div id='errmsg' style='color: #f00'></div>
  <input id='submitid' type='submit' value='Submit Comment'/>
</form>
```

2. Add the following script to the `<head>` section to validate the comments field:

```
$('#main').live('pageinit', function(event) {
  $('#commentform').submit(function() {
    var len = $('#comments').val().length;
    if ( len < 10 || len > 100 ) {
      $('#errmsg').text('Invalid comments. Length must be between
10-100 chars').show().fadeOut(5000);
      return false;
    }
    else
      return true;
  });
});
```

## How it works...

In `main.html`, create the **Blog Comments** form. Set the form `action` to `'/postComment'` and also specify the attribute `data-transition='pop'`. The rest of the code and form validations are the same as in the previous recipe and are explained in detail there. When you launch the application, the form is displayed as shown in the following screenshot:

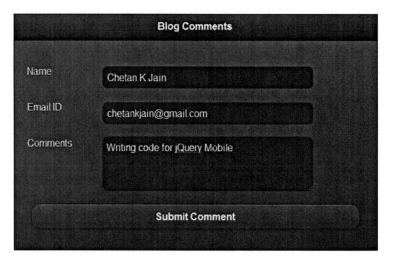

Fill the form and click on **Submit Comment** button. If no errors are found, the form is submitted via Ajax. The custom nodejs web server responds to the `/postComment` request by generating the following HTML content as a response with mime-type `'text/html'`:

```
<div data-role='page' data-theme='a'>
  <div data-role='header'>
    <h1>Comments Added</h1>
  </div>
  <div data-role='content'>
    Hi {User name entered}!
    <p>Your Email ID: {Email ID entered}</p>
    <p>Added your comment: {Comments entered}</p>
    <a href='#' data-role='button' data-rel='back'>Back</a>
  </div>
</div>
```

The response is rendered by the framework as shown in the following screenshot:

The page transition is smooth and it uses the pop animation. You can click on the **Back** button and navigate back to the original page as the data-rel='back' attribute is also specified.

## There's more...

You can submit this form without using Ajax by specifying the data-ajax='false' attribute to the form element. This code is available in the non-ajax.html file in the same folder as main.html:

```
<form id='commentform' action='/postComment' method='post' data-
ajax='false'>
```

When Ajax is not used, the response triggers a full page refresh. The server response in this recipe returns only the page div container and does not return the <head> element with any links to the jQuery Mobile stylesheet. Also, references to the jQuery and jQuery Mobile libraries are missing in the response. So the resultant page is as shown in the following screenshot. Here the response page is not styled and if you click on the **Back** link, it does not work.

# Comments Added

Hi Chetan K Jain!

Your Email ID: chetankjain@gmail.com

Added your comment: Writing code for jQuery Mobile

Back

## The Ajax response

The server response via Ajax replaces the content of the request form as seen in this recipe. You can view this response by using a DOM inspector. But if you view the page source, the original page is still shown. POST requests cannot be bookmarked as they do not contain any query parameters in the hash. The response to a POST request returns with the same URL as the request and it does not update the URL hash.

## Other ways of non-Ajax form submission

This recipe shows you how to submit forms without using Ajax by setting the attribute `data-ajax='false'`. Another way to not use Ajax is to specify a `target` attribute to the form as shown in the following code:

```
<form id='commentform' action='/postComment' method='post'
target='sometarget'>
```

This is applicable to both POST and GET server requests.

Ajax can also be turned off across your application by using the global configuration as shown in the following code in the `mobileinit` event handler:

```
$.mobile.ajaxEnabled = false;
```

## See also

▶  The *Validating forms* recipe

▶  The *Fetching data using GET* recipe

▶  The *Configuring ajaxEnabled* recipe in *Chapter 7, Configurations*

# Fetching data using GET

This recipe shows you how to use an Ajax **GET** request and fetch data from a server. In this recipe, the server sends back soccer scores to a GET request from a **Soccer League Scores** form.

## Getting ready

Copy the full code of this recipe from the `code/05/get-request` sources folder. This code can be launched using the URL `http://localhost:8080/05/get-request/main.html`. To try out this recipe you will need to launch the simple nodejs web server that is shipped along with the source code of this book. Launch the server by using the following command:

```
node jqmserver.js
```

## How to do it...

1. In `main.html`, add the following code to create a form:

```
<div id='scores' data-role='fieldcontain'>
   <form id='scoreform' action='/getScores' method='get'>
      The latest scores are now available!
      <input id='submitid' type='submit' name='submitid' data-
inline='true' value='Fetch Scores' />
   </form>
</div>
```

2. Add the following script to the `<head>` section to fetch and display the scores using Ajax:

```
$('#main').live('pageshow', function(event) {
   $('#scoreform').submit(function() {
      $.get('/getScores').success(showScores).error(errMsg);
      return false; // cancel the default submit
   });
});
function showScores(data) { // on success
   $('#scores').html(data).trigger('create');
}
function errMsg() { // on error
   $('#scores').html('Unable to fetch scores, try later');
}
```

## How it works...

In `main.html`, add a `<div>` container with `id='scores'` and set its attribute `data-role='fieldcontain'`. This `<div>` container will display the scores. Add a form (`id='scoreform'`) to the page and set its `action` to `'/getScores'` and `method` to `'get'`. Add a submit button with text **Fetch Scores** to the form to fetch the scores from the server. You can add a decorated footer using `class='ui-bar ui-bar-e'` to the page. When you load the application the following screen is displayed:

Add an event handler to the `pageshow` event as shown in the previous code. When you click on the `submit` button, it calls the jQuery `submit()` method. The server response to the default form `submit()` would replace the entire page with new content. To get a partial page update, call the jQuery `.get()` Ajax method to fetch data from the `'/getScores'` server URL. Then cancel the default `submit()` method by returning `false`. The `.get()` method specifies the callback functions for `success` and `error` as shown in the previous code. In the success callback function `showScores()`, replace the content of `#scores` div with the HTML response obtained from the server. Trigger the `'create'` method to let the jQuery Mobile framework initialize and enhance the newly added content. Any error is handled by the `errMsg()` error handler as shown in the previous code.

The custom nodejs web server responds to the `/getScores` get request by generating the following HTML content as a response with mime-type `'text/html'`:

```
<ul data-role='listview'>
  <li data-role='list-divider'>Group A</li>
    <li>Team A beat Team B [ 5 - 3 ]</li>
    <li>Team C lost to Team D [ 1 - 2 ]</li>
  <li data-role='list-divider'>Group B</li>
    <li>Team E drew Team F [ 0 - 0 ]</li>
    <li>Team G lost to Team H [ 3 - 4 ]</li>
</ul>
```

Now only the contents of the `#scores` `<div>` container are replaced by this server response. The header and footer remain untouched. The resulting display is as shown in the following screenshot:

## There's more...

You can submit forms without using Ajax by specifying the `data-ajax='false'` attribute to the form element as shown in the following code. When Ajax is not used, the response triggers a full page refresh. So ensure that a proper jQuery Mobile page is returned in the server response or else the resultant page could have styling and other issues.

```
<form action='/someAction' method='get' data-ajax='false'>
```

### The Ajax response

The server response via Ajax replaces the content of the request form completely. You can view the response by using a DOM inspector. But if you view the page source, the original page is still shown. GET requests can be bookmarked as they support query parameters in the hash. The GET response allows the update of the URL hash.

### Form submission defaults

You can also submit a form without any action or method attribute as specified in the following code:

```
<form>
```

The form will use the default values of the action and method attributes. The method will default to `'get '` and the action will default to the current page's relative path. You can access this path via the call to the `$.mobile.path.get()` method.

 Always specify the `action` and `method` attributes for a form.

## See also

▶ The *Validating forms* recipe

▶ The *Submitting a form using POST* recipe

▶ The *Configuring ajaxEnabled* recipe in *Chapter 7, Configurations*

# Creating an accessible form

The jQuery Mobile framework has very good support for the accessibility features, such as **WAI-ARIA**. This provides support for accessibility tools such as screen readers. This enables your application screens to be read out to those users who depend on such assistive technologies. Also speech input controls are now available on a few browsers like Chrome (which uses the webkit engine). These controls accept voice input. This recipe shows you how to generate accessible form controls that accept voice input and also support screen readers.

## Getting ready

Copy the full code of this recipe from the `code/05/accessible-controls` sources folder. You can launch this code by using the URL `http://localhost:8080/05/accessible-controls/main.html`.

## How to do it...

1. In `main.html`, add the following code to create a form:

```
<form action='#' method='post'>
  <div data-role='fieldcontain' class='ui-hide-label'>
    <input type='text' name='username' id='username'
placeholder='Enter Name' speech x-webkit-speech/>
    <label for='username'>Name</label>
  </div>
  <div data-role='fieldcontain'>
    <input type='number' name='age' id='age' placeholder='Enter
Age' speech x-webkit-speech/>
    <label for='age' class='ui-hidden-accessible'>Age</label>
  </div>
  <div data-role='fieldcontain'>
    <input type='text' name='city' id='city' placeholder='Enter
City' class='custom' speech x-webkit-speech/>
    <label for='city' class='ui-hidden-accessible'>City</label>
  </div>
  <input type='submit' name='submit' id='submit' value='Submit' />
</form>
```

## How it works...

In `main.html`, add three fields as follows, **username** (input `type='text'`), **age** (input `type='number'`), and **city** (input `type='text'`). Associate a label to each of these fields and add a `div` container with attribute `data-role='fieldcontain'` for each set of labels and input controls. This helps the framework to realign and adjust the layout dynamically based on the platform and settings. The `placeholder` attribute is used to give an appropriate hint to the user for input.

To enable voice input, add the attributes `speech` and `x-webkit-speech` as shown in the previous code for each of the input controls. The support for voice input is totally dependent on browser implementation and a few browsers still do not implement them. When the page loads, you will see the following screenshot:

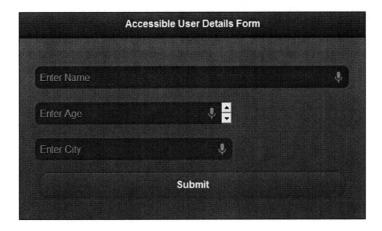

You will see a small microphone icon at the right corner of each input control. The user can tap on this icon and will be prompted to speak in the value for the input. Once the user speaks in, **the speech to text engine** converts the voice to text and displays the input value text in the control. Though not fully accurate the voice to text technologies are improving by the day.

## There's more...

As mentioned earlier, the jQuery Mobile framework has very good support for the accessibility features such as WAI-ARIA. So add meaningful labels to all the form elements. When the page is initialized, the framework exposes these labels to the screen readers automatically. If you are already using placeholders to provide hints to the user, labels might be redundant. But if you are seeking to build an application that supports accessibility, then you should also define labels.

If you want to use the placeholder feature and also support accessibility, then jQuery Mobile provides an easy option to hide the labels by using the style `'ui-hidden-accessible'` on the form control. You can also hide the label by adding the style `'ui-hide-label'` to the form field container as shown in the code. Now the labels are not shown on the display but are still available to screen readers. You can verify this by running your favorite screen reader and accessing the page created.

### Popular voice readers for mobile devices

There are numerous voice readers in the market today and you can try any of the popular ones based on your platform. Apple phones have **VoiceOver** (see `http://www.apple.com/accessibility/iphone/vision.html`), Android has **TalkBack**, **Spiel**, **Mobile Accessibility** for Android, and other applications in the **Android Play Store**.

## Desktop voice readers

For the Chrome desktop browser, the **ChromeVox** extension can be installed from `http://code.google.com/p/google-axs-chrome` and once enabled it will start reading out the form controls for you. You can verify that the hidden label contents are also read out by the screen reader.

# 6
# List Views

In this chapter we will cover:

- ▶ Using inset and non-inset lists
- ▶ Creating a custom numbered list
- ▶ Using a nested list
- ▶ Using a read-only nested list
- ▶ Formatting content in a list
- ▶ Using a split button list
- ▶ Using image icons
- ▶ Creating a custom search filter
- ▶ Modifying a list with JavaScript

## Introduction

A simple list in jQuery Mobile is created using the following code:

```
<ul data-role='listview'>
    <li><a href='link1'>Item 1</a></li>
    <li><a href='link2'>Item 2</a></li>
</ul>
```

The previous code is a regular HTML unordered list to which you add the attribute
`data-role='listview'`. The framework now enhances the list, styles it, and makes it
mobile friendly. It adds a right arrow for the anchor elements and when you tap any of the
list items, the page in the link is loaded into the DOM and opened using AJAX transition
when possible.

# Using inset and non-inset lists

An **inset list** is a list embedded within a container (a page or form or another list). This recipe shows you how to create inset and non-inset lists. The recipe also highlights what you need to take care while using non-inset lists with other form controls.

## Getting ready

Copy the full code of this recipe from the `code/06/inset-list` sources folder. This code can be launched using the URL `http://localhost:8080/06/inset-list/main.html`.

## How to do it...

1. Create `main.html` with three lists and a few buttons as shown in the following code:

```
<div data-role='content'>
  <a href='#' data-role=button data-theme='b'>Button 1</a>
  <ul data-role='listview' data-inset='true'>
    <li data-theme='e'><a href='#'>Item 1</a></li>
    <li data-theme='e'><a href='#'>Item 2</a></li>
  </ul>
  <a href='#' data-role=button data-theme='b'>Button 2</a>
  <ul data-role='listview'>
    <li data-theme='e'><a href='#'>Item A</a></li>
    <li data-theme='e'><a href='#'>Item B</a></li>
  </ul>
  <a href='#' data-role=button data-theme='b'>Button 3</a>
  <ul data-role='listview' style='margin: 15px'>
    <li data-theme='e'><a href='#'>Item 3</a></li>
    <li data-theme='e'><a href='#'>Item 4</a></li>
  </ul>
  <a href='#' data-role=button data-theme='b'>Button 4</a>
</div>
```

## How it works...

In the code, the first list is an inset list and the other two are non-inset lists. You can create an inset list by adding the attribute `data-inset='true'` to a list. This styles the list with rounded corners and gives it a nice margin of 15px on all four sides. If you place buttons or any other form controls next to inset lists, the layout is automatically adjusted.

The next list in the code is a non-inset list and it does not have the `data-inset` attribute. The framework adds a padding of `-15px` to this list and stretches it to fill the entire width of the screen. If you place buttons or any other form controls next to this list, the controls will overlap each other due to the negative padding. This list has rectangular corners.

The third list in the code is also a non-inset list. But the overlapping of controls is handled here by using the attribute `style='margin: 15px'`. This adds a margin of `15px` to the list and negates the default padding. The three lists are displayed as shown in the following screenshot:

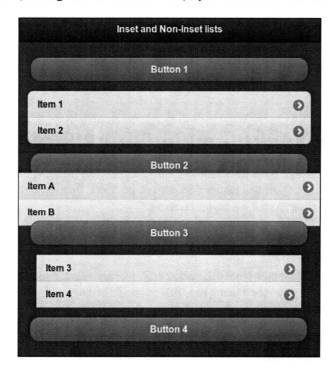

 Add an additional margin when you use non-inset lists with other form controls to avoid overlapping of the controls.

## There's more...

You can configure the framework to use inset lists by default in your app. You can do this by setting the `inset` option of the `listview` plugin to `true` and bind this to the `mobileinit` event as shown in the following code:

```
$(document).bind('mobileinit',function(){
    $.mobile.listview.prototype.options.inset = 'true';
});
```

### Setting the listview theme

You can use the data-theme attribute and set a theme to the list as shown in the following code. The list uses swatch e in the following code:

```
<ul data-role='listview' data-theme='e'>
```

### Setting the theme on list items

You can use the data-theme attribute with each list item and set different themes. The following code sets swatch e to the list item **Item 1**, whereas, the list item **Item 2** will use swatch d.

```
<ul data-role='listview' data-theme='e'>
  <li>Item 1</a>
  <li data-theme='d'>Item 2</li>
</ul>
```

# Creating a custom numbered list

A **numbered list** by default uses decimals in jQuery Mobile. The framework uses CSS to add the numbering. JavaScript is used where CSS cannot be used. This recipe shows you how to add alphabet numbering to your list using JavaScript.

## Getting ready

Copy the full code of this recipe from the code/06/custom-numbered-list sources folder. This code can be launched using the URL http://localhost:8080/06/custom-numbered-list/main.html.

## How to do it...

1. In main.html, create an ordered and an unordered list as shown in the following code:

```
<div data-role='content'>
  <ol data-role='listview' data-theme='e' data-inset='true'>
    <li>Soccer</li>
    <li>Basketball</li>
    <li>Hockey</li>
    <li>Tennis</li>
  </ol>
  <ul id='alphalist' data-role='listview' data-theme='e' data-inset='true'>
    <li>Soccer</li>
    <li>Basketball</li>
    <li>Hockey</li>
    <li>Tennis</li>
```

```
        </ul>
      </div>
```

2. Add the following script to add alphabet numbering to the unordered list:

```
$('#main').live('pageinit', function(event) {
  var alph = 'a';
  $('#alphalist').find('li').each(function() {
    var str = "<span style='font-weight: normal'>" + alph
        + '. </span>' + $(this).html();
    $(this).html(str);
    alph = String.fromCharCode(alph.charCodeAt(0)+1);
  });
});
```

## How it works...

The first list in the code is an ordered list and uses decimal numbers by default. The next list with `id='alphalist'` is an unordered list. Add the given script to the page container or the `<head>` section of `main.html`.

In the script, bind the `pageinit` event to a function that injects the alphabet numbering. In this function, call the jQuery `find('li')` method to fetch all the list items in the list. Loop through each of these items using the jQuery `each()` method. In the callback function of `each()`, get the current text of the list item using `$(this).html()` and prefix the alphabet (with `normal` font weight) to this text. Set this new string (`str`) to the list item by using `$(this).html(str)`. Finally increment the alphabet in the loop by using the `charCodeAt()` and `fromCharCode()` JavaScript methods. When the page is shown, the two lists are now displayed as in the following screenshot:

## There's more...

You can create any type of numbered lists (such as Roman numerals, small or upper case alphabets, bullets and so on) using JavaScript. But you will have to ensure that you handle all the scenarios with these lists (for example, handling the item numbering of nested lists).

# Using a nested list

A **Nested List** is a list that is embedded within the list item of another list. A right arrow icon is shown by default on the list item and when you click on it, the framework opens a separate sub page to display the nested list. The sub page shown uses theme b by default for the page header. The framework can handle nesting to n-levels. This recipe shows you how to use nested lists and also how to fetch the child pages of the nested list using JavaScript.

## Getting ready

Copy the full code of this recipe from the `code/06/nested-list` sources folder. This code can be launched using the URL `http://localhost:8080/06/nested-list/main.html`.

## How to do it...

1. In `main.html`, add the following code to create a list of authors. Add nested lists with book names to some of the authors.

```html
<div data-role='content'>
  <ul data-role='listview' data-theme='b' data-inset='true'>
    <li><a href='#'>H.G. Wells</a></li>
    <li><a href='#'>Rabindranath Tagore</a>
      <ul data-role='listview' data-theme='a' data-inset='true'>
        <li><a href='#'>The Gardener</a></li>
        <li><a href='#'>Gitanjali</a></li>
      </ul>
    </li>
    <li><a href='#'>William Shakespeare</a>
      <ul data-role='listview' data-theme='a' data-inset='true'>
        <li><a href='#'>Merchant of Venice</a></li>
        <li><a href='#'>Romeo and Juliet</a></li>
      </ul>
    </li>
  </ul>
  <div id='nestedlists'></div>
</div>
```

2. Add the following script to fetch the child pages of the nested list:

```
$('#main').live('pageinit', function(event) {
  var str = '';
  $('ul').listview('childPages').each(function() {
    str = $(this).find("div[class$='ui-title']").html() + ', ' +
str;
  });
  $('#nestedlists').html('Books available for authors : ' + str);
});
```

## How it works...

In the code, add author names as list items with anchor links. Add nested lists with book names for the authors **Rabindranath Tagore** and **William Shakespeare**. The author **H.G. Wells** does not have a nested list.

Add the given script to the page container or the `<head>` tag in `main.html`. In the script bind the `pageinit` event to an event handler to call the `childPages` method of the **listview plugin**. Iterate through the array of child pages using the jQuery `each()` method. In the callback function of `each()`, get the header text of the sub pages using the jQuery `find()` method. Find the header div that has the attribute `class='ui-title'`. Concatenate this text to a string and once all the author sub pages are fetched, set this string as the content of the empty `'nestedlists'` div. This will display the list of authors who have a nested list of books. The author **H.G. Wells** does not have a nested list and is not shown.

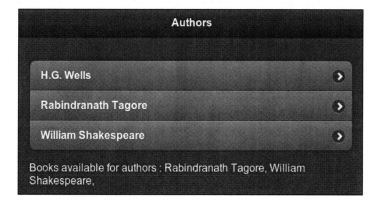

The nested lists are embedded after the anchor link `<a>` tag inside the list item `<li>` tag in a list. When you click on this list item, it opens the sub page as shown in the following screenshot. The anchor link text is set as the header of the sub page and the header uses theme b by default.

## There's more...

You will notice the difference in the theme of the sub page compared to the main page. The main page uses theme a for the page content and header. It uses theme b for the list. The sub page header is set to theme b by default. Since the nested list used the `data-theme='a'` attribute, the entire sub page, including the nested list, is themed with swatch a. This might not be ideal while using nested lists in your app. Refer to the recipe *Theming a nested list* in *Chapter 10, The Theme Framework* on how to theme a nested list properly.

### Theming the header of the sub page of a nested list

As seen in this recipe, by default the header of the sub page of a nested list is set to swatch b. You can use the attribute `data-header-theme` as shown in the following code to set the header theme of the sub page:

```
<ul data-role='listview' data-theme='d' data-header-theme='a'>
```

### Configuring the header theme option of a list view

You can configure the default header theme of nested lists across your app by setting the `headerTheme` option of the `listview` plugin. The following code sets this to theme a and binds it to the `mobileinit` event:

```
$(document).bind('mobileinit',function(){
    $.mobile.listview.prototype.options.headerTheme = 'a';
});
```

## See also

- ▸ The *Using a read-only nested list* recipe
- ▸ The *Theming a nested list* recipe in *Chapter 10, The Theme Framework*

# Using a read-only nested list

A **read-only list** is a list that contains non interactive items or items that do not have anchor links in them. The framework styles read-only items differently compared to the regular items. The read-only items have a lighter or paler shade of the theme color and they also have a smaller size as the user is not expected to tap on them.

This recipe shows you how to create a read-only nested list and also use **Options** to configure list views. It also shows you how to display a nested list as an inset list.

## Getting ready

Copy the full code of this recipe from the `code/06/read-only-list` sources folder. This code can be launched using the URL `http://localhost:8080/06/read-only-list/main.html`.

## How to do it...

1. In `main.html`, add the following code to create a list of authors. Add nested lists with book names to some of the authors.

```
<div data-role='content'>
  <ul data-role='listview'>
    <li>H.G. Wells</li>
    <li><a href='#'>Mark Twain</a></li>
    <li>Rabindranath Tagore
      <ul data-role='listview'>
        <li>The Gardener</li>
        <li>Gitanjali</li>
      </ul>
    </li>
    <li>William Shakespeare
      <div><ul data-role='listview'>
        <li>Merchant of Venice</li>
        <li>Romeo and Juliet</li>
      </ul></div>
    </li>
  </ul>
</div>
```

2. Add the following script to the page to configure the list view options:

```
<script>
  $.mobile.listview.prototype.options.theme = 'e';
  $.mobile.listview.prototype.options.headerTheme = 'a';
  $.mobile.listview.prototype.options.inset = true;
</script>
```

## How it works...

In the code, add author names as list items without any anchor links. Add nested lists with books for authors **Rabindranath Tagore** and **William Shakespeare**. Author **H.G. Wells** does not have a nested list. Author **Mark Twain** has an anchor link. The list uses theme e, that is, a yellow color. Items that do not have nested lists or anchor links are displayed in a lighter shade and a smaller font. Items with nested lists or with anchor links are displayed in a regular color and have a bigger font.

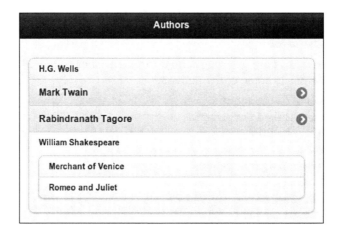

Add the previous script to the page or the <head> tag of main.html as shown in the code. The script configures the default options of the listview plugin. In this recipe, the theme, headerTheme, and inset options are configured. Use the headerTheme option to set the theme of the sub page header to a as shown in the previous code. Now when you click the list item **Rabindranath Tagore**, the sub page is opened for the nested list. The nested list with the header theme a is displayed as shown in the following screenshot:

## There's more...

There may be instances when you want to display the nested list as an inset list. You can do this by wrapping the inner list within a `<div>` tag. The framework now will not create a sub page for the nested list.

 Calling the `childPages` method on the `listview` plugin will not return the lists that are embedded with the `<div>` tag.

The list of books of **William Shakespeare** are embedded within the `<div>` tag in this recipe and so a nested list is not created.

 Using inset nested lists will stretch your list vertically and the user will have to scroll the page to view all the contents. So use them selectively.

## See also

- ▶ The *Using a nested list* recipe
- ▶ The *Theming a nested list* recipe in *Chapter 10, The Theme Framework*

# Formatting content in a list

This recipe shows you how to format text in a list item. It also shows you how to use collapsible items and **count bubbles** within the list item.

## Getting ready

Copy the full code of this recipe from the `code/06/format-content` sources folder. This code can be launched using the URL `http://localhost:8080/06/format-content/main.html`.

## How to do it...

1. In `main.html`, add the following code to create a list of modes of transport:

```
<div data-role='content'>
  <ul data-role='listview'>
    <li>
      <p class='ui-li-aside' style='font-size: 15px'>
          <strong>High Speed</strong></p>
      <div data-role='collapsible' data-theme='e'>
```

```
        <h2>Air</h2>
        <ul data-role='listview'>
          <li>Aeroplane</li><li>Helicopter</li>
        </ul>
      </div>
      <p class='ui-li-count'>2</p>
    </li>
    <li  data-theme='e'>
      <p class='ui-li-aside' style='font-size: 15px'>
          <strong>Moderate Speed</strong></p>
      <div data-role='collapsible' data-theme='e'>
        <h2>Land</h2>
        <ul data-role='listview'>
          <li>Bus</li><li>Car</li><li>Bike</li><li>Train</li>
        </ul>
      </div>
      <p class='ui-li-count'>4</p>
    </li>
    <li>
      <p class='ui-li-aside' style='font-size: 15px'>
          <strong>Slow Speed</strong></p>
      <div data-role='collapsible' data-theme='e'>
        <h2>Water</h2>
        <ul data-role='listview'>
          <li>Ship</li><li>Submarine</li><li>Boat</li>
        </ul>
      </div>
      <p class='ui-li-count'>3</p>
    </li>
  </ul>
</div>
```

2. Add the following script to the page to configure the list view options:

```
<script>
  $.mobile.listview.prototype.options.theme = 'e';
  $.mobile.listview.prototype.options.countTheme = 'a';
  $.mobile.listview.prototype.options.inset = true;
</script>
```

## How it works...

Add the three modes of transport as list items as shown in the previous code. Add a collapsible block with `data-role='collapsible'` to each of the list items. Add a heading text to each of the collapsible block and create a list with different vehicle types as its content. Add a string with the style set to `class='ui-li-aside'`. This creates a string and positions it on the top right corner of the list item. Finally, add the number of vehicles listed and set its style to a **count bubble** by using `class='ui-li-count'`. Do this for each of the list items.

Add the script shown in the code to the page or the `<head>` tag of `main.html` to configure the default values for list options `theme`, `inset`, and `countTheme`. The list is now displayed as shown in the following screenshot:

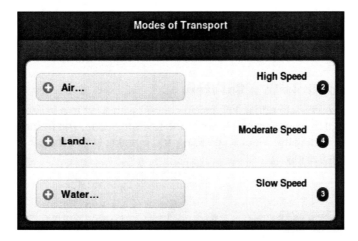

The following image shows the list with one collapsible block expanded:

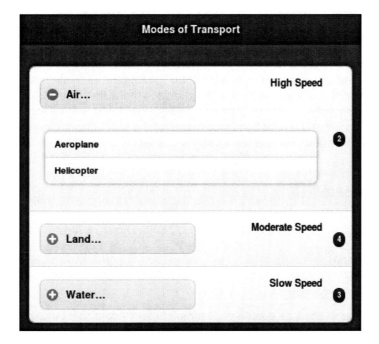

## There's more...

You can theme the count bubble using the option `countTheme` as already mentioned in this recipe. You can also set the attribute `data-count-theme` on the list as shown in the following code:

```
<ul data-role='listview' data-count-theme='a'>
```

### Using form controls in a list item

This recipe shows you how to add a collapsible content with a list to a list item. You can also add any form control to a list item as shown in the following code. The framework enhances the form control by adding the required padding and margins within the list item and makes the form control tap friendly.

```
<li><input type='text' name='username' placeholder='Enter name'/></li>
```

## See also

▸    The *Using a split button list* recipe

# Using a split button list

A **split button list** is a list that provides two different actions for the same list item. This is created by adding two anchor links to a list item. The framework then automatically converts the list item to a split button. Any image added to the first link gets scaled down to a thumbnail with a size of 80 x 80px. The second link is replaced with an icon called the **split icon** and is positioned at the right-hand side corner of the split button. This recipe shows you how to create a split button list to display images in a list.

## Getting ready

Copy the full code of this recipe from the `code/06/split-button-list` sources folder. This code can be launched using the URL `http://localhost:8080/06/split-button-list/main.html`.

## How to do it...

1.    Create `main.html` as a multi-page template app. Add a split button list in the `#main` page as shown in the following code:

```
<div data-role='content'>
    <ul data-role='listview' data-inset='true' data-theme='b'
        data-split-theme='e' data-split-icon='arrow-d'>
        <li>
```

```
        <a href='#viewphoto' data-rel='dialog'>
          <img style='margin: 10px'
              src='../../resources/images/img1.png' />
          <h3>Lal Bagh</h3>
          <p>Bangalore, India</p>
        </a>
        <a href='#download' data-rel='dialog'>Lal Bagh, Bangalore</
    a>
      </li>
      <li>
        <a href='#viewphoto' data-rel='dialog'>
          <img style='margin: 10px'
              src='../../resources/images/img2.png' />
          <h3>Peacock</h3>
          <p>Mysore, India</p>
        </a>
        <a href='#download' data-rel='dialog'>Peacock, Mysore</a>
      </li>
      <li>
        <a href='#viewphoto' data-rel='dialog'>
          <img style='margin: 10px' height=75%
            src='../../resources/images/img3.png' />
          <h3>Ganesha</h3>
          <p>Bangalore, India</p>
        </a>
        <a href='#download' data-rel='dialog'>Ganesha, Bangalore</a>
      </li>
    </ul>
  </div>
```

2. Add the #viewphoto page that will be opened on tapping the left part of the split button.

```
<div id='viewphoto' data-role='page' data-theme='e' >
  <div data-role='header' data-theme='e'>
    <h1>Photo View</h1>
  </div>
  <div data-role='content'>
    Showing photo here ...
  </div>
</div>
```

3. Add the #download page that will be opened on tapping the split icon.

```
<div id='download' data-role='page' data-theme='e' >
   <div data-role='header' data-theme='e'>
     <h1>Download</h1>
   </div>
   <div data-role='content'>
       Downloading file ...
   </div>
</div>
```

## How it works...

Add list items to the list in the #main page as shown in the previous code. Each list item has two links and both the links are opened as dialogs by setting the data-rel='dialog' attribute. Point the first link to the #viewphoto page. Add an image pointing to the photo and add a formatted description to the anchor link text. Depending on the size of the thumbnail image, you can add padding to the image as shown in the previous code.

Point the second link to the #download page. The second link is automatically converted to a split icon. The right arrow is used by default for the split icon. You can configure this by using the data-split-icon attribute on the list view. Use the data-split-theme attribute to theme the split icon. The split button list is displayed as shown in the following screenshot:

Tapping on the photo image or the left button in the list item opens the **Photo View** dialog as shown in the following screenshot:

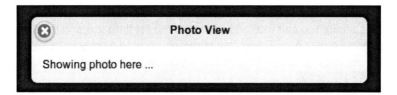

Tapping on the split icon opens the **Download** dialog as shown in the following screenshot:

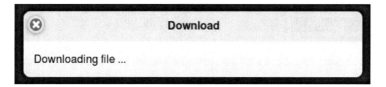

## There's more...

To display the photo image in the `#viewphoto` dialog you will have to write some JavaScript code to handle the `pagechange` event. This is covered in the recipe *Using changePage() to change a page* in *Chapter 9, Methods and Utilities*.

### Configuring the split button list using listview options

You can configure the default values for the split icon and the split icon theme using the `splitTheme` and `splitIcon` options of the `listview` plugin and bind it to the `mobileinit` event. The following code sets the star icon and theme `e` as default values for the list view options:

```
$(document).bind('mobileinit',function(){
    $.mobile.listview.prototype.options.splitIcon = 'star';
    $.mobile.listview.prototype.options.splitTheme = 'e';
});
```

## See also

- ▸ The *Formatting content in a list* recipe
- ▸ The *Using image icons* recipe
- ▸ The *Using changePage( )to change a page* recipe in *Chapter 9, Methods and Utilities*

# Using image icons

The jQuery Mobile framework adds an icon to the right-hand side of an interactive list item (a list item having a link). You can also add an icon to the list item text and the framework sizes this icon to fit within `40 x 40px`. This recipe shows you how to display icons with list items.

## Getting ready

Copy the full code of this recipe from the `code/06/list-icons` sources folder. This code can be launched using the URL `http://localhost:8080/06/list-icons/main.html`.

## How to do it...

1.  In `main.html`, add a list with list items as shown in the following code:

```
<div data-role='content'>
  <ul data-role='listview' data-theme='b' data-inset='true'>
    <li data-icon='star'>
      <a href='#'>
        <img src='../../resources/images/img1.png' class='ui-li-
icon'
            alt='Lal Bagh'/>
        <h3 style='margin-left: 25px'>Lal Bagh, Bangalore</h3>
      </a>
    </li>
    <li data-icon='star'>
      <a href='#'>
        <img src='../../resources/images/img2.png' class='ui-li-
icon'
            alt='Peacock'/>
        <h3 style='margin-left: 25px'>Peacock, Mysore</h3>
      </a>
    </li>
    <li data-icon='star'>
      <a href='#'>
        <img src='../../resources/images/img3.png' class='ui-li-
icon'            alt='Ganesha'/>
        <h3 style='margin-left: 25px'>Ganesha, Bangalore</h3>
      </a>
    </li>
  </ul>
</div>
```

## How it works...

Add an image to each of the list items in the list within the anchor link of the list item. Set the attribute `class='ui-li-icon'` to this image element. This instructs the framework to style the image as an icon and the image is automatically scaled down to fit inside the list item. You can set the required margin to the text so that it gets displayed correctly after adjusting for the image size. The list is displayed as shown in the following screenshot:

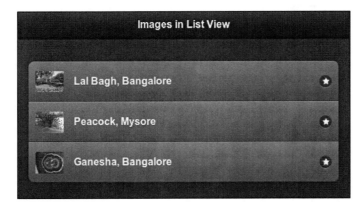

## There's more...

For an interactive list item, that is, an item with a link, the framework adds a right arrow icon by default at the right-hand side of the list item. This can be changed by using the `data-icon` attribute on the list item. The code in this recipe uses the `star` icon for the list item.

## See also

- ▸ The *Formatting content in a list* recipe
- ▸ The *Using a split button list* recipe

# Creating a custom search filter

When a **List Search Filter** is used, the framework runs through the list items and displays the items that match the filter text. Alternate text can also be used with the search filter. The list item text is ignored when alternate text is used. The search is a generic match and any occurrence of the search value within the text is displayed in the result.

This recipe shows you how to use a search filter that can search both the list item text and alternate text. It also shows you how to configure search filters and also how to implement a custom search callback function that uses a custom search logic.

## Getting ready

Copy the full code of this recipe from the `code/06/custom-search` sources folder. This code can be launched using the URL `http://localhost:8080/06/custom-search/main.html`.

## How to do it...

1. In `main.html`, create the following list of Mobile platforms. The list items also contain the OS manufacturer names in the attribute `data-filtertext`.

```
<div data-role='content' data-theme='e'>
  <ul id='oslist' data-role='listview'>
    <li data-role='list-divider'>Open Source</li>
    <li data-filtertext='Google'>Android</li>
    <li data-filtertext='HP'>WebOS</li>
    <li data-filtertext='Samsung Intel'>Tizen</li>
    <li data-filtertext='Linux Foundation'>LiMo</li>
    <li data-filtertext='Mozilla'>Boot2Gecko</li>
    <li data-role='list-divider'>Closed</li>
    <li data-filtertext='Apple'>iOS</li>
    <li data-filtertext='Nokia'>Symbian</li>
    <li data-filtertext='Nokia'>S40</li>
    <li data-filtertext='RIM'>Blackberry OS</li>
    <li data-filtertext='Microsoft'>Windows Phone</li>
    <li data-filtertext='Samsung'>Bada</li>
  </ul>
</div>
```

2. Add the following script to the page to configure the default list options:

```
$.mobile.listview.prototype.options.theme = 'e';
$.mobile.listview.prototype.options.inset = true;
$.mobile.listview.prototype.options.dividerTheme = 'e';
$.mobile.listview.prototype.options.filter = true;
$.mobile.listview.prototype.options.filterTheme = 'e';
$.mobile.listview.prototype.options.filterPlaceholder = 'Search
for ...';
$.mobile.listview.prototype.options.filterCallback = customFilter;
```

3. The following code snippet includes the list item text in the search text:

```
$('#main').live('pageinit', function(event) {
  $('#oslist').find('li').each(function() {
    $(this).attr('data-filtertext',
        $(this).attr('data-filtertext') + ' ' + $(this).html());
  });
});
```

4. The custom search callback is defined as in the following code:

```
function customFilter(text, searchValue) {
  var regx='\\b'+searchValue;
  return !(text.match(new RegExp(regx, 'i')));
}
```

## How it works...

In `main.html`, create a list with `id='oslist'`. Add list items for the various Mobile OS platforms as shown in the code. Create list items with the attribute `data-role='list-divider'` and separate the list items as **Open Source** and **Closed**. Add the OS manufacturer name as alternate search text by using the `data-filtertext` attribute.

Add the given script to the page or the `<head>` tag of `main.html`. Set the various list view configuration options like `theme='e'` and `inset='true'`. This is a **read-only list** and the list items are shaded with a light yellow color. Use the `dividerTheme='e'` option to theme the list divider items. The list divider items are styled with a darker shade by the framework.

Next, add the `filter='true'` and `filterTheme='e'` options to add a search filter to the list and theme it with swatch e. Use the `filterPlaceholder` option to specify a custom text for the search filter text control (the default is `'Filter Items...'`). Finally set a custom search call back function by setting the option `filterCallback=customFilter`. The list is displayed as shown in the following screenshot:

The default search function in a list matches any occurrence of the search string in the text. To override this, define the custom filter callback as shown in the previous code. The function accepts two parameters, `text` and `searchValue`. Create a regular expression to search for the occurrence of the `searchValue` at the start of the word in the given text. The occurrence of the search value in between a word is ignored. The regular expression is matched with the text using the `match()` method. The `i` parameter makes it case insensitive.

If the `filtertext` attribute is used with a list item, the default search uses only this text and ignores the list item text. To use both the list item text and the filter text, add a `pageinit` event handler as shown in the previous code. In this function, find each list item using the jQuery `find('li').each()` method and in the callback of `each()`, fetch the list item text and add it to the filter text. This will not have any visible impact on the list item. But the list item text is now part of the filter text and is thus available for the search filter. So a search for **a** will list **Android** and **iOS** (the filtertext has the value **Apple**). But this will not list **Symbian** or **Bada** which contain **a** in between words as seen in the following screenshot:

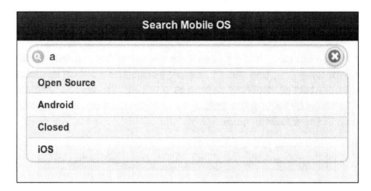

If you search for **Bo** it shortlists only **Boot2Gecko** as seen in the following screenshot:

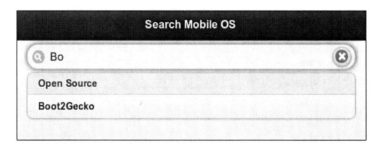

## There's more...

The search callback function returns a Boolean value and this indicates if the text should be hidden by the search filter. So the search filter callback should return `false` for all matching elements. Unmatched text elements return `true` and get hidden by the search filter.

### Using data-attribute to configure list divider themes

The recipe uses the `dividerTheme` option to theme the list divider item. You can also use the `data-divider-theme` attribute as shown in the following code:

```
<ul data-role='listview' data-theme='e' data-divider-theme='e'>
```

### Using data-attribute to configure list search filters

The recipe shows you how to use the `filter`, `filterTheme` and `filterPlaceholder` options to configure the list view. These can also be set using the `data-filter`, `data-filter-theme`, and `data-filter-placeholder` attributes as shown in the following code:

```
<ul data-role='listview' data-filter='true' data-filter-theme='e'
data-filter-placeholder='Search for...'>
```

## Modifying a list with JavaScript

You can use JavaScript to dynamically modify a list and its contents. This recipe shows you how to use JavaScript to add or remove list items in a read-only list.

### Getting ready

Copy the full code of this recipe from the `code/06/scripting-lists` sources folder. This code can be launched using the URL `http://localhost:8080/06/scripting-lists/main.html`.

### How to do it...

1. In `main.html`, add the following code to create an empty list in a layout grid:

```
<div data-role='content'>
  <div data-role='fieldcontain'>
    <fieldset class='ui-grid-b'>
      <div class='ui-block-a' style='width: 65%'>
        <ul id='numlist' data-role='listview' data-theme='e'
            data-inset='true'>
        </ul>
      </div>
      <div class='ui-block-b'>
        <button data-theme='b' id='addBtn'>Add</button>
        <button data-theme='b' id='removeBtn'>Remove</button>
      </div>
    </fieldset>
  </div>
</div>
```

2. Add the following script to dynamically add or remove list items:

```
var count = 0;
$('#main').live('pagecreate', function(event) {
  $('#numlist').listview({create: function(event, ui) {
    $('#addBtn').bind('click', function(event, ui) {
      var str = "<li><a href='#'>Item " + (++count) + '</a></li>';
      $('#numlist').append(str);
      $('#numlist').listview('refresh');
    });
    $('#removeBtn').bind('click', function(event, ui) {
      if (--count < 0) {
        count = 0;
        return;
      }
      $('#numlist').find('li').last().remove();
      $('#numlist').listview('refresh');
    });
  }});
});
```

## How it works...

Add a two column layout grid to `main.html` using the attribute `class='ui-grid-b'` on a `fieldset` container. Add an empty list with `id='numlist'` to the first column. Add two buttons with the IDs `addBtn` and `removeBtn` to the second column. On clicking these buttons, list items are dynamically updated to the empty list in the first column.

Add the given script to the page or the `<head>` section of `main.html`. In the script, create an event handler for the `pagecreate` event which gets fired before the page is fully initialized. Here, add an event handler for the `create` event of the `listview` element. When the `listview` element is created, this event is fired. In its callback function, bind the `click` event of the `addBtn` and `removeBtn` buttons as shown in the previous code.

The `addBtn`, when pressed, adds a list item to the list. The list item text is kept in memory and incremented on adding new elements. The `removeBtn` when pressed, fetches the most recent list item element that was added by calling the jQuery `find('li').last()` method. This last element is removed by calling the `remove()` method. Call the `refresh()` method on the **listview plugin** after any modification to update the list.

When the app is started, the display looks like the following screenshot with an empty list:

Pressing the **Add** button adds new list items to the list, as in the following screenshot:

Pressing the **Remove** button removes the recently added list item.

## There's more...

As mentioned in this recipe, you have to call the `refresh()` method on the **listview plugin** after any modification. On adding new list items or on removing list items, the `refresh()` method triggers an update of the list and applies the necessary styles and enhancements on the list items.

```
$('#numlist').listview('refresh');
```

# 7

# Configurations

In this chapter, we will cover the following recipes:

- ▶ Configuring the active classes
- ▶ Configuring `ajaxEnabled`
- ▶ Configuring `autoInitializePage`
- ▶ Configuring the default transitions
- ▶ Configuring `ignoreContentEnabled`
- ▶ Configuring the page loading and error messages
- ▶ Configuring the default namespace
- ▶ Configuring `hashListeningEnabled` and `subPageUrlKey`
- ▶ Configuring `pushStateEnabled` and `linkBindingEnabled`

## Introduction

The jQuery Mobile framework enhances the markup and elements in a document as soon as the document is loaded. You can tweak the default configurations used for these enhancements by setting their values in the `mobileinit` event handler, which gets fired at startup on the document object. This chapter shows you how to use the various configurations available in the framework.

## Configuring the active classes

The jQuery Mobile framework uses the CSS class `activeBtnClass` to style a button in an active state with theme b by default. The `activeBtnClass` class has a default string value `ui-btn-active`. To style the active page (the page in view or in transition), the framework uses the CSS class `activePageClass`, which has a default string value `ui-page-active`. This recipe shows you how to configure the framework to use custom classes instead of these default classes.

## Getting ready

Copy the full code of this recipe from the `code/07/active-class` sources folder.
You can launch this code using the URL: `http://localhost:8080/07/active-class/main.html`.

## How to do it...

1. In `main.html`, add the following style to the `<head>` tag of the page to define your own custom active button class and active page class:

```
<link rel="stylesheet"
  href="http://code.jquery.com/mobile
  /1.1.1/jquery.mobile-1.1.1.min.css" />
<style>
  .ui-custom-btn-active {
    background: #53C584;
    background-image: -webkit-gradient(linear, left top,
      left bottom, from( #53C584 ), to( #6FD598 ));
    background-image: -webkit-linear-gradient( #53C584 ,
      #6FD598 );
    background-image: -moz-linear-gradient( #53C584 ,
      #6FD598 );
    background-image: -ms-linear-gradient( #53C584 ,
      #6FD598 );
    background-image: -o-linear-gradient( #53C584 ,
      #6FD598 );
    background-image: linear-gradient( #53C584 ,
      #6FD598 );
  }
  .ui-mobile .ui-custom-page-active {
    border: 3px;
    border-style: dotted;
    width: 99%;
    display: block;
    overflow: visible;
  }
</style>
```

2. Add the following script before including the jQuery Mobile script:

```
$(document).bind("mobileinit", function() {
  $.mobile.activePageClass = "ui-custom-page-active";
  $.mobile.activeBtnClass = "ui-custom-btn-active";
});
```

3. Create the #main page with a link to open #page1 as follows:

```
<div id="main" data-role="page" data-theme="e">
  <div data-role="header" data-theme="e">
    <h1>Active Classes</h1>
  </div>
  <div data-role="content">
    <a href="#page1" data-role="button">Open Page 1</a>
  </div>
</div>
```

4. Create #page1 with a link to go back to the #main page as follows; this is a multi-page document:

```
<div id="page1" data-role="page" data-theme="e">
  <div data-role="header" data-theme="e">
    <h1>Page 1</h1>
  </div>
  <div data-role="content">
    <a href="#main" data-rel="back" data-role="button">
      Go Back
    </a>
  </div>
</div>
```

## How it works...

In main.html, add a style tag and define the class ui-custom-btn-active to set a different gradient background (green shade) on the active button. The default active button background is a bright blue shade. Also add a ui-custom-page-active class that sets a 3px thick-dotted border for the page. Next, add the given script in the code before including the reference to jquery.mobile.js. In the script, add an event handler for the mobileinit event that gets triggered at the start of the app. Here, set the $.mobile.activePageClass and $.mobile.activeBtnClass properties to the two new classes. Finally, add the #main and #page1 page containers. When you launch the app, the #main page is now displayed with a dotted border as shown in the following screenshot:

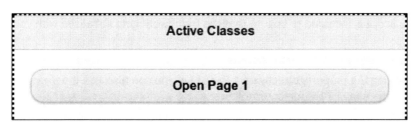

When you click on the **Open Page 1** button, the active state of the button shows the green shade when pressed, as shown in the following screenshot:

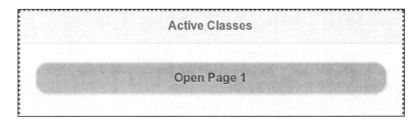

Next, the page #page1 opens and it too has the dotted border:

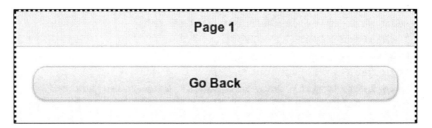

The **Go Back** button also gets a green shade when you click on it:

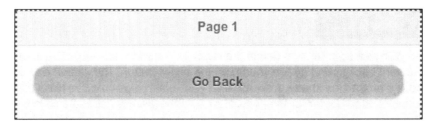

## There's more...

You can customize and configure the default settings for the jQuery Mobile framework using the mobileinit event handler. You have to add this custom script before the jquery. mobile.js script is included to ensure that the framework gets initialized with your settings.

### Using the jQuery .extend() call

Instead of setting the property directly on $.mobile, you can also use the .extend() jQuery call to extend the $.mobile object, as follows:

```
$.extend( $.mobile, {
    $.mobile.activeBtnClass = "ui-custom-btn-active";
});
```

▶  *Chapter 2, Pages and Dialogs, Using CSS to create a bouncing page transition*: This
   recipe provides and overview of vendor prefixes

# Configuring ajaxEnabled

Whenever possible, the jQuery Mobile framework automatically uses Ajax for handling link
clicks and form submissions. This can be configured using the $.mobile.ajaxEnabled
property, which has a Boolean value of true by default. If Ajax is disabled or if its not
supported, then an ordinary HTTP request is used and a full page load occurs. URL
hash listening is also disabled. This recipe shows you how to configure the $.mobile.
ajaxEnabled property.

## Getting ready

Copy the full code of this recipe from the code/07/ajax-enabled sources folder. You can
launch this code using the URL: http://localhost:8080/07/ajax-enabled/main.html.

## How to do it...

1. In main.html, add the following script before including jquery.mobile.js:

```
$(document).bind("mobileinit", function() {
  $.mobile.ajaxEnabled = true;
});
```

2. Create the main page with a link to open page1.html:

```
<div id="main" data-role="page" data-theme="e">
  <div data-role="header" data-theme="a">
    <h1>Ajax Enabled</h1>
  </div>
  <div data-role="content">
    <p>This is the main page</p>
    <a href="page1.html" data-role="button">
      <p>Open Page 1</p>
    </a>
  </div>
</div>
```

3. Finally, create page1.html with a link to go back to main.html, as follows:

```
<div data-role="page" data-theme="e" data-add-back-
  btn="true">
  <div data-role="header">
    <h1>Page 1</h1>
```

```
      </div>
      <div data-role=content>
        <p>Sub Page Contents</p>
        <a href="main.html" data-role="button">Go back</a>
      </div>
    </div>
```

## How it works...

Add the given script in the code before including the reference to jquery.mobile.js. In the script, add an event handler for the mobileinit event that gets triggered at the start of the app. Here, set the configuration $.mobile.ajaxEnabled=true.

 Since $.mobile.ajaxEnabled is true by default, you don't have to explicitly set it in your code. It is included in this recipe, because you will be changing this value to false later in the code.

Add the #main page. Create page1.html as shown in the code (note that the <head> element is not present in page1.html). The #main page is displayed, as shown in the following screenshot:

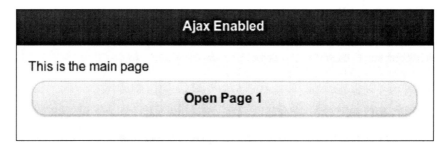

Click on the **Open Page 1** button to open page1.html as follows. This page gets loaded via Ajax, and the framework enhances the controls.

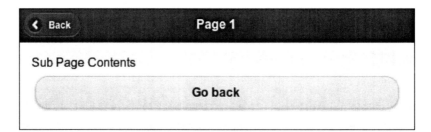

Next, set the `ajaxEnabled` property to `false` in `main.html`, and reload the page. Now, when `page1.html` is opened, the elements are not enhanced, as shown in the following screenshot:

# Page 1

Sub Page Contents Go back

## There's more...

When Ajax is disabled, the entire page is loaded. In `page1.html`, since the `<head>` element with the links to the jQuery Mobile framework library is missing, the page does not get any style or enhancements.

# Configuring autoInitializePage

When you navigate to a new page or when a page is loaded in the DOM, the framework initializes the page and makes it visible. This is controlled by the `$.mobile.intializePage` property, which has a Boolean value of `true` by default. If this is set to `false`, the page is not shown. You will have to manually set this back to `true` to show the page. This recipe shows you how to do the same.

## Getting ready

Copy the full code of this recipe from the `code/07/auto-initialize` sources folder. You can launch this code by using the URL: `http://localhost:8080/07/auto-initialize/main.html`.

## How to do it...

1. In `main.html`, add the following script before including `jquery.mobile.js`:

```
$(document).bind("mobileinit", function() {
  $.mobile.autoInitializePage = false;
});
```

2. Create the main page with the following content:

```
<div data-role="content">
  <a href="#" data-role="button">A button</a>
  <script>
    $.mobile.autoInitializePage = true;
  </script>
</div>
```

## How it works...

Add the given `autoInitializePage` script to the code before including the reference to `jquery.mobile.js`. In the script, add an event handler for the `mobileinit` event that gets triggered at the start of the app. Here, set the configuration `$.mobile.autoInitializePage=false`. Finally, add the `#main` page. The page content will be similar to the following screenshot:

The contents are initialized and visible as the value of `$mobile.autoInitializePage` is manually set to `true`, as shown in the code. You can comment this line (in the page content section) and reload the page to find that nothing gets shown.

## There's more...

You can use this feature to delay displaying the page while you do some background work or while you fetch data in the background from a server. It is useful when you manually handle the changing of pages.

# Configuring the default transitions

By default, the jQuery Mobile framework uses the **fade** transition while loading pages with Ajax. The **pop** transition is used by default while opening dialogs with Ajax. This recipe shows you how to set different default transitions for your app.

## Getting ready

Copy the full code of this recipe from the `code/07/default-transitions` sources folder. You can launch this code using the URL: `http://localhost:8080/07/default-transitions/main.hml`.

## How to do it...

1. In `main.html`, add the following script before including `jquery.mobile.js`:

```
$(document).bind("mobileinit", function() {
  $.mobile.defaultDialogTransition = "flow";
  $.mobile.defaultPageTransition = "turn";
});
```

2. Create the `#main` page as follows:

```
<div id="main" data-role="page" data-theme="e">
  <div data-role="header">
    <h1>Configure Transitions</h1>
  </div>
  <div data-role=content>
    <a href="#page1" data-role="button">Open as Page</a>
    <a href="#page1" data-rel="dialog" data-role="button">Open as
Dialog</a>
  </div>
</div>
```

3. Create `#page1` as follows; this is a multi-page document:

```
<div id="page1" data-role="page" data-theme="e" data-add-back-
btn="true">
  <div data-role="header">
    <h1>Page 1</h1>
  </div>
  <div data-role=content>
    <p>Page 1 Content</p>
  </div>
</div>
```

## How it works...

Create `main.html` and add the given script in the code before including the reference to `jquery.mobile.js`. In the script, add an event handler for the `mobileinit` event that gets triggered at the start of the app. Here, set the default transitions for pages and dialogs using the `$.mobile.defaultDialogTransition` and `$.mobile.defaultPageTransition` properties. Finally, add the `#main` and `#page1` page containers as shown.

In `#main`, there are two buttons. The first one opens `#page1` as a page and the second one opens it as a dialog. You will see that the default transitions are changed. The page now uses the `turn` transition and the dialog uses the `flow` transition.

## There's more...

You can also set both the page and the dialog default transitions to `none`. This will just load the pages or dialogs without using any transitions:

```
$.mobile.defaultDialogTransition = "none";
$.mobile.defaultPageTransition = "none";
```

### Using custom transitions

You can configure the framework to use your own custom transitions as default transitions. You have to set the transition name as follows:

```
$.mobile.defaultDialogTransition = "myDialogTransition";
$.mobile.defaultPageTransition = "myPageTransition";
```

### Transition fallbacks

The `fade` transition is the default transition and it uses 2D. All other transitions use 3D. Older browsers and devices that do not support 3D transformations will fall back to using `fade`. You can configure this default fall back transition to `none` or you can set it to your own custom 2D transition. This can be done for each of the individual 3D transitions, as follows:

```
$.mobile.transitionFallbacks.slideout = "none";
$.mobile.transitionFallbacks.flip = "myCustom2DTransition";
```

## See also

▸ *Chapter 2, Using CSS to create a bouncing page transition*
▸ *Chapter 2, Using JS to create a Slide 'n Fade transition*

# Configuring ignoreContentEnabled

The jQuery Mobile framework automatically enhances controls and markup found in a page. To skip enhancing certain sections of markup, you can use the `$.mobile.ignoreContentEnabled` configuration (which is `false` by default). This recipe shows you how to do the same.

## Getting ready

Copy the full code of this recipe from the `code/07/content-enabled` sources folder. You can launch this code using the URL: `http://localhost:8080/07/content-enabled/main.html`.

## How to do it...

1. In `main.html`, add the following script before including `jquery.mobile.js`:

```
$(document).bind("mobileinit", function() {
    $.mobile.ignoreContentEnabled = true;
});
```

2. Create the `#main` page with the following content :

```
<div data-role="content">
  <div data-enhance="false">
    <input type="checkbox" name="chkbox1" id="chkbox1"
      checked />
    <label for="chkbox1">Checkbox</label>
    <input type="radio" name="radiobtn1" id="radiobtn1"
      checked />
    <label for="radiobtn1">Radio Button</label>
  </div>
  <div>
    <input type="checkbox" name="chkbox2" id="chkbox2"
      checked />
    <label for="chkbox2">Enhanced Checkbox</label>
    <input type="radio" name="radiobtn2" id="radiobtn2"
      checked />
    <label for="radiobtn2">Enhanced Radio Button</label>
  </div>
</div>
```

## How it works...

Create `main.html` and add the given script in the code before including the reference
to `jquery.mobile.js`. In the script, add an event handler for the `mobileinit`
event that gets triggered at the start of the app. Here, set the property `$.mobile.`
`ignoreContentEnabled=true`. In `#main`, add two divs. Add a checkbox and a radio button
to each `div`. Set the attribute `data-enhance=false` to the first `div`. Now, the elements
added to this `div` are not enhanced by the framework. The elements in the second `div` are
automatically enhanced. The page is displayed as shown in the following screenshot:

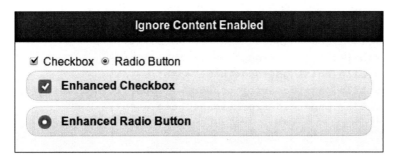

## There's more...

When you use the $.mobile.ignoreContentEnabled=true configuration, it tells the framework to avoid enhancing certain sections of markup. This is done by using the data-enhance="false" attribute as shown in this recipe. Now, when the framework encounters each control or markup, it first checks if the parent element has the data-enhance attribute set to false. If so, it skips applying the style or any enhancements to the control.

 Using $.mobile.ignoreContentEnabled and data-enhance could cause performance degradation while the pages are enhanced.

# Configuring the page loading and error messages

By default, the jQuery Mobile framework shows a spinning animation with theme a and without any text when loading a new page. If there is an error, the page load times out and an error message Error Loading Page is shown, with theme e. This recipe shows you how to change and customize the page loading and error messages.

## Getting ready

Copy the full code of this recipe from the sources code/07/load-message folder. To try out this recipe, launch the simple nodejs web server that is available in the folder code, by using the following command:

```
node jqmserver.js
```

Then you can launch the code by using the URL: http://localhost:8080/07/load-message/main.hml.

## How to do it...

1. In main.html, add the following script before including jquery.mobile.js:

```
$(document).bind("mobileinit", function() {
    $.mobile.loadingMessage = "Fetching it...";
    $.mobile.loadingMessageTextVisible = true;
    $.mobile.loadingMessageTheme = "b";
    $.mobile.pageLoadErrorMessage = "Oops, it's missing!";
    $.mobile.pageLoadErrorMessageTheme = "b";
});
```

2. Create the #main page with the following content:

```
<div data-role="content">
  <a href="/delay" data-role="button">Dummy page</a>
</div>
```

## How it works...

Create main.html, and add the given script before including the reference to jquery. mobile.js. In the script, add an event handler for the mobileinit event that gets triggered at the start of the app. Here, set the default page load messages and error messages as shown in the code.

In #main, there is a link that tries to open the "/delay" page. This is a GET operation on the nodejs server. The server handles this request and returns an error code after pausing for a few seconds. The spin control with a text message is shown for this duration, as shown in the following screenshot:

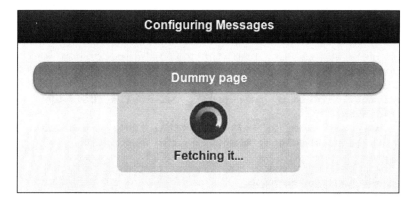

The error response causes the following error message to be shown:

# Configuring the default namespace

This recipe shows you how to configure the jQuery Mobile framework to use your custom namespace for the `data-` attributes.

## Getting ready

Copy the full code of this recipe from the `code/07/namespace` sources folder. You can launch this code using the URL: `http://localhost:8080/07/namespace/main.html`.

## How to do it...

1. In `main.html`, add the following script before including `jquery.mobile.js`:

```
$(document).bind("mobileinit", function() {
  $.mobile.ns = "my-";
});
```

2. Add the following style to the `<head>` tag:

```
<link rel="stylesheet" href="http://code.jquery.com/mobile/1.1.1/
jquery.mobile-1.1.1.min.css" />
<style>
  .ui-mobile [data-my-role=page], .ui-mobile [data-my-
role=dialog],
    .ui-page { top: 0; left: 0; width: 100%; min-height: 100%;
    position: absolute; display: none; border: 0; }
</style>
```

3. Create the main page as follows:

```
<div id="main" data-my-role="page" data-my-theme="e">
  <div data-my-role="header" data-my-theme="a">
    <h1>Configure Namespace</h1>
  </div>
  <div data-my-role="content">
    <p>This is the main page</p>
    <a href="#dialog" data-my-role="button">
      Open Dialog
    </a>
  </div>
</div>
```

4. Create the `#dialog` page as follows; this is a multi-page document:

```
<div id="dialog" data-my-role="dialog" data-my-theme="e">
  <div data-my-role="header" data-my-theme="a">
    <h1>Dialog</h1>
  </div>
```

```
    <div data-my-role="content">
      <p>This is a dialog</p>
      <a href="#" data-my-role="button" data-my-
        rel="back">Go Back</a>
    </div>
  </div>
```

## How it works...

To use a custom namespace, you will have to override one specific selector in the
jquery.mobile.css file, the .ui-mobile [data-my-role=page], and the
.ui-mobile [data-my-role=dialog] selector. Override this style as shown in
the code. Using data-my-role means that the namespace is set to my.

Create main.html, and set this configuration by adding the preceding script before
including the reference to jquery.mobile.js. In the script, add an event handler for the
mobileinit event that gets triggered at the start of the app. Here, set the default namespace
by using the $.mobile.ns="my-"configuration . Add the #main and #dialog pages.

The following screenshot shows the page as seen through a DOM inspector:

You will note that the code also used the data-my- attributes. You will also observe that
the framework has added enhancements, and even these enhancements use the custom
namespace all across the page.

 Use a trailing hyphen as in "my-" for the custom namespace.
It is easier to read the enhanced code this way.

# Configuring hashListeningEnabled and subPageUrlKey

When you use a nested `listview`, the jQuery Mobile framework generates a sub page in the form of `pagename.html&ui-page=subpageidentifier`. The hash segment before the sub page URL key (`&ui-page`) is used by the framework for navigation. This recipe shows you how to use a custom sub page URL key. It also shows you how to use the `$.mobile.hashListeningEnabled` configuration.

## Getting ready

Copy the full code of this recipe from the sources folder `code/07/sub-page`. You can launch this code using the URL: `http://localhost:8080/07/sub-page/main.html`.

## How to do it...

1. In `main.html`, add the following script before including `jquery.mobile.js`:

```
$(document).bind("mobileinit", function() {
  $.mobile.subPageUrlKey = "my-page";
  $.mobile.hashListeningEnabled = false;
});
```

2. Create the `#main` page with a nested list in its content as follows:

```
<div data-role="content">
  <ul data-role="listview" data-theme="e">
    <li>Main Page Item 1</li>
    <li>Sub Page Items
      <ul data-role="listview">
        <li>Sub Page Item A</li>
        <li>Sub Page Item B</li>
      </ul>
    </li>
  </ul>
</div>
```

## How it works...

Create `main.html`, and add the given script in the code before including the reference to `jquery.mobile.js`. In the script, add an event handler for the `mobileinit` event that gets triggered at the start of the app. Here, set the `$.mobile.subPageUrlKey="my-page"` and `$.mobile.hashListeningEnabled=false` configurations. Finally, add the `#main` page with a nested list as shown in the code. The output will be similar to the following screenshot:

Click on **Sub Page Items,** and open the nested list in a sub page. The address bar shows the custom sub page URL key `my-page`, as shown in the following screenshot:

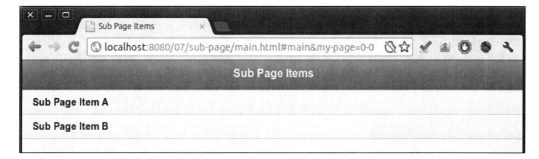

Now, go back using the browser **Back** button. The URL in the address bar gets updated, but the page does not change back to the previous screen, as shown in the following code:

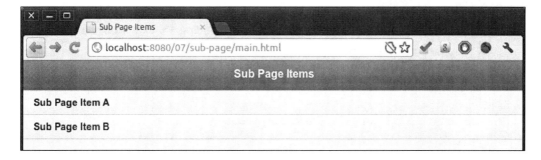

This is because `hashListeningEnabled` was configured to `false` at startup. This will prevent the framework from listening and handling the location hash changes. If you set the `hashListeningEnabled` to `true` (the default value) and reload the page, the page navigation will work fine and the main list is shown again from the nested list.

Configure `hashListeningEnabled` only if you want to custom manage the hash changes instead of allowing the framework to handle it.

## See also

▶   *Chapter 7, Configurations, Configuring pushStateEnabled and linkBindingEnabled*

# Configuring pushStateEnabled and linkBindingEnabled

When you click on a link, navigation happens and the URL hash is updated. The framework allows you to replace the URL hash to a full path in browsers that support the `history.replaceState` API. This recipe shows you how to do this using the `$.mobile.pushStateEnabled` configuration. It also shows you how to use the `$.mobile.linkBindingEnabled` configuration that allows the framework to automatically bind the clicks on the anchor links in a document. Both these are `true` by default.

## Getting ready

Copy the full code of this recipe from the sources `code/07/push-state` folder. You can launch this code using the URL: `http://localhost:8080/07/push-state/main.html`.

## How to do it...

1.  In `main.html`, add the following script before including `jquery.mobile.js`:

    ```
    $(document).bind("mobileinit", function() {
      $.mobile.linkBindingEnabled = true;
      $.mobile.pushStateEnabled = false;
    });
    ```

2.  Create the `#main` page with the following content:

    ```
    <div data-role="content">
      <a href="page1.html" data-role="button">Go to Page 1</a>
    </div>
    ```

3.  Create `page1.html` as follows:

    ```
    <div id="page1" data-role="page" data-theme="e">
      <div data-role="header">
        <h1>Header of Page 1</h1>
      </div>
      <div data-role="content">
    ```

```
            <a href="#" data-role="button" data-rel="back">Go Back</a>
        </div>
    </div>
```

## How it works...

Create `main.html`, and add the given script in the code before including the reference to `jquery.mobile.js`. In the script, add an event handler for the `mobileinit` event that gets triggered at the start of the app. Here, set the `$.mobile.pushStateEnabled=false` and `$.mobile.linkBindingEnabled=true` configurations. Finally, add the `#main` page contents and `page1.html`, as shown in the code. The output will be similar to the following screenshot:

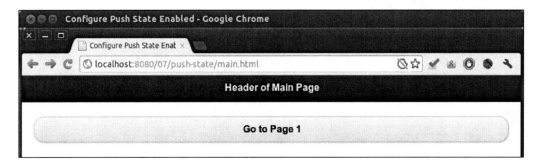

When you open **Page 1**, the URL address bar has the full path appended to `main.html`, as shown in the following screenshot:

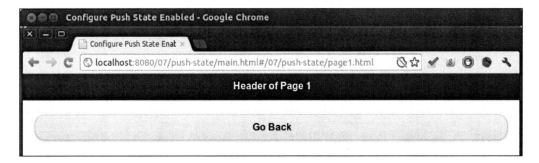

This is because `pushStateEnabled` was set to `false` at startup. If you set this to `true` (the default value) and reload the page, the URL hash is replaced and is shown as `http://localhost:8080/07/push-state/page1.html`.

 Set the `pushStateEnabled` configuration to `false` when Ajax is not used or when external links are used extensively in your app.

## There's more...

In this recipe, the `linkBindingEnabled` configuration was set to `true` at startup (its default value). If you set this to `false` and reload the page, you will notice that the **Go to Page 1** button does not get the active state when clicked. The framework does not automatically bind the link clicks in this case.

>  Use the `linkBindingEnabled` configuration only if you want your custom code (or another library) to handle the link clicks.

## See also

▶ *Chapter 7, Configurations, Configuring hashListeningEnabled and subPageUrlKey*

# 8
# Events

In this chapter, we will cover:

- ► Using orientation events
- ► Using scroll events
- ► Using touch events
- ► Using virtual mouse events
- ► Using page initialization events
- ► Using page load and remove events
- ► Using page change events
- ► Using page transition and animation events
- ► Using layout events

## Introduction

The jQuery Mobile framework provides specific events in addition to the default native events for both desktop and mobile platforms. It allows you to bind to these events using the jQuery `bind()` or `live()` method, and thus allows you to perform custom actions. This chapter shows you how to use the events that are available in the jQuery Mobile framework.

## Using orientation events

The jQuery Mobile framework triggers an `orientationchange` event when the orientation (**portrait** or **landscape**) of the mobile device is changed. This recipe shows you how to use the `orientationchange` event.

## Getting ready

Copy the full code of this recipe from the `code/08/orientation` sources folder. You can launch this code by using the URL `http://localhost:8080/08/orientation/main.html`

## How to do it...

Carry out the following steps:

1. Create `main.html` as follows:

```
<div id="main" data-role="page" data-theme="e">
  <div data-role="header" data-theme="a">
    <h1>Orientation Events</h1>
  </div>
  <div data-role="content">
    <p>Change orientation</p>
  </div>
</div>
```

2. Add script to handle the `orientationchange` event in the `<head>` section:

```
$(window).bind("orientationchange", function(event, data) {
  $("h1").html(data.orientation);
});
```

## How it works...

Create `main.html` with page content, as shown in the preceding code snippet. Add the given script and bind the `orientationchange` event to a callback function. Here, set the current orientation of the device to the  h1 header of the page. You can get the device orientation by using the `data.orientation` property of the callback function.

When the page loads, change the orientation of the device; the header text will show **portrait** or **landscape** based on the current orientation.

## There's more...

In platforms where the orientation property is not supported (`$.support.orientation` is `false`), or when the `$.mobile.orientationChangeEnabled` global configuration is set to `false`, the framework binds the resize event handler to handle the orientation change of the device.

## The orientationChangeEnabled global configuration

You can configure the `$.mobile.orientationChangeEnabled` configuration in the `mobileinit` event handler, which gets invoked at the start of your app. This must be done before including the `jquery.mobile.js` script.

```
$(document).bind("mobileinit", function() {
  $.mobile.orientationChangeEnabled = false;
});
```

# Using scroll events

When you scroll, the jQuery Mobile framework fires the scrollstart event. When you stop scrolling the `scrollstop` event is triggered. This recipe shows you how to use these two events.

## Getting ready

Copy the full code of this recipe from the `code/08/scroll` sources folder. You can launch this code by using the URL `http://localhost:8080/08/scroll/main.html`

## How to do it...

Carry out the following steps:

1. Create `main.html` with the page content `div` styled with a large value for its height, so that the scroll bars appear:

```
<div id="main" data-role="page" data-theme="e">
  <div data-role="header" data-theme="a" data-
  position="fixed">
    <h1>Scroll Events</h1>
  </div>
  <div data-role="content">
    <div style="height: 1000px">Scroll now</div>
  </div>
</div>
```

2. Add the following script to the `<head>` section to handle the `scroll` events:

```
$(window).bind("scrollstart", function(event) {
  $("h1").html("Scrolling now...");
});
$(window).bind("scrollstop", function(event) {
  $("h1").html("Scrolling done!");
});
```

## How it works...

Create `main.html` as shown in the preceding code. Add a `div` container with a `height` of `1000px` to the page content. This will make the vertical scroll bars appear. Now, add the given script to the `<head>` section of the page. Bind the `scrollstart` event to a callback function that updates the page header text. Similarly bind the `scrollstop` event to a callback function that updates the header text. Now, scroll the page holding the vertical scroll bar handle. You can see the page header text showing `"Scrolling now..."`, and when you stop or pause scrolling, the text is updated to `"Scrolling done!"`.

## There's more...

There is an issue as to how the `scrollstart` event works on iOS devices. DOM manipulation is not allowed during scroll, and the event gets queued and triggered as soon as the scrolling stops. So keep this in mind when you work with scroll events on iOS devices. You will have to have to make your changes before scrolling starts and not as soon as it starts.

# Using touch events

The jQuery Mobile framework provides five touch events. They are the `tap`, `taphold`, `swipe`, `swipeleft`, and `swiperight` events. The tap event is fired when you tap the screen. If the tap duration is longer, the `taphold` event is fired first and then the `tap` event is fired after you lift your finger. When you swipe across the screen, the `swipe` event is fired first and then the `swipeleft` or `swiperight` events are fired, based on the direction of your swipe action. This recipe shows you how to use these touch events.

In this recipe, a yellow box is shown where you last tapped the screen. A green box is created each time you tap and hold. You can also see how the swipe action works by swiping a blue bar to the left or right edge of the screen.

## Getting ready

Copy the full code of this recipe from the `code/08/touch` sources folder. You can launch this code by using the URL `http://localhost:8080/08/touch/main.html`.

## How to do it...

The steps to be followed are

1. In `main.html`, define the following styles in the `<head>` tag:

```
<style>
    .box { width:60px; height:60px; position:fixed }
    .yellow { background-color:yellow; z-index:1 }
```

```
.green { background-color:green; z-index:2 }
.blue { background-color: blue; z-index:3; height:100% }
</style>
```

2. Add the page content with two `<div>` tags styled with the blue bar and yellow box:

```
<div id="content" data-role="content">
  <div id="movingbox" class="box yellow" style="top:0px;
left:0px"></div>
  <div id="edgebar" class="box blue" style="top:0px; left:0px"></
div>
</div>
```

3. Add the following script to the `<head>` section, to handle the `tap` and `taphold` events:

```
var tapholdflag = false;
$("#main").live("tap", function(event) {
  var stylestr = "left:" + event.clientX + "px; top:"
    + event.clientY + "px;"
  if (tapholdflag) {
    var str = "<div class=''box green'' style=''" +
      stylestr + "''></div>";
    $("#content").append(str).trigger("create");
  } else {
    $("#movingbox").attr("style",
      stylestr).trigger("refresh");
  }
  tapholdflag = false;
});
$("#main").live("taphold", function(event) {
  tapholdflag = true;
});
```

4. Finally, handle the `swipe`, `swipeleft`, and `swiperight` events:

```
$("#main").live("swipe", function(event) {
  $.event.special.swipe.scrollSupressionThreshold = 15;
  $.event.special.swipe.durationThreshold = 1250;
  $.event.special.swipe.horizontalDistanceThreshold = 25;
  $.event.special.swipe.verticalDistanceThreshold = 50;
});
$("#main").live("swipeleft", function(event) {
  $("#edgebar").attr("style", "top:0px;
    left:0px").trigger("refresh");
});
$("#main").live("swiperight", function(event) {
  $("#edgebar").attr("style", "top:0px;
    right:0px").trigger("refresh");
});
```

## How it works...

In `main.html`, add the `style` tag and define the `box`, `yellow`, `green`, and `blue` classes. Add an empty `div` tag with `id="movingbox"`, and set the attribute `class="box yellow"`. This creates a `60px` wide yellow-colored square. Next, add an empty `div` tag with `id="edgebar"`, and set the attribute `class="box blue"`. This creates a `60px` wide blue bar on the edge of the screen as shown in the following screenshot. The yellow box is hidden below the blue bar as it has a lower `z-index` value.

Now add the given script to the `<head>` section of `main.html`. Bind each of the five touch events to callback functions as shown. If the tap duration is long, then it is `taphold`. So, define a Boolean `tapholdflag` to track whether the `tap` event was `taphold` or not. Set this to `true` in the `taphold` event handler, and clear it after the `tap` event is fired.

In the callback of the `tap` event, first check if `tapholdflag` is already set. If so, then this is a `taphold` event. Create a new green box and call the `"create"` method as shown. If the `tapholdflag` is `false`, then this is a simple tap. Update the new position of the yellow box, and trigger the `"refresh"` method. Finally, clear `tapholdflag` and set it to `false`.

You can get the tap location by using the `event.clientX` and `event.clientY` parameters. Set these values to the `left` and `top` style attributes of the box to update its position. The screen looks similar to the following screenshot after a few `tap` and `taphold` events:

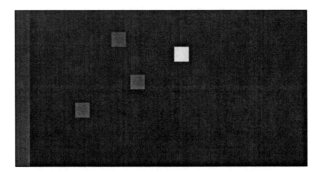

Now, bind the `swipe` event to a callback function and configure the `swipe` event properties as shown in the code. The code shows you how to configure the `scrollSupressionThreshold`, `durationThreshold`, `horizontalDistanceThreshold`, and `verticalDistanceThreshold` properties.

Bind the `swipeleft` event to a callback to set the `left` and `top` style attributes of the blue bar and call the `"refresh"` method. This will move the bar to the left edge of the screen. Similarly, bind the `swiperight` event to a callback to set the `right` and `top` style attributes of the blue bar, and call `"refresh"`. This will move the bar to the right edge of the screen. Now, when you swipe towards the right side of the screen, the bar moves to the right edge, as shown in the following screenshot; swipe towards the left side, and the bar moves back to the left edge:

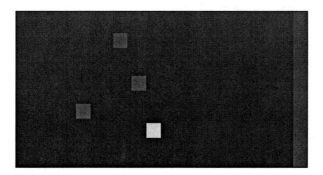

## There's more...

In the code, the callback for the `swipe` event shows you how to configure the `swipe` event properties. The available configurations are as follows:

- `scrollSupressionThreshold` (`10px` by default): The swipe distance must be more than this value for the event to be fired, else it is a `scroll` event

- `durationThreshold` (`1000ms` by default): If the swipe duration is more than this value, then the `swipe` event is prevented from being fired

- `horizontalDistanceThreshold` (`30px` by default): The horizontal swipe distance must be more than this value for the event to be fired

- `verticalDistanceThreshold` (`75px` by default): The vertical swipe distance must be less than this value for the event to be fired

### The tapholdThreshold property

The `tap` event is fired whenever you tap the screen. If the tap duration exceeds a certain value (`750ms` by default), then this is treated as a `taphold` event. You can configure this duration by setting the `$.event.special.tap.tapholdThreshold` property as follows:

```
$("#main").live("tap", function(event) {
  $.event.special.tap.tapholdThreshold = 1000;
});
```

 The default `tap` event configurations work well for most of the platforms. So modify them only if you have a very strong reason to do so.

## See also

▸ The *Using virtual mouse events* recipe

# Virtual mouse events

The jQuery Mobile framework provides virtual `mouse` or `vmouse` events to abstract the mouse and touch events.

You don't have to write separate handlers for the touch and mouse events for each of the supported platforms or devices. You just have to write the event handlers for the `vmouse` events and this will work across various platforms. There are seven `vmouse` events supported by the framework: `vmousemove`, `vmouseover`, `vmouseout`, `vmousedown`, `vmouseup`, `vclick`, and `vmousecancel`. This recipe shows you how to use these `vmouse` events.

## Getting ready

Copy the full code of this recipe from the `code/08/vmouse` sources folder. You can launch this code by using the URL `http://localhost:8080/08/vmouse/main.html`.

## How to do it...

The steps to be followed are:

1. Create `main.html` with content having seven `div` tags for the seven `vmouse` events, as follows:

```
<div data-role="content">
  <div id="move"></div>
  <div id="over"></div>
```

```
<div id="out"></div>
<div id="down"></div>
<div id="up"></div>
<div id="click"></div>
<div id="cancel"></div>
</div>
```

2.  Add the following script to the `<head>` section to handle the `vmousemove`, `vmouseover`, and `vmouseout` events:

```
$("#main").live("pageinit", function(e) {
  $("#main").bind("vmousemove", function(e) {
    $("#move").html("<p>Move: " + e.clientX + ", "
      + e.clientY + "</p>");
  });
  $("#main").bind("vmouseover", function(e) {
    $("#over").html("<p>Over: " + e.clientX + ", "
      + e.clientY + "</p>");
  });
  $("#header").bind("vmouseout", function(e) {
    $("#out").html("<p>Out: " + e.clientX + ", " +
      e.clientY + "</p>");
  });
```

3.  Next, handle the `vmousedown`, `vmouseup`, and `vclick` events:

```
$("#main").bind("vmousedown", function(e) {
  var whichbtn;
  switch (e.which) {
    case 1: whichbtn = "Left Button"; break;
    case 2: whichbtn = "Center Button"; break;
    case 3: whichbtn = "Right Button"; break;
    default: whichbtn = "Tap"; break;
  }
  $("#down").html("<p>Down: " + e.clientX + ", "
    + e.clientY + " - " + whichbtn + " </p>");
});
$("#main").bind("vmouseup", function(e) {
  $("#up").html("<p>Up: " + e.clientX + ", " +
    e.clientY + "</p>");
});
$("#main").bind("vclick", function(e) {
  $("#click").html("<p>Click: " + e.clientX + ",
    " + e.clientY + "</p>");
});
```

4. Finally, handle the `vmousecancel` event, as follows:

```
$("#main").bind("vmousecancel", function(e) {
    $("#cancel").html("<p>Cancel: " + e.clientX + ",
      " + e.clientY + "</p>");
    });
});
```

## How it works...

Create `main.html`, and add seven empty `divs` to display the event locations for each of the seven `vmouse` events. Add the given script and bind the callback functions for each of the `vmouse` events, as shown in the `pageinit` event handler. Use the `e.clientX` and `e.clientY` values of the event parameter passed to the callback function to get the location of the `vmouse` event. When you load the page and move the mouse around performing various mouse actions described, the screen is displayed as follows:

| Virtual Mouse Events |
| --- |
| Move: 561, 638 |
| Over: 280, 119 |
| Out: 135, 20 |
| Down: 204, 273 - Tap |
| Up: 561, 638 |
| Click: 204, 273 |
| Cancel: 204, 285 |

When the mouse is moved (or on a `touchmove` event), the `vmousemove` event is triggered. The `vmouseover` event is triggered when the move action is done over an element to which the event is bound. The `vmouseout` event is triggered when the `move` action goes out of the element to which the event is bound. In the preceding code, the `vmouseout` event is bound to the `h1` header. Move your mouse over the header and out of it to see this parameter get updated on the screen. The `vmousedown` event is triggered when the mouse is clicked (or on a `touchstart` event). The `vmouseup` event follows the `down` event when the click is over (`touchend` event). The `vclick` event is triggered along with the `vmousedown` and `vmouseup` event on the click or tap action. In the `vmousedown` event handler, you can use the `event.which` attribute to find which mouse button was clicked. This value is `0` for a `tap` event. You can try and click the different buttons on your mouse to see the screen update accordingly. Finally, the `vmousecancel` event is triggered when there is a mouse or touch event that is canceled.

## There's more...

The framework provides the following three configurations for the vmouse events:

- $.vmouse.moveDistanceThreshold (10px by default): If the move is more than this value, then it is a scroll event. The vmousecancel event gets called and the TouchMove event gets canceled.

- $.vmouse.clickDistanceThreshold (10px by default): If a vmouse click event was already captured, it is in the block list. Then, all vmouse clicks less than this distance are ignored.

- $.vmouse.resetTimerDuration (1500ms by default): If the interval between vmouse clicks is more than this duration, then it is not a touch event. Scroll, TouchMove, and TouchEnd events use this. The block list is cleared.

 The default vmouse configurations work well for most of the platforms. So modify them only if you have a very strong reason to do so.

## Mouse coordinates

This recipe shows you to use the event.clientX and event.clientY properties to get the mouse coordinates. You can also get the screen and page coordinates using the event.pageX, event.pageY, screen.pageX, and screen.pageY attributes.

## Using vclick events on touch devices

On touch devices, the webkit browsers are known to process click events after a lag of about 300ms after the touchend event is triggered. This delay could result in a different target being selected if the underlying object or background were to change within this gap. Another issue would be to match the event with the corresponding target due to the time lag; for example, when using event.preventDefault(). To avoid these issues on touch devices, use the click event instead of the vclick event.

## See also

- The *Using touch events* recipe

# Page initialization events

The jQuery Mobile framework provides the **page plugin** which automatically handles page initialization events. The `pagebeforecreate` event is fired before the page is created. The `pagecreate` event is fired after the page is created but before the widgets are initialized. The `pageinit` event is fired after the complete initialization. This recipe shows you how to use these events.

## Getting ready

Copy the full code of this recipe from the `code/08/pageinit` sources folder. You can launch this code using the URL `http://localhost:8080/08/pageinit/main.html`

## How to do it...

Carry out the following steps:

1. Create `main.html` with three empty `<div>` tags as follows:

   ```
   <div id="content" data-role="content">
     <div id="div1"></div>
     <div id="div2"></div>
     <div id="div3"></div>
   </div>
   ```

2. Add the following script to the `<head>` section to handle the `pagebeforecreate` event:

   ```
   var str = "<a href='#' data-role='button'>Link</a>";
   $("#main").live("pagebeforecreate", function(event) {
     $("#div1").html("<p>DIV1 :</p>"+str);
   });
   ```

3. Next, handle the `pagecreate` event:

   ```
   $("#main").live("pagecreate", function(event) {
     $("#div1").find("a").attr("data-icon", "star");
   });
   ```

4. Finally, handle the `pageinit` event:

   ```
   $("#main").live("pageinit", function(event) {
     $("#div2").html("<p>DIV 2 :</p>"+str);
     $("#div3").html("<p>DIV 3 :</p>"+str);
     $("#div3").find("a").buttonMarkup({"icon": "star"});
   });
   ```

## How it works...

In `main.html`, add three empty `divs` to the page content as shown. Add the given script to the page. In the script, `str` is an HTML string for creating an anchor link with the `data-role="button"` attribute.

Add the callback for the `pagebeforecreate` event, and set `str` to the `div1` container. Since the page was not yet created, the button in `div1` is automatically initialized and enhanced as seen in the following image.

Add the callback for the `pagecreate` event. Select the previous anchor button in `div1` using the jQuery `find()` method, and set its `data-icon` attribute. Since this change was made after page initialization but before the button was initialized, the `star` icon is automatically shown for the `div1` button as shown in the following screenshot. Finally, add the callback for the `pageinit` event and add `str` to both the `div2` and `div3` containers. At this point, the page and widgets are already initialized and enhanced. Adding an anchor link will now show it only as a native link without any enhancement for `div2`, as shown in the following screenshot. But, for `div3`, find the anchor link and manually call the `buttonmarkup` method on the button plugin, and set its icon to `star`. Now when you load the page, the link in `div3` gets enhanced as follows:

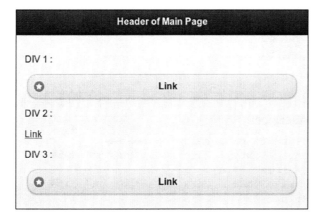

## There's more...

You can trigger `"create"` or `"refresh"` on the plugins to let the jQuery Mobile framework enhance the dynamic changes done to the page or the widgets after initialization.

### Page initialization events fire only once

The page initialization events fire only once. So this is a good place to make any specific initializations or to add your custom controls.

## Do not use $(document).ready()

The `$(document).ready()` handler only works when the first page is loaded or when the DOM is ready for the first time. If you load a page via Ajax, then the `ready()` function is not triggered. Whereas, the `pageinit` event is triggered whenever a page is created or loaded and initialized. So, this is the best place to do post initialization activities in your app.

```
$(document).bind("pageinit", callback() {…});
```

# Page load and remove events

The jQuery Mobile framework triggers the page load events whenever an external page is loaded into the DOM. It fires the `pagebeforeload` event before loading the page and then fires either the `pageload` or `pageloadfailed` event based on the status of the page load. The `pageremove` event is fired when a page is removed from the DOM. This recipe shows you how to use the page load and page remove events.

## Getting ready

Copy the full code of this recipe from the `code/08/pageload` sources folder. You can launch this code using the URL `http://localhost:8080/08/pageload/main.html`.

## How to do it...

Carry out the following steps:

1. Create `main.html` with four buttons and an empty `div` element, as shown in the following code snippet:

```
<div id="content" data-role="content">
  <a href="page1.html" data-role="button" data-
    inline="true">Page 1</a>
  <a href="page2.html" data-role="button" data-
    inline="true">Page 2</a>
  <a href="page3.html" data-role="button" data-
    inline="true">Page 3</a>
  <a href="page4.html" data-role="button" data-
    inline="true">Page 4</a>
  <div id="msgdiv"></div>
</div>
```

2. Add the following script to the `<head>` section to handle the `pagebeforeload` event:

```
$(document).bind("pagebeforeload", function(event, data) {
  var str = "<p>LOADING PAGE ...</p>"
    + "<p>url: " + data.url + "</p>"
    + "<p>absUrl : " + data.absUrl + "</p>"
    + "<p>dataUrl : " + data.dataUrl + "</p>"
    + "<p>options.type: " + data.options.type + "</p>";
  var re = /page2.html/;
  if ( data.url.search(re) !== -1 ) {
    str += "<p>ABORTED!!! page2.html does not
      exist.</p>";
    event.preventDefault();
    data.deferred.reject( data.absUrl, data.options);
  }
  re = /page4.html/;
  if ( data.url.search(re) !== -1 ) {
    str += "<p>ABORTED!!! error dialog shown
      instead.</p>";
    event.preventDefault();
    data.deferred.resolve( data.absUrl, data.options,
      $("#subpage"));
  }
  $("#msgdiv").html(str).trigger("refresh");
});
```

3. Next, handle the `pageload` event:

```
$(document).bind("pageload", function(event, data) {
  var str = "<p>PAGE LOADED!</p><p>textStatus: " + data.textStatus
    +    "</p><p>xhr.status : " + data.xhr.status + "</p>";
  $("#msgdiv").append(str).trigger("refresh");
});
```

4. Next, handle any error with the `pageloadfailed` event:

```
$(document).bind("pageloadfailed", function(event,
  data) {
  var str = "<p>PAGE LOAD FAILED!</p>"
    + "<p>textStatus: " + data.textStatus + "</p>"
    + "<p>xhr.status : " + data.xhr.status + "</p>"
    + "<p>errorThrown : " + data.errorThrown + "</p>";
  $("#msgdiv").append(str).trigger("refresh");
});
```

5. Also handle the `pageremove` event:

```
$("#page1").live("pageremove", function(event) {
  $("#msgdiv").append("<p>PAGE
    REMOVED!</p>").trigger("refresh");
});
```

6. Now, create a dialog with `id="dialog"` as follows:

```
<div id="dialog" data-role="dialog" data-theme="e" data-add-back-
btn="true">
  <div data-role="header">
    <h1>Page Load Failed!</h1>
  </div>
  <div data-role="content">
    <p>There was an error</p>
  </div>
</div>
```

7. Finally, create `page1.html` with a button to go back to #main, as shown in the following code snippet:

```
<div id="page1" data-role="page" data-theme="e">
  <div data-role="header">
    <h1>Header of Page 1</h1>
  </div>
  <div data-role="content">
    <a href="#" data-role="button" data-
      rel="back">Go to Main Page</a>
  </div>
</div>
```

## How it works...

In `main.html`, create the #main page and add four anchor links with the `data-role="button"` and `data-inline="true"` attributes, to create four inline buttons. These links point to `page1.html`, `page2.html`, `page3.html`, and `page4.html`. Also add an empty `div` container with `id="msgdiv"` to display the messages. Next, add a dialog with `id="dialog"` to `main.html`. Finally, create only `page1.html`, as shown, with a link to return back to the main page. The other three pages are not created. Bind the page load and page remove events to callback functions as given in the script. These callback functions have two parameters available. The first is the `event` object and the second is the `data` object.

In the callback of the `pagebeforeload` event, get the `url`, `absUrl` (absolute URL), `dataUrl` (the data URL), and `options.type` properties from the `data` object. Display them in the `msgdiv` container. The `options` object is the same that gets passed into the `$.mobile.loadPage()` call.

In the callback of the `pageload` event, get the `xhr.status` (the jQuery `XMLHttpRequest` object) and `textStatus` attributes that indicate page load success and display them in the `msgdiv` container.

Add the `pageloadfailed` callback function to display the `data.xhr.status` and `data.errorThrown` properties on page load error. Finally, add the `pageremove` callback function and display a message that the page was removed.

Now, when you initially load the app and click on the **Page 1** button to open `page1.html`, the `pagebeforeload` event is triggered first, then the `pageload` event is fired after the page is fully loaded. Navigate back to the main page and this triggers the `pageremove` event. You can see these messages displayed, as shown in the following screenshot:

Next, in the `pagebeforeload` event handler, use a regular expression search to check whether the page requested or the `data.url` is `page2.html` (which does not exist). Display a custom error message if `page2.html` was requested. Also prevent any further action on this request by calling `event.preventDefault()`. The `data.deferred.reject()` method must be finally called to reject the deferred object reference contained in the data object. Now, when you click on the **Page 2** button, the `pageloadfailed` event is not triggered, as shown in the following screenshot, and the custom error message **ABORTED!!! page2.html does not exist.** is displayed:

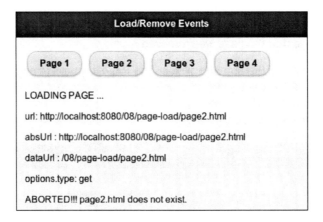

Click on the **Page 3** button; it now tries to load `page3.html`, which is not present, and displays an **Error Loading Page** default error message overlaid on the current page, as shown in the following screenshot. You can also see the messages from the `pageloadfailed` event handler here. There was no custom event handling done in this case.

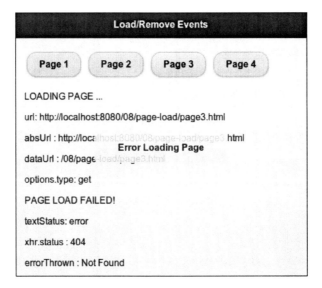

Finally, add code in the `pagebeforeload` callback function to search for `page4.html` in the `data.url` object. If the string was found, redirect the request to load the `#dialog` dialog. Also, display a custom message if `page4.html` was requested. Now, to prevent the default action on `pagebeforeevent`, call the `event.preventDefault()` method. You must also call the `data.deferred.resolve()` method to resolve the deferred object reference contained in the `data` object. Then, open the `#dialog` page by passing it as the parameter to the `resolve` method, as shown in the code. Now, when you click on the **Page 4** button, the custom error dialog popup is displayed. When you close the dialog, your custom message **ABORTED!!! error dialog shown instead.** is displayed, as shown in the following screenshot. You will note that the `pageloadfailed` event callback function did not get called.

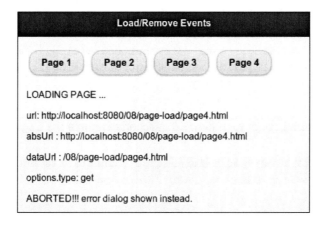

## There's more...

If you prevent the default page load events by calling the `event.preventDefault()` method, then you must inform the framework to resume processing other `changePage()` requests once you are done. You can do this by calling the `reject()` or `resolve()` methods on the `data.deferred` object passed to the callback function of the event.

## See also

▸ The *Using loadPage() to load a page* recipe in *Chapter 9, Methods and Utilities*

# Page change events

The jQuery Mobile framework triggers page change events whenever a page is loaded by the `$.mobile.changePage()` method into the DOM. The `pagebeforechange` event is fired first, before the page changes. Then, either the `pagechange` event (on success) or the `pagechangefailed` event (on failure) is fired. This recipe shows you how to use the page change events.

## Getting ready

Copy the full code of this recipe from the `code/08/pagechange` sources folder. You can launch this code using the URL `http://localhost:8080/08/pagechange/main.html`.

## How to do it...

Carry out the following steps:

1.  Create `main.html` with two links to open two dialogs and an empty `div` element in its page content, as follows:

    ```
    <div id="content" data-role="content">
      <a href="#dialog1" data-role="button">Dialog 1</a>
      <a href="#dialog2" data-role="button">Dialog 2</a>
      <div id="msgdiv"></div>
    </div>
    ```

2.  Add the following script to the `<head>` section to handle the `pagebeforechange` event:

    ```
    $(document).bind("pagebeforechange", function(event, data) {
      var str = "<p>CHANGING PAGE ...</p><p>toPage: ";
      str += (!!data.toPage.attr)? data.toPage.attr("data-
        url") : data.toPage;
      str += "</p>";
      $("#msgdiv").html(str).trigger("refresh");
      $("#dialogdiv").html(str).trigger("refresh");
    });
    ```

3.  Next, handle the `pagechange` event:

    ```
    $(document).bind("pagechange", function(event, data) {
      var str = "<p>CHANGED PAGE ...</p><p>fromPage: ";
      str += (!!data.options.fromPage && !!data.options.fromPage.
    attr)?
      data.options.fromPage.attr("data-url") : "none";
      str += "</p><p>options.transition: " + data.options.transition +
    "</p>";
      $("#msgdiv").append(str).trigger("refresh");
      $("#dialogdiv").append(str).trigger("refresh");
    });
    ```

4. Next, handle any error with the `pagechangefailed` event:

```
$(document).bind("pagechangefailed", function(event,
  data) {
  var str = "<p>PAGE CHANGE FAILED ...</p>";
  $("#msgdiv").append(str).trigger("refresh");
});
```

5. Finally, create the `#dialog1` dialog as follows. The second dialog, `#dialog2`, is not created.

```
<div id="dialog1" data-role="dialog" data-theme="e"
  data-add-back-btn="true">
  <div data-role="header">
    <h1>Dialog Header</h1>
  </div>
  <div data-role="content">
    <div id="dialogdiv"></div>
  </div>
</div>
```

## How it works...

In `main.html`, add two anchor links with `data-role="button"` to the content of the `#main` page. These links point to the `#dialog1` and `#dialog2` dialogs. Also, add an empty `div` container with `id="msgdiv"` to display the messages. Finally, add only one dialog with `id="dialog1"` to `main.html`. Add an empty `div` container with `id="dialogdiv"` to this dialog. The other dialog is not created. Bind the page change events to the callback functions as given in the script. These call back functions have two parameters available. The first is the `event` object and the second is the `data` object.

In the callback of the `pagebeforechange` event, get the `data.toPage` (target page) attribute. This can either be a string or an object. Check if this is an object (if it has the `toPage` attribute) and then use the `data.toPage.data-url` string. Display the `toPage` message in both the message `div` containers.

In the callback of the `pagechange` event, get the `data.fromPage` (source page) attribute. Check again whether this is an object or a string and display the `data.fromPage.data-url` string if it is an object in both the message `div` containers. Also, the `data.options` object has properties, such as `transition`, that you can use.

Finally, in the callback for the `pagechangefailed` event, display a custom error message. When the page loads for the first time, you can see the following image. The text **main** is shown for **toPage**; there is no **fromPage** here:

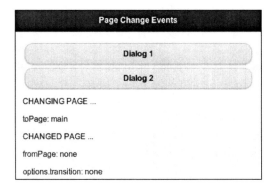

Click on the **Dialog 1** button and the following dialog box will be shown. The **toPage** value is **dialog1** and **fromPage** is **main**. The transition that was used is shown as **pop**, which is the default transition for the dialog:

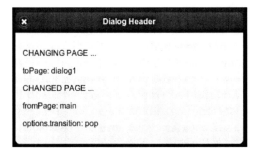

Close this dialog box, and the `#main` page opens , which displays a message similar to the one shown in the following screenshot. **toPage** is **main** and **fromPage** is **dialog1**. The transition used is again shown as **pop**:

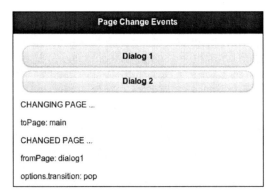

Finally, click on **Dialog 2** button; since `#dialog2` does not exist, the custom error message **PAGE CHANGE FAILED** is shown, as you can see in the following screenshot, from the `pagechangefailed` callback:

## There's more...

You can prevent the default page change action by calling the `event.preventDefault()` method in the `pagebeforechange` event handler. You can redirect the navigation to another page here using the `$.mobile.changePage()` method.

### Sequence of pagechange event

After the `pagebeforechange` event is triggered, the `changePage()` request loads the page into the DOM, and then the transition of the page occurs. The `pageshow` and `pagehide` events are triggered at this point. Finally, the `pagechange` event is fired only after this.

## See also

> ▸ The _Using changePage() to change a page_ recipe in _Chapter 9, Methods and Utilities_

# Page transition and animation events

During page navigation, the current page transitions out and the new active page transitions in. Animation is used where supported. The jQuery Mobile framework triggers four page transition events during page navigation, which are listed as follows:

> ▸ `pagebeforehide`: This event is triggered before the current page is hidden
>
> ▸ `pagehide`: This event is fired once the current page is hidden
>
> ▸ `pagebeforeshow`: This event is fired before the new active page is shown
>
> ▸ `pageshow`: This event is triggered once the active page is shown

You can also access the `animationComplete` plugin to perform custom actions as soon as the animation is completed. This recipe shows you how to use the page transition events and also how to use the `animationComplete` plugin.

## Getting ready

Copy the full code of this recipe from the `code/08/transition` sources folder. You can launch this code using the URL `http://localhost:8080/08/transition/main.html`.

## How to do it...

Carry out the following steps:

1. Create `main.html`, and add `#main` page with a link to open the `#page` page and an empty `div` container, as shown in the following code snippet:

```
<div id="main" data-role="page" data-theme="e">
  <div data-role="header">
    <h1>Page Transition and Animation Events</h1>
  </div>
  <div id="content" data-role="content">
    <a href="#page" data-role="button" data-
      transition="slide">Page 1</a>
  <div id="msgdiv"></div>
  </div>
</div>
```

2. Create the `#page` page, as follows, with a button to go back to `#main` and an empty `div` container to display messages:

```
<div id="page" data-role="page" data-theme="e">
  <div data-role="header">
    <h1>Page Header</h1>
  </div>
  <div data-role="content">
    <a href="#" data-rel="back" data-role="button">Go Back</a>
  <div id="pagediv"></div>
  </div>
</div>
```

3. Add the following script to the `<head>` section, to clear the message `div` containers whenever a link is clicked:

```
$("#main").live("pageinit", function(event) {
  $("a").bind("click", function(event, ui) {
    $("#msgdiv").html("");
    $("#pagediv").html("");
  });
});
```

4. Handle the `pagebeforeshow` event:

```
$(document).bind("pagebeforeshow", function(event, data) {
  var str = "<p>BEFORE PAGE SHOW ...</p><p>Previous
    Page: ";
  str += (!!data.prevPage.attr)?
    data.prevPage.attr("data-url") : "none";
  str += "</p>";
  $("#msgdiv").append(str).trigger("refresh");
  $("#pagediv").append(str).trigger("refresh");
});
```

5. Handle the `pagebeforehide` event:

```
$(document).bind("pagebeforehide", function(event,
  data) {
  $(data.nextPage).animationComplete(anim);
  var str = "<p>BEFORE PAGE HIDE ...</p><p>Current Page: ";
  str += (!!data.nextPage.attr)?
    data.nextPage.attr("data-url") : "none";
  str += "</p>";
  $("#msgdiv").append(str).trigger("refresh");
  $("#pagediv").append(str).trigger("refresh");
});
```

6. Handle the `pageshow` event:

```
$(document).bind("pageshow", function(event, data) {
  var str = "<p>PAGE SHOW!</p><p>Previous Page: ";
  str += (!!data.prevPage.attr)?
    data.prevPage.attr("data-url") : "none";
  str += "</p>";
  $("#msgdiv").append(str).trigger("refresh");
  $("#pagediv").append(str).trigger("refresh");
});
```

7. Handle the `pagehide` event:

```
$(document).bind("pagehide", function(event, data) {
  var str = "<p>PAGE HIDE!</p><p>Current Page: ";
  str += (!!data.nextPage.attr)?
    data.nextPage.attr("data-url") : "none";
  str += "</p>";
  $("#msgdiv").append(str).trigger("refresh");
  $("#pagediv").append(str).trigger("refresh");
});
```

8. Add the callback function for the `animationComplete()` method:

```
anim = function() {
  $("#msgdiv").append("ANIMATION
    DONE!!!").trigger("refresh");
  $("#pagediv").append("ANIMATION
    DONE!!!").trigger("refresh");
}
```

## How it works...

Create `main.html` and add an anchor link with `data-role="button"` to the content of the `#main` page. This link opens the `#page` page in `main.html`. Create the `#page` page, as shown with a link to go back to `#main`. Add empty `#msgdiv` and `#pagediv` containers to the pages respectively, to display messages. Bind the `click` event of the anchor link in the `pageinit` event handler, and clear any previously displayed messages. This callback is triggered whenever you click on the links in the app.

Now, bind the four page transition events to their callback functions as given in the script. These callback functions have two parameters available. The first is the `event` object and the second is the `data` object.

In the callback of the `pagebeforeshow` event, get the `data.prevPage` (previous page) object. This can be empty on first load. Check if it is available (if it has the `prevPage` attribute) and use the `data.prevPage.data-url` string. Display the `prevPage` message in both the message `div` containers. Use similar logic in the callback for the `pagehide` event.

Similarly, in the callback of the `pagebeforehide` and `pagehide` events, obtain and display the `data.toPage` (source page) property. Finally, invoke the `animationComplete` plugin and define the `anim` callback function, as shown in the `pagebeforehide` event handler. Write code in the `anim()` function to display a simple **ANIMATION DONE!!!** message in both the div containers, as shown.

When the page loads for the first time, you can see the following image with the `pagebeforeshow` and `pageshow` event handlers being called. `prevPage` is undefined at this point of time.

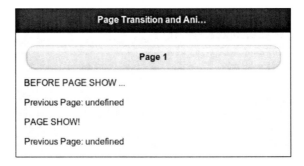

Click on the **Page 1** button to open #page. You can see messages from the `pagebeforehide` and `pagebeforeshow` event handlers saying that **Current Page** is **page** and **Previous Page** is **main**. Then, you can see the **ANIMATION DONE!!!** message from the `animationComplete()` callback. The page is visible at this point, and the messages from the `pagehide` and `pageshow` events can also be seen:

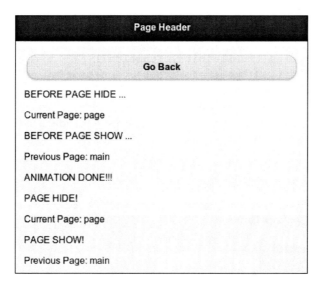

Click on the **Go Back** button. Now, #main is shown and the messages are displayed as before. This time, **Current Page** is **main** and **Previous Page** is **page**:

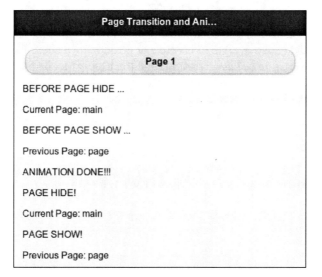

## There's more...

On first load, the `pagebeforeshow` and `pageshow` event handlers show an empty `data.nextPage` object. To display proper values on first load, these two events must be bound to their callback functions in the `mobileinit` handler, when the page loads and before loading the `jquery.mobile.js` script file, as shown in the following code snippet:

```
<script>
  $(document).bind("mobileinit", function() {
    $(document).bind("pagebeforeshow", function(event, data) {
      alert(data.nextPage);
    });
    $(document).bind("pageshow", function(event, data) {
      alert(data.nextPage);
    });
  });
</script>
<script src="http://code.jquery.com/mobile/1.1.1/jquery.mobile-
1.1.1.min.js"></script>
```

## See also

▸  The *Configuring the default transitions* recipe in *Chapter 7, Configurations*

# Using layout events

Components, such as list views and collapsible blocks, are dynamically resized by user interactions. This could cause overlap of controls or positioning issues. To prevent this, these components trigger the `updatelayout` event, and the jQuery Mobile framework updates the entire document and ensures that all components are laid out correctly. This recipe shows you how to use the `updatelayout` event.

## Getting ready

Copy the full code of this recipe from the `code/08/layout` sources folder. You can launch this code by using the URL `http://localhost:8080/08/layout/main.html`.

## How to do it...

Carry out the following steps:

1. Create `main.html` with three collapsible blocks and a `<div>` container, as shown in the following code snippet:

```
<div data-role="content">
  <div id="msgdiv">Collapsible Blocks</div>
  <div data-role="collapsible" data-theme="a" data-
    collapsed="false">
   <h3>Tallest Mountain</h3>
   Mt. Everest
  </div>
  <div data-role="collapsible" data-theme="a" data-
    collapsed="false">
   <h3>Longest River</h3>
   R. Nile
  </div>
  <div data-role="collapsible" data-theme="a" data-
    collapsed="false">
   <h3>Largest Ocean</h3>
   Pacific
  </div>
</div>
```

2. Add the following script to the `<head>` section, to handle the `updatelayout` event:

```
$("#main").live("pageshow", function(event, ui) {
  $("div").bind("updatelayout", function(event) {
    $("#msgdiv").html("updatelayout on : " + event.target.
innerHTML);
  });
});
```

## How it works...

In `main.html`, add a div container with `id="msgdiv"` to the page content. Add three collapsible blocks with the `data-collapsed="false"` attribute. Add the given script to bind the `pageshow` event (which gets fired on page show), to an event handler. Here, bind the `updatelayout` event to a callback function. In this callback, use the `event.target.innerHTML` property to get the text of the collapsible block on which the `updatelayout` event was called. Display it in the `msgdiv` block as shown. Now, when you load the page, the three collapsible blocks are seen expanded.

Click on the first block that says **Tallest Mountain**. You will see it collapse and `msgdiv` text being updated to show **updatelayout on: Mt. Everest**, as shown in the following screenshot:

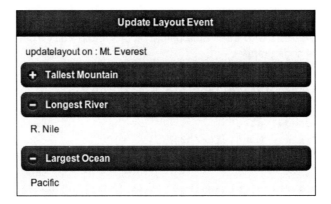

## There's more...

The jQuery Mobile framework updates the layout and adjusts the positions as required for most of the scenarios when you add or manipulate components or toggle their visibility in your page. You have to trigger the `create` or `refresh` method on these elements. But there may be occasions in which the framework does not handle the positioning properly when you add or manipulate controls or toggle their visibility. In such cases, you can trigger the `updatelayout` event and inform the framework to update all components and reposition them. You can do this by using the following code:

```
(yourselector).trigger("updatelayout");
```

# 9

# Methods and Utilities

In this chapter, we will cover the following recipes:

- ▶ Using `loadPage()` to load a page
- ▶ Using `changePage()` to change a page
- ▶ Using `jqmData()` and `jqmRemoveData()`
- ▶ Using `jqmEnhanceable()`
- ▶ Using `jqmHijackable()`
- ▶ Using `$.mobile.base`
- ▶ Parsing an URL
- ▶ Using `$.mobile.path` utility methods
- ▶ Using silent scrolling

## Introduction

The jQuery Mobile framework provides numerous methods and utilities that work on the `$.mobile` object. This chapter shows you how to use these methods and utilities.

The source files for all the recipes in this chapter are available under the `code/09` folder of the archive. Each recipe is listed in its own sub-folder, which is named accordingly.

## Using loadPage() to load a page

Using the `$.mobile.loadPage()` method, you can load an external page in the background into the DOM and enhance its contents without affecting the current page. This recipe shows you how to do the same.

## Getting ready

Copy the full code of this recipe from the `code/09/loadpage` source folder. You can launch this code by using the URL: `http://localhost:8080/09/loadpage/main.html`.

## How to do it...

1. Create `main.html` with the page `id="main"`, and add an empty `div` tag and a link to #page1, shown as follows:

```
<div data-role="content">
  <div id="msgdiv"></div>
  <a href="#page1" data-role="button">Show Page 1</a>
</div>
```

2. Add an event handler for the `pagebeforeshow` event of #main, and load #page1 using the `loadPage()` method:

```
$("#main").live("pagebeforeshow", function(event, data) {
  $("#msgdiv").html("<p>Current Active Page : "
    + $.mobile.activePage.attr("data-url") + "</p>");
  $.mobile.loadPage( "page1.html", {role: "dialog"});
});
```

3. Add an event handler for the `pagebeforeshow` event of #page1 to update the displayed message:

```
$("#page1").live("pagebeforeshow", function(event, data) {
  $("#page1content").html("<p>Current Active Page : "
    + $.mobile.activePage.attr("data-url") + "</p>");
});
```

4. Finally, create `page1.html`, shown as follows:

```
<div id="page1" data-role="page" data-theme="e">
  <div data-role="header">
    <h1>Header of Page 1</h1>
  </div>
  <div id="page1content" data-role="content"></div>
</div>
```

## How it works...

Create main.html with #main page, and add an empty `div` with `id="msgdiv"` and a link to open #page1 in it. The #page1 reference is not yet available during `pageinit`, as it comes from the external `page1.html` file. Add the event handler for the `pagebeforeshow` event on the #main page. Here, obtain the current active page using the `$.mobile.activePage()` method, and display its `data-url` attribute in #msgdiv using the jQuery `attr()` method. Next, load `page1.html` using the `$.mobile.loadPage()` call. Also, set the `loadPage()` options, and set the `role` attribute to `dialog`. The page now gets loaded in the background.

Add an event handler for the `pagebeforeshow` event of #page1. Obtain `data-url` of the active page, as done previously, and display it in the #page1content div container. Finally, create `page1.html` with an empty div with `id="page1content"`.

When `main.html` loads, you will see the **Show Page 1** button. Click on it, and `page1.html` will be shown as a dialog box using the default pop transition. Also, the active page data URL will be correctly shown in both the pages.

## There's more...

`$.mobile.loadPage()` returns a deferred `promise` object, which automatically gets resolved once the page is enhanced and loaded into the DOM.

### The loadPage() options

The `loadPage()` method takes in an optional `options` object as the second argument. The following properties can be set on the `options` object:

- ▶ `data`: This is the data for the Ajax page request
- ▶ `loadMsgDelay` (50 seconds by default): This is the delay before the page load message is shown
- ▶ `pageContainer`: This is the element that contains the loaded page
- ▶ `reloadPage` (`false` by default): This forces the page to be reloaded
- ▶ `role`: This is the `data-role` value for the page load
- ▶ `showLoadMsg` (`false` by default): This decides whether to display the page load message or not
- ▶ `type` (`get` by default): This specifies the type of Ajax request (`get` or `post`)

## See also

- ▶ The *Using changePage() to change a page* recipe
- ▶ The *Using page load and remove events* recipe in *Chapter 8, Events*

# Using changePage() to change a page

This recipe shows you how to use the $.mobile.changePage() method to change from one page to another using JavaScript. This recipe extends the *Using a split button list* recipe from *Chapter 6, List Views*, and displays the selected image from the list item in a new page.

## Getting ready

Copy the full code of this recipe from the code/09/changepage source folder. Also, revisit the *Using a split button list* recipe from *Chapter 6*. You can launch this code by using the URL: http://localhost:8080/09/changepage/main.html.

## How to do it...

1. Create main.html with a split button list, with the href attribute for the <img> tag having a file parameter, with the path for the image file in the left button, as follows:

```html
<div data-role="content">
  <ul data-role="listview" data-inset="true"
    data-theme="b" data-split-theme="e"
    data-split-icon="arrow-d">
    <li>
      <a href="#viewphoto&file=img1.png">
        <img style="margin: 10px"
          src="../../resources/images/img1.png" />
          <h3>Lal Bagh</h3>
      </a>
      <a href='#' data-rel='dialog'>Download</a>
    </li>
    <li>
      <a href="#viewphoto&file=img2.png">
        <img style="margin: 10px"
          src="../../resources/images/img2.png" />
          <h3>Peacock</h3>
      </a>
      <a href='#' data-rel='dialog'>Download</a>
    </li>
    <li>
      <a href="#viewphoto&file=img3.png">
        <img style="margin: 10px"
          src="../../resources/images/img3.png"
          height=75% />
          <h3>Ganesha</h3>
      </a>
      <a href='#' data-rel='dialog'>Download</a>
```

```
      </li>
    </ul>
  </div>
```

2. Add the `#viewphoto` page, and open it when the left part of the split button is clicked:

```
<div id="viewphoto" data-role="page" data-theme="e" data-add-back-
btn="true">
…. . . . .
  <div data-role="content">
    <div id="imgid">
    <p>Displaying Image ...</p>
    </div>
  </div>
</div>
```

3. Add the following script to the `<head>` section, and call `$.mobile.changePage()` in the `pagebeforechange` event handler:

```
$(document).live( "pagebeforechange", function( e, data ) {
  if ( typeof data.toPage === "string" ) {
    var u = $.mobile.path.parseUrl( data.toPage );
    var re = /^#viewphoto&file/;
    if ( u.hash.search(re) !== -1 ) {
      $.mobile.changePage("main.html#viewphoto",
      {
        transition: "pop",
        dataUrl: u.hash.split("=")[1],
        type: "get"
      });
      e.preventDefault();
    }
  }
});
```

4. Display the image in the `pagebeforeshow` event handler of the `#viewphoto` page:

```
$("#viewphoto").live( "pagebeforeshow", function( e, data ) {
  var u = $.mobile.path.parseUrl( document.location.href );
  var re = /^#img/;
  if ( u.hash.search(re) !== -1 ) {
    var str="<img src='../../images/" + u.hash.substr(1) + "' />";
    $("#imgid").html(str).trigger("refresh");
  }
});
```

## How it works...

Add the split button list and the `#viewphoto` page in `main.html`, as shown in the code. Add an empty `#imgid` attribute to the `div` tag in the `#viewphoto` page, to show the full image. The split button list and the `#viewphoto` page code are already explained in *Chapter 6*. The `href` attribute of the right button just points to #, as it is not used in this recipe. Change the list item `href` attribute in the left buttons to include the file parameter; for example, `href="#viewphoto&file=img1.png"`. When the app is launched, the following screen is displayed with thumbnails, as shown in the split button list.

But, nothing happens when you click on the split list buttons, as the framework does not understand the file parameter with the `href` attribute. To open and display the image, you will have to manually handle the page change. To manually invoke `pageChange()`, add an event handler for the `pagebeforechange` event. Here, check if the target page (`data.toPage`) is an URL string, and obtain the URL components using the `$.mobile.path.parseUrl()` method. Now, search for the file parameter in the URL hash using the regular expression— `#viewphoto&file`. If it is found, then it is a request to view the image. You must now handle the page change.

Call the `pageChange()` method and pass it the `main.html#viewphoto` URL. Also, set the `options` argument with custom values for `transition`, `type`, and `dataUrl`. You can store the filename information in `dataUrl` by splitting the URL hash as shown. Finally, prevent the default `pagebeforechange` event handling, as you are already handling the page change here.

Next, you will have to query the URL string provided to `pageChange()` for the `file` parameter, and display the image. To do this, add an event handler for the `pagebeforeshow` event of the #`viewphoto` page. Get the URL components using the `$.mobile.path. parseUrl()` method. Search for the `img` expression; if found, get the filename from the URL hash and display the image in the #`imgid` div container, as shown in the code. Now, if you click on any list item, the corresponding image is displayed in a larger size in the #`viewphoto` page, as shown in the following screenshot:

## There's more...

The `$.mobile.changePage()` method uses the `$.mobile.loadPage()` method internally to fetch the new page during the page change.

### The changePage() options

The `changePage()` method takes in an optional `options` object as the second argument. The following properties can be set on the `options` object:

- `allowSamePageTransition` (`false` by default): Transitions to the current active page are ignored by default, but can be enabled by using the `allowSamePageTransition` option
- `changeHash` (`true` by default): This updates hash in the location bar
- `data`: This is the data for the Ajax page request
- `dataUrl`: This is the URL to update the browser location after page change
- `pageContainer`: This is the element that contains the loaded page

- ▸ reloadPage (false by default): This forces the page to be reloaded
- ▸ reverse (false by default): This is the direction of transition for page show
- ▸ role: This provides the data-role value for showing the page
- ▸ showLoadMsg (false by default): This decides whether or not to display the page load message
- ▸ transition: This is the transition to be used for page change
- ▸ type (get by default): This specifies the type of Ajax request (get or post)

## See also

- ▸ The *Using loadPage() to load a page* and *Parsing a URL* recipes
- ▸ The *Using a split button list* recipe, in *Chapter 6, List Views*
- ▸ The *Using page load and remove events* recipe in *Chapter 8, Events*

# Using jqmData() and jqmRemoveData()

The jqmData() and jqmRemoveData() methods are available to add or remove data attributes to the elements of a jQuery mobile app. They automatically handle custom namespaces. This recipe shows you how to use these methods.

## Getting ready

Copy the full code of this recipe from the code/09/jqmdata source folder. You can launch this code by using the URL: http://localhost:8080/09/jqmdata/main.html.

## How to do it...

1. Add the following script to main.html before including jquery.mobile.js:

```
$(document).bind("mobileinit", function() {
  $.mobile.ns = "my-";
});
```

2. Add two text inputs and a button to the page, as follows:

```
<div data-my-role="content">
  <div data-role="fieldcontain">
    <label for="pgtheme">Page Theme : </label>
    <input type="text" id="pgtheme" />
  </div>
  <div data-role="fieldcontain">
    <label for="customdata">Custom Data : </label>
```

```
      <input type="text" id="customdata" />
    </div>
    <button id="clearbtn">Clear Custom Data</button>
  </div>
```

3. Add the following script to the `<head>` section to invoke the `jqmData()` and `jqmRemoveData()` methods:

```
$("#main").live("pageinit", function(event) {
    var pg = $("div:jqmData(role='page')");
    pg.jqmData("custom", "Custom data text");
    $("#pgtheme").attr("value", pg.jqmData("theme"));
    $("#customdata").attr("value", pg.jqmData("custom"));
    $("#clearbtn").bind("click", function(event, ui) {
        pg.jqmRemoveData("custom");
        $("#customdata").attr("value",
          ""+pg.jqmData("custom"));
    });
});
```

## How it works...

In `main.html`, add an event handler for the `mobileinit` event, before including the reference to `jquery.mobile.js`. This is invoked at the start of the app. Here, set the `$.mobile.ns="my-"` namespace configuration.

Add two text inputs with `id="pgtheme"` and `id="customdata"` to display the page theme and custom data, respectively. Add a button with `id="clearbtn"`. Next, bind the `pageinit` event to a callback function. In this function, get the `page` element using the `div:jqmData(role='page')` custom selector. Using `jqmData()` ensures that the lookup of the data attribute (`data-my-role`) with a custom namespace is automatically handled.

Set a **Custom Data** attribute on the page with the value **Custom data text** using the `jqmData()` method, as shown in the following screenshot. Finally, display the **Page Theme** and **Custom Data** attributes in the two text inputs. The page is displayed as follows:

Next, add a `click` event handler for `#clearbtn` to remove the custom data attribute set on the page using the `jqmRemoveData()` method, and update the value of the **Custom Data** text field. Now, when you click on the **Clear Custom Data** button, the text input will display **undefined**.

## There's more...

The jQuery methods `data()`, `hasData()`, and `removeData()`, do not take the namespace of the `data-` attributes into consideration. You will have to write a custom code to handle it. Instead, use the `jqmData()` and `jqmRemoveData()` methods, as shown in this recipe. You can inspect the code using a DOM inspector to verify the use of a custom namespace.

## See also

▸ The *Configuring the default namespace* recipe in *Chapter 7, Configurations*

# Using jqmEnhanceable()

When `data-enhance="false"` is set on a parent element, it is inherited by all the child elements. To search for elements that can use manual enhancements or for custom plugin authoring, the jQuery Mobile framework provides a filter method called `jqmEnhanceable()`. This recipe shows you how to use it.

## Getting ready

Copy the full code of this recipe from the `code/09/jqmenhance` source folder. You can launch this code using the URL `http://localhost:8080/09/jqmenhance/main.html`.

## How to do it...

1. Add the following script to `main.html` before including `jquery.mobile.js`:

```
$(document).bind("mobileinit", function() {
  $.mobile.ignoreContentEnabled = true;
});
```

2. Add two anchor buttons to the page as shown. The second button is within a `div` tag which has `data-enhance="false"`.

```
<div data-role="content">
  <div>
    <a href="#">Link 1</a>
  </div>
  <div data-enhance="false">
    <a href="#">Link 2</a>
  </div>
</div>
```

3. Add the following script to the `<head>` section to invoke the `jqmEnhanceable()` method:

```
$("#main").live("pagecreate", function(event) {
  $("a").jqmEnhanceable().attr("data-role", "button");
});
```

## How it works...

In `main.html`, add an event handler for the `mobileinit` event before including the reference to `jquery.mobile.js`, which is invoked at the start of the app. Set the `$.mobile.ignoreContentEnabled=true` configuration.

Add two `div` tags to the content of `#main`. Add a # link to both these `div` tags. Do not set the `data-role="button"` attribute on either of the links. The second `div` tag has the `data-enhance="false"` attribute set. Next, bind the `pagecreate` event to an event handler. At this point, the page is already `initialzied`, but the widgets are yet to be enhanced. Now invoke the `jqmEnhanceable()` method on the anchor element, as shown. This filters and provides only those anchor elements that do not have `data-enhance="false"` inherited from its parent. So, in the code, Link 1 is made available. Set its `data-role` attribute to `button` using the jQuery `attr()` call, as shown in the code.

Now, when you open the app, only **Link 1** is enhanced to a button and **Link 2** is not enhanced, as shown in the following screenshot:

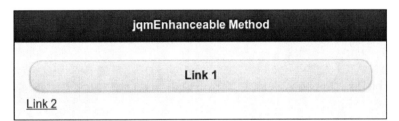

## There's more...

The `jqmEnhanceable()` method works only when the `$.mobile.ignoreContentEnabled=true` configuration is set. The parent node of each element is visited and checked for the `data-enhance` value, and any parent that has a `false` setting is removed with its child elements from the filtered set.

 Using `jqmEnhanceable()` on even a small set of elements is costly, as all the parent elements are checked for the `data-enhance` value.

## See also

▸ The *Using jqmHijackable() recipe*

# Using jqmHijackable

When `data-ajax="false"` is set on a parent element, this is inherited by all the child elements. A filter method called `jqmHijackable()` is available to search for child elements that can use custom forms and link binding. This recipe shows you how to use this method.

## Getting ready

Copy the full code of this recipe from the `code/09/jqmhijack` source folder. You can launch this code by using the URL: `http://localhost:8080/09/jqmhijack/main.html`.

## How to do it...

1. Add the following script to `main.html` before including `jquery.mobile.js`:

```
$(document).bind("mobileinit", function() {
  $.mobile.ignoreContentEnabled = true;
});
```

2. Add two anchor buttons to the page, as shown. The second button is within a `div` tag, which has `data-ajax="false"`:

```
<div data-role="content">
  <div>
    <a href="page1.html" data-role="button">Link 1</a>
  </div>
  <div data-ajax="false">
    <a href="page1.html" data-role="button">Link 2</a>
  </div>
</div>
```

3. Add the following script to the `<head>` section to invoke the `jqmHijackable()` method:

```
$("#main").live("pageinit", function(event) {
  $("a").jqmHijackable().each(function() {
    $(this).attr("data-transition", "flip");
  });
});
```

4. Finally, create `page1.html`, as shown in the following code snippet:

```
<div id="page1" data-role="page" data-theme="e">
.... . . . .
  <div data-role="content">
    <p>Page 1 Content</p>
    <a href="main.html" data-direction="reverse" data-ajax="false"
      data-role="button">Go Back</a>
  </div>
</div>
```

## How it works...

In `main.html`, add an event handler for the `mobileinit` event before including the reference to `jquery.mobile.js`. This is invoked at the start of the app. Set the `$.mobile.ignoreContentEnabled=true` configuration.

Add two `div` tags to the content of `#main`. Add a link to the external `page1.html` file in both these `div` tags. The second `div` tag has the `data-ajax="false"` attribute set. Next, bind the `pageinit` event to an event handler, and invoke the `jqmHijackable()` method on the anchor element, as shown. This filters and provides only those anchor elements that do not have `data-ajax="false"` inherited from their parent. So, in the code, Link 1 is made available. Set its `data-transition` attribute to `flip` using the jQuery `attr()` call, as shown in the code. Finally, create `page1.html`, and add the **Go Back** link to return to the `#main` page.

Now, when you click on **Link 1**, `page1.html` opens with the flip transition. But, if you click on **Link 2**, `page1.html` is opened without the flip.

## There's more...

In this recipe, **Link 2** opens `page1.html` using `data-ajax="false"`. This will clear `main.html` from the DOM. Returning back to `main.html` will load `main.html` into the DOM, but will not trigger the `mobileinit` event. This will cause **Link 1** to not use the flip transition when opening `page1.html`. To work around this issue, add the `data-ajax="false"` attribute to return the link in `page1.html`. This will reload `main.html` into DOM freshly and trigger the `mobileinit` event. Now, moving from `main.html` to `page1.html` via both links works smoothly any number of times.

### $.mobile.ignoreContentEnabled configuration

The `jqmHijackable()` method works only when the `$.mobile.ignoreContentEnabled=true` configuration is set. The parent node of each element is visited and checked for the `data-ajax` value, and any parent that has a `false` setting is removed with its child elements from the filtered set.

> Using jqmHijackable() on even a small set of elements is costly, as all the parent elements are checked for the data-ajax value.

## See also

▶ The *Using jqmEnhanceable()* recipe

# Using $.mobile.base

The $.mobile.base object provides the reference to the original document base. You can set a custom value on the base object using the set() method. You can use the reset() method to revert to the original value. This recipe shows you how to use these utility methods.

## Getting ready

Copy the full code of this recipe from the code/09/base source folder. You can launch this code by using the URL: http://localhost:8080/09/base/main.html.

## How to do it...

1.  Create main.html with two buttons, as shown in the following code snippet:

    ```
    <div id="content" data-role="content">
      <div id="dispdiv"></div>
      <button id="changebtn">Set Document Base</button>
      <button id="resetbtn">Reset Document Base</button>
    </div>
    ```

2.  Add the following script to display the document base object values:

    ```
    function disp() {
      var str = "<p>Original Document Base: " + $.mobile.
    getDocumentBase()
          + "</p>" + "<p>Document Base set to : "
          + $.mobile.base.element.attr("href");
      $("#dispdiv").html(str);
    }
    ```

3.  Invoke the $.mobile.base utility methods in the pageinit event handler:

    ```
    $("#main").live("pageinit", function(event) {
      disp();
      $("#changebtn").bind("click", function(event, ui) {
        $.mobile.base.set("http://localhost:8080/");
    ```

```
      disp();
    });
    $("#resetbtn").bind("click", function(event, ui) {
      $.mobile.base.reset();
      disp();
    });
  });
```

## How it works...

Add an empty `div` tag with `id="dispdiv"`, and add two buttons (`#changebtn` and `#resetbtn`) to `main.html`, as shown. Add a `disp()` function to display the current document base and the original document base values in the `#dispdiv` div container. You can get the original document base using the `$.mobile.getDocumentBase()` method. Invoke the `disp()` function on the `pageinit` event. On first load, the base values are displayed as follows:

Now, bind the click event of the `#changebtn` to an event handler, and set the document base to a custom value using the `$.mobile.base.set()` method. Click on the **Set Document Base** button now, and the custom base is displayed, as shown in the following screenshot:

Bind `#resetbtn` to an event handler, and reset the document base by calling the `$.mobile.base.reset()` method. Click on the **Reset Document Base** button and you will see that the base value has been reverted.

# Parsing an URL

The `$.mobile.path` object provides properties and methods that you can use to work with URLs. This recipe shows you how to fetch the components of a URL using the `$.mobile.path.parseUrl()` method.

## Getting ready

Copy the full code of this recipe from the `code/09/parseurl` source folder. You can launch this code by using the URL: `http://localhost:8080/09/parseurl/main.html`.

## How to do it...

1. Create `main.html` with an empty `div` tag and an anchor link, as shown in the following code snippet:

```
<div data-role="content">
  <div id="msgdiv"></div>
  <a href="http://user:pwd@localhost:8080/09/main.html?img=img1.
png#imgview"
      data-role="button">Link 1</a>
</div>
```

2. Add the following script to the `<head>` section to fetch the URL of the anchor button when it is clicked:

```
$("#main").live("pageinit", function(event) {
  dispPath($.mobile.getDocumentUrl());
  $("a").bind("click", function(event, ui) {
    dispPath($(this).attr("href"));
    event.preventDefault();
    event.stopPropagation();
  });
```

3. Add the following method to display the various components of the URL:

```
function dispPath(urlstr) {
  var urlcomp = $.mobile.path.parseUrl(urlstr);
  var str = "<p>href: " + urlcomp.href + "</p>"
    + "<p>hrefNoHash: " + urlcomp.hrefNoHash + "</p>"
    + "<p>hrefNoSearch: " + urlcomp.hrefNoSearch + "</p>"
    + "<p>domain: " + urlcomp.domain + "</p>"
    + "<p>protocol: " + urlcomp.protocol + "</p>"
    + "<p>authority: " + urlcomp.authority + "</p>"
```

```
            + "<p>username: " + urlcomp.username + "</p>"
            + "<p>password: " + urlcomp.password + "</p>"
            + "<p>host: " + urlcomp.host + "</p>"
            + "<p>hostname: " + urlcomp.hostname + "</p>"
            + "<p>port: " + urlcomp.port + "</p>"
            + "<p>pathname: " + urlcomp.pathname + "</p>"
            + "<p>directory: " + urlcomp.directory + "</p>"
            + "<p>filename: " + urlcomp.filename + "</p>"
            + "<p>hash: " + urlcomp.hash + "</p>"
            + "<p>search: " + urlcomp.search + "</p>";
        $("#msgdiv").html(str);
    }
});
```

## How it works...

Add an empty `div` tag with `id="msgdiv"` to `main.html`. Add a link with a complex `href` string, as shown in the code. Create a `dispPath` function that takes in a URL string. Here, call the `$.mobile.path.parseUrl` method to obtain an object (`#urlcomp`) that contains the various components of the URL. Display these URL components in the `#msgdiv` div container. When the app is first loaded, call the `dispPath()` method in the `pageinit` event handler, and pass it to the document URL parameter `got`, by calling the `$.mobile.getDocumentUrl()` method. The following screenshot is displayed on first load:

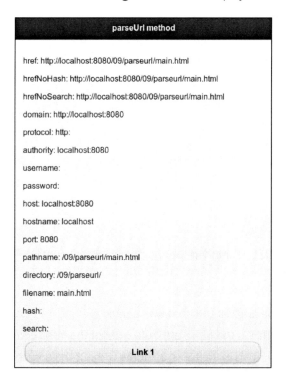

Next, add an event handler for the `click` event of the anchor link. Invoke the `dispPath()` function, and pass it the `href` attribute as the parameter. Get the `href` attribute by calling the jQuery `attr("href")` method on the anchor object. Finally, call the `event.preventDefault()` and `event.stopPropagation()` methods to prevent the default action of the click event. Now, when you click on **Link 1**, the URL components of the complex `href` attribute are displayed as follows:

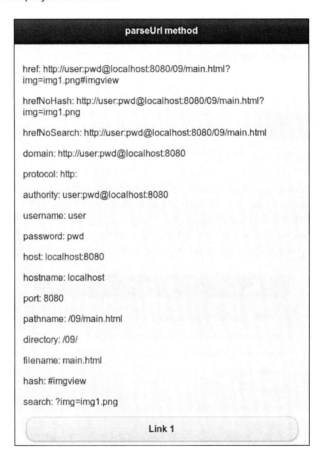

## There's more...

The `$.mobile.parseUrl()` method returns an object that contains the string values of the various URL components as follows; empty strings are stored when a particular URL component is not used:

- `href`: This is the original URL that was parsed
- `hrefNoHash`: This is the `href` attribute without the hash component
- `hrefNoSearch`: This is the `href` attribute without the search query and hash

- ▸ `domain`: This has the protocol and authority components

- ▸ `protocol`: This is the protocol (includes the `:` character)

- ▸ `authority`: This has the username, password, and host components

- ▸ `username`: This is the username

- ▸ `password`: This is the password

- ▸ `host`: This is the host and port

- ▸ `hostname`: This is the name of the host

- ▸ `port`: This is the port (can be empty if the protocol uses its default port)

- ▸ `pathname`: This is the path of the file or directory referenced

- ▸ `directory`: This is the directory part of the pathname without filename

- ▸ `filename`: This is the filename part of the pathname without directory

- ▸ `hash`: This is the hash component (includes the `#` character)

- ▸ `search`: This is the query component (includes the `?` character)

## See also

- ▸ The *Using $.mobile.path utility methods* recipe

# Using $.mobile.path utility methods

This recipe shows you how to use the utility methods provided by the `$.mobile.path` object in your app.

## Getting ready

Copy the full code of this recipe from the `code/09/path` source folder. You can launch this code by using the URL: `http://localhost:8080/09/path/main.html`.

## How to do it...

1. Create the `main.html` page with four anchor links, as shown in the following code snippet:

```
<div data-role="content">
  <div id="msgdiv"></div>
  <a href="http://localhost:8080/09/base/main.html"
    data-role="button">
    1: http://localhost:8080/09/base/main.html
  </a>
```

```
    <a href="http://localhost:8080/09/base/" data-
      role="button">
      2: http://localhost:8080/09/base/
    </a>
    <a href="page1.html" data-role="button">
      3: page1.html
    </a>
    <a href="../" data-role="button">4: ../</a>
  </div>
```

2. Add the following script to the `<head>` section to get the URL of the link clicked.

```
$("#main").live("pageinit", function(event) {
  var docurl = $.mobile.getDocumentUrl();
  $("a").bind("click", function(event, ui) {
    dispPath($(this).attr("href"));
    event.preventDefault();
    event.stopPropagation();
  });
```

3. Add the `disppath()` function to display the output of the `$.mobile.path` utility methods:

```
function dispPath(urlstr) {
  var urlcomp = $.mobile.path.parseUrl(urlstr);
  var str = "<p>Base: " + docurl + "</p>"
    + "<p>Page: " + urlcomp.href + "</p>"
    + "<p>Same Domain: " + $.mobile.path.isSameDomain(
    docurl, urlcomp) + "</p>"
    + "<p>is Absolute: "
    + $.mobile.path.isAbsoluteUrl(urlcomp) + "</p>"
    + "<p>is Relative: "
    + $.mobile.path.isRelativeUrl(urlcomp) + "</p>";
  if ($.mobile.path.isRelativeUrl(urlcomp)) {
    str += "<p>Make Absolute Path: "
        + $.mobile.path.makePathAbsolute(urlcomp.href,
          $.mobile.path.parseUrl(docurl).pathname) + "</p>"
        + "<p>Make Absolute Url: "
        + $.mobile.path.makeUrlAbsolute(urlcomp.href,
        docurl) + "</p>"
  }
  $("#msgdiv").html(str);
}
});
```

## How it works...

Add an empty div tag with `id="msgdiv"` to `main.html`. Add four links with different URLs, as shown in the code. Add script to the `<head>` section to obtain the original document URL (#docurl) of the page using the `$.mobile.getDocumentUrl()` method in the `pageinit` event handler. Use this URL as the reference point for comparison in this recipe.

Next, add an event handler for the `click` event of the four anchor links. Invoke the `dispPath()` function, and pass it the `link` href attribute as the parameter. You can obtain the `href` attribute by calling the jQuery `attr("href")` method on the anchor object. Also call the `event.preventDefault()` and `event.stopPropagation()` methods in this event handler to prevent any further action on the `click` event.

In the `dispPath` function, call the `$.mobile.path.parseUrl` method to obtain the `href` component of the URL passed in. Now, invoke the various `$.mobile.path` utility methods, and display their outputs in the #msgdiv div container, as shown in the code. Call the `isRelativeUrl()` method to check if the URL passed in is relative. Convert it to an absolute value using the `makePathAbsolute()` and `makeUrlAbsolute()` methods. The original document URL is used as reference for these conversions.

When the page loads, you will see four link buttons. Click on the first link `http://localhost:8080/09/path/main.html`, and an output similar to the following screenshot will be shown. The URL is in the same domain as the reference URL, and the URL is also absolute.

Base: http://localhost:8080/09/path/main.html

Page: http://localhost:8080/09/base/main.html

Same Domain: true

is Absolute: true

is Relative: false

The second link, `http://localhost:8080/09/base/`, points to a folder. The following output is seen; the domain is same and the URL is absolute:

Base: http://localhost:8080/09/path/main.html

Page: http://localhost:8080/09/base/

Same Domain: true

is Absolute: true

is Relative: false

The third link, `page1.html`, is a relative URL. The absolute path and the absolute URL are computed using the reference URL and displayed, as shown in the following screenshot; the **Same Domain** value is **false** here.

> Base: http://localhost:8080/09/path/main.html
>
> Page: page1.html
>
> Same Domain: false
>
> is Absolute: false
>
> is Relative: true
>
> Make Absolute Path: /09/path/page1.html
>
> Make Absolute Url: http://localhost:8080/09/path/page1.html

The final link points to the parent directory, `../`, and is again a relative URL. The absolute path and URL is computed using the reference URL, and is displayed as shown in the following screenshot; the **Same Domain** value is **false** again:

> Base: http://localhost:8080/09/path/main.html
>
> Page: ../
>
> Same Domain: false
>
> is Absolute: false
>
> is Relative: true
>
> Make Absolute Path: /09/
>
> Make Absolute Url: http://localhost:8080/09/

## There's more...

The `$.mobile.path` utility methods used in this recipe are as follows:

- ▶ `isAbsoluteUrl`: Checks if a given URL is absolute
- ▶ `isRelativeUrl`: Checks if a given URL is relative
- ▶ `makePathAbsolute`: Converts a relative path to absolute; the method uses a reference path argument for the conversion
- ▶ `makeUrlAbsolute`: Converts a relative URL to absolute; the method uses a reference URL argument for the conversion
- ▶ `isSameDomain`: Checks if two URLs belong to the same domain

See also

▶ The *Parsing an URL* recipe

# Using silent scrolling

You can use the `$.mobile.silentScroll` method to scroll to any vertical position on your page, without triggering the scroll event listeners. This recipe shows you how to use silent scrolling.

## Getting ready

Copy the full code of this recipe from the `code/09/silentscroll` source folder. You can launch this code by using the URL: `http://localhost:8080/09/silentscroll/main.html`.

## How to do it...

1. Create `main.html` with an empty `div` tag and two buttons that will be used to scroll to the top and bottom of the page:

```
<div data-role="content">
  <button id="bottombtn">Page Bottom</button>
  <div id="dispdiv"></div>
  <button id="topbtn">Page Top</button>
</div>
```

2. Add the following script to the `<head>` section to create a lengthy page:

```
$("#main").live("pageinit", function(event) {
  var str="";
  for (var i=0; i<100; i++) {
    str += i + "<br/>";
  }
  $("#dispdiv").html(str);
```

3. Now, based on the button clicked, scroll to the top or bottom of the page:

```
$("#topbtn").bind("click", function(event, ui) {
  $.mobile.silentScroll($.mobile.defaultHomeScroll);
});
$("#bottombtn").bind("click", function(event, ui) {
  $.mobile.silentScroll(2000);
});
});
```

## How it works...

Add two buttons with IDs `bottombtn` and `topbtn` to `main.html`. Create an empty `div` tag with `id="dispdiv"`, and populate it with some lengthy content. Here, a script is used on the `pageinit` event to add 100 lines of text in a loop to `#dispdiv`. The page is initially displayed as follows:

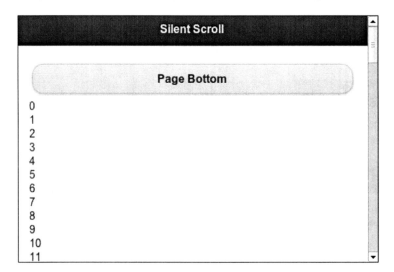

Bind the `click` event of the `#bottombtn` button to call `$.mobile.silentScroll` with a large value (2000px here) as the Y parameter. Now, when you click on the **Page Bottom** button, the page scrolls to the Y position (2000px) which is at the bottom of the document, as shown in the following screenshot:

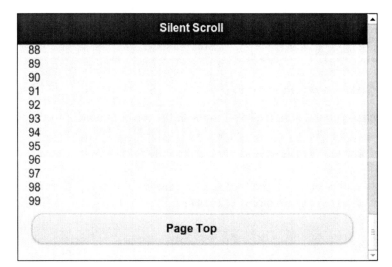

Next, bind the `click` event of the `#topbtn` button, and pass the `$.mobile.defaultHomeScroll` property as a parameter to `$.mobile.silentScroll`. Now, click on the **Page Top** button, and the page scrolls back to the top.

## There's more...

The `silentScroll` method does not invoke the scroll event listeners. Add the following code to verify that the alert is not shown when you click on any of the buttons. But the alert is shown when you use the scrollbar.

```
$(window).bind("scrollstop", function(event) {
  alert("Scroll event was fired");
});
```

### The $.mobile.defaultHomeScroll Property

The `$.mobile.defaultHomeScroll` property used in this recipe is internally used by the jQuery Mobile framework to scroll to the top of the page. This value is obtained from the browser using the `$.support.scrollTop` property. If this value is not `0`, the framework sets it to `0`.

## See also

▸   The *Using Scroll Events* recipe in *Chapter 8, Events*

# 10
# The Theme Framework

In this chapter, we will cover the following recipes:

- ▸ Theming a nested list
- ▸ Using a custom background
- ▸ Using custom fonts
- ▸ Styling corners
- ▸ Overriding the global Active State theme
- ▸ Overriding an existing swatch
- ▸ Using the ThemeRoller tool to create a swatch

## Introduction

The jQuery Mobile framework provides a lightweight theming system, which supports many CSS3 properties, such as rounded corners, shadows, and gradients. It also provides a lightweight icon set in a sprite that you can use in your mobile apps (Icon Sprites are covered in *Chapter 4, Buttons and Content Formatting*). The framework provides five default swatches (**a** to **e**) and can support up to 26 swatches. These swatches can provide a different look and feel to your apps.

## Theming a nested list

When you theme a nested list differently from the page theme, the list sub page will look inconsistent compared to the main page. This is described in the *Using a Nested List* recipe, in *Chapter 6, List Views*. This recipe shows you how to theme a nested list in a consistent manner.

## Getting ready

Copy the full code of this recipe from the `code/10/nested-list` folder. You can launch this code using the URL `http://localhost:8080/10/nested-list/main.html`.

## How to do it...

1. Create `main.html` with the `#main` page having a nested list, as follows:

```
<div id='main' data-role='page' data-theme='a'>
  <div data-role='header' data-theme='a'>
    <h1>Movies</h1>
  </div>
  <div data-role='content'>
    <ul data-role='listview' data-header-theme='a' data-
      theme='b' data-inset='true'>
      <li><a href='#'>Director 1</a>
        <ul data-role='listview' data-inset='true'>
          <li><a href='#'>Movie 1</a></li>
          <li><a href='#'>Movie 2</a></li>
          <li><a href='#'>Movie 3</a></li>
        </ul>
      </li>
      <li><a href='#'>Director 2</a>
        <ul data-theme='a' data-role='listview' data-
          inset='true'>
          <li data-theme='b'><a href='#'>Movie A</a></li>
          <li data-theme='b'><a href='#'>Movie B</a></li>
          <li data-theme='b'><a href='#'>Movie C</a></li>
        </ul>
      </li>
    </ul>
  </div>
</div>
```

## How it works...

In `main.html`, add the `#main` page with `data-theme='a'` to give it a black theme. Add a black colored header with `data-theme='a'`. Add a blue colored list view to the page content with `data-theme='b'`. Set its header to have a black color with `data-header-theme='a'`. Add two items, **Director 1** and **Director 2**, to this list. The list will now appear as shown in the following screenshot:

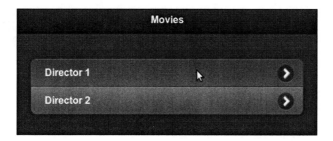

Add nested lists to both these list items. The first nested list does not specify any additional theme attributes. When you click on the first list item, the subpage with movies for **Director 1** is shown. You will notice that the subpage has a background of `data-theme='b'`, and it does not look consistent with the main page, as shown in the following screenshot:

Now, set `data-theme='a'` on the second nested list. Add the `data-theme='b'` attribute to each of the nested list items. This will create the subpage with a black background. The nested list items get the blue color. The subpage appears, as shown in the following screenshot; it is now consistent with the main page:

## See also

▸  The *Using a nested list* recipe in *Chapter 6, List Views*

# Using a custom background

This recipe shows you how to use a custom background in your app.

## Getting ready

Copy the full code of this recipe from the `code/10/custom-background` source folder. You can launch this code using the URL: `http://localhost:8080/10/custom-background/main.html`.

## How to do it...

1. Create `main.html` and define the `orangebar` and `orangebody` classes in the `<head>` section, as follows:

```
<style>
  .orangebar {
    border: 1px solid #e3b264;
    background: #f7e0bb;
    color: #000;
    text-shadow: 0 1px 0 #bfbfbf;
    background-image: -webkit-gradient(linear, left top,
      left bottom,
      from( #f7e0bb ), to( #f7bd5e ));
    background-image: -webkit-linear-gradient( #f7e0bb ,
      #f7bd5e );
    background-image: -moz-linear-gradient( #f7e0bb ,
      #f7bd5e );
    background-image: -ms-linear-gradient( #f7e0bb ,
      #f7bd5e );
    background-image: -o-linear-gradient( #f7e0bb ,
      #f7bd5e );
    background-image: linear-gradient( #f7e0bb , #f7bd5e );
  }
  .orangebody {
    border: 1px solid #e3b264;
    background: #f4ffde;
    color: #000;
    text-shadow: 0 1px 0 #bfbfbf;
    background-image: -webkit-gradient(linear, left top,
      left bottom,
      from( #fef9f1 ), to( #f2d5a6 ));
    background-image: -webkit-linear-gradient( #fef9f1 ,
      #f2d5a6 );
```

```
        background-image: -moz-linear-gradient( #fef9f1 ,
          #f2d5a6 );
        background-image: -ms-linear-gradient( #fef9f1 ,
          #f2d5a6 );
        background-image: -o-linear-gradient( #fef9f1 ,
          #f2d5a6 );
        background-image: linear-gradient( #fef9f1 , #f2d5a6 );
      }
    </style>
```

2. Add the #main page with the following content:

```
<div id='main' data-role='page' class='orangebody'>
  <div data-role='header' class='orangebar'>
    <h1>Orange Background</h1>
  </div>
  <div data-role='content'>
    <p>Page Content</p>
  </div>
</div>
```

## How it works...

In main.html, define the orangebar and orangebody classes in the <style> tag. Define the values for the border, background, and background-image CSS properties. Specify a linear gradient with multiple vendor-specific values for the background-image attribute. Create the #main page and style the page to use the orangebody class. Style the header to use the orangebar class. The page is now displayed with an orange background, as shown in the following screenshot:

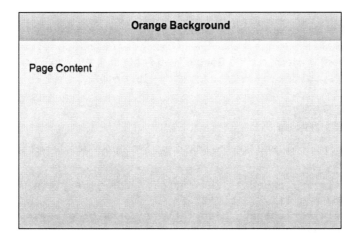

## There's more...

This recipe shows you how to quickly change the background of your page and its header. But if you add a button or any control to this page, the control would get the default theme and would look out of place. You will have to theme the controls to match the page. Instead of manually setting the theme for each and every element, you can create themes or modify the existing themes using the jQuery Mobile **ThemeRoller** tool available at http://www.jquerymobile.com/themeroller.

 It is better to use a separate CSS file to store the style info. In this way the style is kept separate from the HTML or document structure, making it easier to maintain and upgrade the styles later.

## See also

▸ The *Theming the active state* and *Using the ThemeRoller tool to create a swatch* recipes

▸ The *Using CSS to create a bouncing page transition* recipe in *Chapter 2, Pages and Dialogs*: This recipe provides details on vendor prefixes

# Using custom fonts

The jQuery Mobile framework uses Helvetica, Arial, and Sans Serif fonts by default. This recipe shows how to include and use other fonts in your app.

## Getting ready

Copy the full code of this recipe from the code/10/custom-font source folder. The **Komika TrueType Font** used in this recipe is available in the code/resources/font folder. The **Syncopate Web Font** is used from the **Google Web Fonts** site. You can launch this code using the URL: http://localhost:8080/10/custom-font/main.html.

## How to do it...

1. Create main.html, and add the link to the Syncopate Google web font stylesheet, as follows:

```
<link rel='stylesheet' href='http://code.jquery.com/mobile/1.1.1/
jquery.mobile-1.1.1.min.css' />
<link rel='stylesheet' href='http://fonts.googleapis.com/css?famil
y=Syncopate:400,700'/>
```

2. Define style classes to use the two custom fonts in the `<style>` tag:

```
<style>
  h1 {font-family: 'Syncopate', sans-serif; }
  .divstyle {font-family: 'Syncopate'; font-weight: 400; }
  @font-face {
    font-family: KomikaDisplay;
    src: url('../../resources/font/Komika_display.ttf');
  }
  .komikafont { font-family: KomikaDisplay; }
</style>
```

3. Add the `#main` page container using the custom fonts as follows:

```
<div id='main' data-role='page' data-theme='a'>
  <div data-role='header'>
    <h1>Custom Font</h1>
  </div>
  <div data-role='content'>
    <p>In Default font</p>
    <div class='komikafont'><p>In Komika Display Font</p></div>
    <div class='divstyle'><p>In Syncopate Font</p></div>
  </div>
</div>
```

## How it works...

Create `main.html`, and add the link to the Syncopate stylesheet from the Google Web Fonts site after including the jQuery Mobile stylesheet, as shown. Define the header `h1` to use Syncopate and `sans-serif` fonts using the `font-family` CSS attribute. Create a CSS class called `divstyle`, and set the `font-family` attribute to `Syncopate` with `font-weight` of `400`. To include the Komika Display TrueType Font, define the font family using the CSS `@font-face` feature. Point its source to the location of the `.ttf` file. Finally, define a `komikafont` class, and set its `font-family` to `KomikaDisplay`.

Now, create the `#main` page with header `h1`. The header will now use the Syncopate web font. Add a `div` tag with `class='komikafont'` to the page content, and the text in this `div` tag will use the Komika Display font. Finally, add another `div` tag with `class='divstyle'`, and this will use the Syncopate font with a font weight of `400`. The screen will be displayed as follows:

## There's more...

This recipe shows you how to use custom fonts for specific elements. To globally change fonts across your entire application, use the jQuery Mobile `ThemeRoller` tool available at `http://www.jquerymobile.com/themeroller`. The following screenshot shows you the **Verdana** font being set globally:

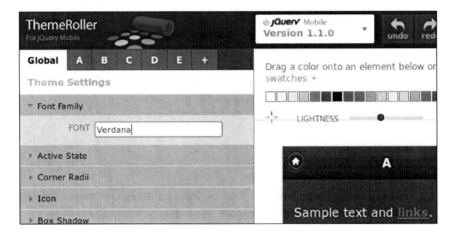

## Using TrueType fonts

**TrueType** (**TTF**) or **OpenType** fonts are mostly supported in all the modern browsers. You will have to take care if you are targeting older browsers or most of the older devices and feature phones, as the fonts might not be supported with `@font-face`. You can refer to `http://www.caniuse.com/#search=ttf` to get the updated status of support for TTF in various browsers. You will note that older versions of iOS do not support TTF. You might have to use SVG fonts instead.

## Downloading the fonts

You can visit and use other web fonts from the Google Web Fonts page at `http://www.google.com/webfonts`. All the fonts are open source and can be used freely. The Komika Display font designed by Apostrophic Labs, is available at the Font Squirrel web page (`http://www.fontsquirrel.com/fonts/Komika-Display`). The Font Squirrel website has a large number of fonts available, all as freeware.

## See also

▸   The *Using the ThemeRoller tool to create a swatch* recipe

# Styling corners

This recipe shows you how to use different corner styles that are readily available with jQuery Mobile.

## Getting ready

Copy the full code of this recipe from the `code/10/corner-styles` source folder.
You can launch this code using the URL: `http://localhost:8080/10/corner-styles/main.html`.

## How to do it...

1. Create `main.html`, and add the following `<style>` tag to its `<head>` section:

```
<style>
  .mydiv { border: 2px solid #000; margin: 5px; text-align:
center; }
</style>
```

2. Create the `#main` page with four `div` elements in a layout grid, as follows:

```
<div id='main' data-role='page' data-theme='a'>
  <div data-role='header' data-theme='e'  class='ui-
    corner-top' style='margin-top: 10px'>
    <h1>Header Text</h1>
  </div>
  <div id='content' data-theme='e' data-role='content'>
    <fieldset data-role='controlgroup' data-
      type='horizontal' class='ui-grid-a'>
      <div class='ui-block-a ui-corner-tl mydiv'
        style='width: 45%'><p>Top Left</p></div>
      <div class='ui-block-b ui-corner-tr mydiv'
        style='width: 45%'><p>Top Right</p></div>
      <div class='ui-block-a ui-corner-bl mydiv'
        style='width: 45%'><p>Bottom Left</p></div>
      <div class='ui-block-b ui-corner-br mydiv'
        style='width: 45%'><p>Bottom Right</p></div>
    </fieldset>
  </div>
  <div data-role='footer' class='ui-corner-bottom' data-
    theme='e'>
    <h4>Footer Text</h4>
  </div>
</div>
```

## How it works...

In `main.html`, define the `.mydiv` class with a border, margin, and center aligned text as shown. Create the #main page and style the header with `class='ui-corner-top'`. This will add corners on the top side of the header. Define the footer with `class='ui-corner-bottom'`, to add bottom corners to the footer. Do not add any style to the content `div`, so the `class='ui-corner-none'` style is used by default. Now, add four `div` tags in two rows using a two column layout grid (`grid-a`). Style these `div` tags using the `mydiv` class. Also, add the different corner styles (`ui-corner-tl`, `ui-corner-tr`, `ui-corner-bl`, and `ui-corner-br`) to these `div` tags respectively. The four `div` tags are now styled as follows:

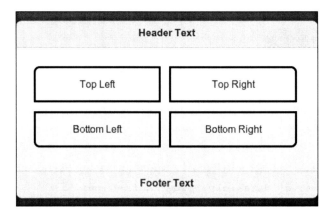

## There's more...

You can globally set the corner radius using the jQuery Mobile `ThemeRoller` tool available at `http://www.jquerymobile.com/themeroller`.

## See also

▸ The *Using the ThemeRoller tool to create a swatch* recipe

▸ The *Grouping Radio Buttons in a Grid* recipe in *Chapter 5, Forms*

# Overriding the global Active State theme

The jQuery Mobile framework uses a bright blue color to indicate the active state for buttons and other controls. This **Active State** theme is consistent for all the default swatches and cannot be overridden via markup. This recipe shows you how to override the Active State theme.

## Getting ready

Copy the full code of this recipe from the `code/10/active-state` source folder. You can launch this code using the URL: `http://localhost:8080/10/active-state/main.html`.

## How to do it...

1. Create the `active-state.css` stylesheet to style the active state, as follows:

```css
.ui-btn-active {
    border: 1px solid #137000;
    background: #93ff86;
    font-weight: bold;
    color: #000;
    text-shadow: 0 1px 1px #eee;
    cursor: pointer;
    text-decoration: none;
    background-image: -webkit-gradient(linear, left top,
        left bottom, from( #a1ff93), to( #14b800));
    background-image: -webkit-linear-gradient( #a1ff93,
        #14b800);
    background-image: -moz-linear-gradient( #a1ff93,
        #14b800);
    background-image: -ms-linear-gradient( #a1ff93,
        #14b800);
    background-image: -o-linear-gradient( #a1ff93,
        #14b800);
    background-image: linear-gradient( #a1ff93, #14b800);
    font-family: Helvetica, Arial, sans-serif;
}
```

2. Specify the style for the on focus event:

```
.ui-focus, .ui-btn:focus {
  -moz-box-shadow: 0px 0px 12px #37bf37;
  -webkit-box-shadow: 0px 0px 12px #37bf37;
  box-shadow: 0px 0px 12px #37bf37;
}
```

3. Specify the on state style for the checkbox and radio button controls:

```
.ui-checkbox-on .ui-icon, .ui-radio-on .ui-icon {
  background-color: #50cf44;
}
```

4. Include the preceding stylesheet in `main.html`:

```
<link rel='stylesheet' href='http://code.jquery.com/mobile/1.1.1/
jquery.mobile-1.1.1.min.css' />
<link rel='stylesheet' href='./active-state.css' />
```

5. Now, create a header with a `navbar` control in the `#main` page:

```
<div id='main' data-role='page' data-theme='a'>
  <div data-role='header'>
    <h1>Active State</h1>
    <div data-role='navbar'>
      <ul>
        <li><a href='#'>Nav1</a></li>
        <li><a href='#' class='ui-btn-
          active'>Nav2</a></li>
        <li><a href='#'>Nav3</a></li>
      </ul>
    </div>
  </div>
```

6. Finally, add the page content with a horizontal checkbox, a vertical checkbox, and a slider, as follows:

```
    <div data-role='content'>
      <div data-role='fieldcontain'>
        <fieldset data-role='controlgroup' data-
          type='horizontal'>
          <legend>CheckBox</legend>
          <input type='checkbox' name='hchkbox'
            id='hchkbox'/>
          <label for='hchkbox'>Horizontal</label>
        </fieldset>
      </div>
      <div data-role='fieldcontain'>
        <fieldset data-role='controlgroup'>
```

```
         <legend>CheckBox</legend>
         <input type='checkbox' name='vchkbox'
           id='vchkbox'/>
         <label for='vchkbox'>Vertical</label>
      </fieldset>
    </div>
    <div data-role='fieldcontain'>
      <label for='sldr'>Input slider:</label>
      <input type='range' name='sldr' id='sldr'
        value='50' min='0' max='100' data-
        highlight='true' />
    </div>
  </div>
</div>
```

## How it works...

Create the `active-state.css` stylesheet to keep the style info separate from the HTML file. The active state, the on focus event, and the on state style of the checkbox and radio button controls use the bright blue theme by default. You can override them in the CSS file, as shown in the code. First, override the `.ui-btn-active` class, and specify your settings for the `border`, `background`, `color`, and `background-image` CSS attributes. Next, override the `.ui-focus` and `.ui-btn:focus` classes, and specify the color for the box-shadow `.ui-checkbox-on` and `.ui-radio-on` styles, as shown in the code.

Create `main.html`, and add a `navbar` control to the header. Add the `ui-btn-active` class to the second link in `navbar`. You will see the active state set on the second link when the page loads. Next, add a horizontal and vertical group of checkbox controls. Finally, add an input slider to the page. The page now loads, as displayed in the following screenshot, with the default bright blue active state theme replaced with a fluorescent green theme:

## There's more...

You can also globally set the active status theme using the jQuery Mobile ThemeRoller tool available at `http://www.jquerymobile.com/themeroller`.

## See also

▸ The *Using the ThemeRoller tool to create a swatch* recipe

▸ The *Using CSS to create a bouncing page transition* recipe in *Chapter 2, Pages and Dialogs*: This recipe provides a note on vendor prefixes

▸ The *Configuring the active classes* recipe in *Chapter 7, Configurations*

# Overriding an existing swatch

The jQueryMobile framework uses the `ui-btn-hover` class to theme the **button hover** event. This recipe shows you how to override the style for the button hover event of an existing swatch.

## Getting ready

Copy the full code of this recipe from the `code/10/button-hover` source folder. You can launch this code using the URL: `http://localhost:8080/10/button-hover/main.html`.

## How to do it...

1. Create `main.html`, and add the following `<style>` tag to the `<head>` section:

```
<link rel='stylesheet' href=
   'http://code.jquery.com/mobile/1.1.1/jquery.mobile-
   1.1.1.min.css' />
<style>
   .ui-btn-hover-a {
      border: 1px solid #115e00;
      background: #51b54a;
      font-weight: bold;
      color: #fff;
      text-shadow: 0 1px 1px #197d19;
      background-image: -webkit-gradient(linear, left top,
         left bottom, from( #7ad66f), to( #41a343));
      background-image: -webkit-linear-gradient( #7ad66f,
         #41a343);
      background-image: -moz-linear-gradient( #7ad66f,
         #41a343);
      background-image: -ms-linear-gradient( #7ad66f,
         #41a343);
      background-image: -o-linear-gradient( #7ad66f,
         #41a343);
      background-image: linear-gradient( #7ad66f, #41a343);  }
</style>
```

2. Create the `#main` page and add a button to the page content:

```
<a href='#' data-role='button'>button</a>
```

## How it works...

In `main.html`, define the override for the `.ui-btn-hover-a` class after linking the jQuery Mobile stylesheet, as shown in the code. Specify the `border`, `background`, `color`, `text-shadow`, and `background-image` CSS attributes. Create the `#main` page with `data-theme='a'`, and add a button to the page content. Load the page, and on button hover you will see that the button gets a bright green color instead of the default hover style, as shown in the following screenshot:

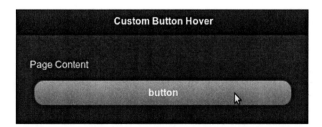

## There's more...

You can also theme the button hover for **swatch A** using the jQuery Mobile ThemeRoller tool available at `http://www.jquerymobile.com/themeroller`.

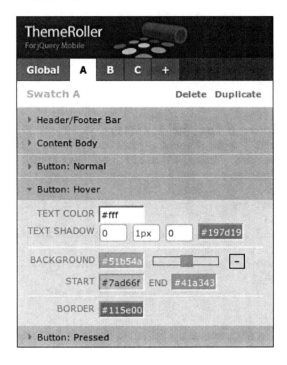

### The buttonMarkup.hoverDelay configuration

You can configure the delay for the button hover by setting the `buttonMarkup.hoverDelay` (defaults to `200` ms) configuration on `mobileinit`. But take care, as using values that are too large or too small will impact the user experience. You can use the following code to configure this property:

```
$(document).bind('mobileinit', function() {
  $.mobile.buttonMarkup.hoverDelay = 500;
});
```

## See also

▶ The *Using the ThemeRoller tool to create a swatch* recipe

▶ The *Using CSS to create a bouncing page transition* recipe in *Chapter 2, Pages and Dialogs*: This recipe provides a note on vendor prefixes

# Using the ThemeRoller tool to create a swatch

This recipe shows you how to create a swatch using the jQueryMobile ThemeRoller web tool.

## Getting ready

The code in this recipe was created using the the jQueryMobile ThemeRoller web tool available at `http://www.jquerymobile.com/themeroller`. The code is available in the `code/10/myTheme` source folder. You can launch this code using the URL `http://localhost:8080/10/myTheme/index.html`.

## How to do it...

1.  Generate the `myTheme.css` file using the jQueryMobile ThemeRoller tool. It gets included in the generated `index.html` file, as follows:

    ```
    <link rel='stylesheet' href='themes/myTheme.min.css' />
    <link rel="stylesheet"
      href="http://code.jquery.com/mobile
      /1.1.1/jquery.mobile.structure-1.1.1.min.css" />
    <script src="http://code.jquery.com/jquery-1.7.1.min.js">
    </script>
    <script src="http://code.jquery.com/mobile/
        1.1.1/jquery.mobile-1.1.1.min.js"></script>
    ```

2.  The `<body>` content in `index.html` gets generated as follows:

    ```
    <div data-role="page" data-theme="a">
      <div data-role="header" data-position="inline">
        <h1>It Worked!</h1>
      </div>
      <div data-role="content" data-theme="a">
        <p>
          Your theme was successfully downloaded. You can use
            this page as a reference for how to link it up!
        </p>
        <pre> .... </pre>
        <p>
          This is content color swatch "A" and a preview of a
            <a href="#" class="ui-link">link</a>.
        </p>
        <label for="slider1">Input slider:</label>
        <input type="range" name="slider1" id="slider1"
    ```

```
            value="50" min="0" max="100" data-theme="a" />
        <fieldset data-role="controlgroup"  data-
          type="horizontal" data-role="fieldcontain">
          <legend>Cache settings:</legend>
          <input type="radio" name="radio-choice-a1" id=
            "radio-choice-a1" value="on" checked="checked" />
          <label for="radio-choice-a1">On</label>
          <input type="radio" name="radio-choice-a1" id=
            "radio-choice-b1" value="off"  />
          <label for="radio-choice-b1">Off</label>
        </fieldset>
      </div>
    </div>
```

## How it works...

Launch the jQuery Mobile ThemeRoller web tool. You will see the available swatches in the left pane called the **Inspector pane**. The swatch always starts with **A**, and you can add, duplicate, or delete swatches. The other swatches are immediately sorted alphabetically. You can create up to 26 swatches (**A** to **Z**). You can directly modify the CSS properties in the **Inspector** pane.

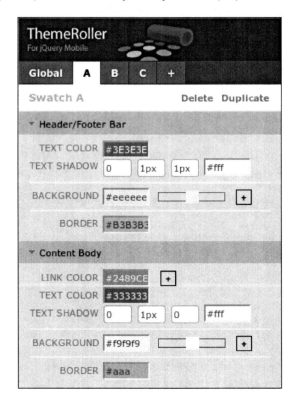

Instead of manually entering the colors, you can also use the **Adobe Kuler** swatch bar available at the top of the screen. Drag-and-drop the color of your choice directly on a component in the preview screen. The component gets updated immediately with the new color.

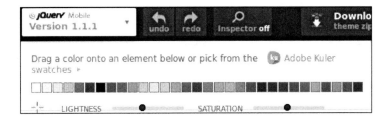

You can click the Kuler Swatches link, and access multiple ready-to-use color combinations that are available online.

Now, drag-and-drop the colors of your choice on the screen components. You will see that the screen preview(shown in the following image), instantly reflects the theme change. You can also theme the active state here.

Once the theme is ready, you can download it by clicking on the **Download** button at the top of the screen. Provide a name and download the zip file. The zip file contains the required icons, CSS files, and also a sample `index.html` file. The new theme is displayed when you extract these files and open the `index.html` file.

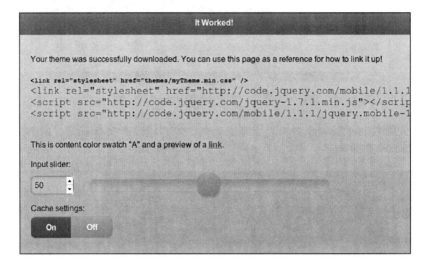

 The `jquery.mobile.css` file is not used in the generated `index.html` file. Instead, it contains the links to `myTheme.css` (for the custom theme) and `jquery.mobile.structure.css` (structure-related CSS properties). Keeping the theme-able properties separate makes it easier to maintain, upgrade, and also to share your themes.

## There's more...

You can synchronize the **Preview** pane and the **Inspector** pane using the **Inspector on/off** button at the top of the ThemeRoller tool. Hovering on any control in the **Preview** pane highlights the control with a blue border. Click on the control to open its CSS settings in the **Inspector** pane. This is very handy while developing themes.

## Importing and upgrading themes

You can import your existing CSS themes into the ThemeRoller tool and extend them to create new themes. You can also upgrade the older versions of jQuery Mobile themes to the latest v1.1.1 using ThemeRoller. Click on the **Import** or **Upgrade** button at the top of the **ThemeRoller** screen to open the **Import Theme** dialog box.

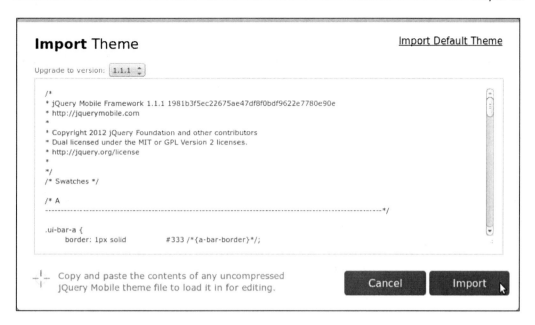

You can copy-paste your existing theme and click on the **Import** button. The new upgraded theme is ready and loaded in the tool. You can also load the default theme provided by the jQuery Mobile framework by clicking on the **Import Default Theme** option at the top of the **Import** dialog box. This loads the five default swatches into ThemeRoller. You can now use this set as a starting point to create fresh themes.

## Sharing themes

The ThemeRoller tool also provides a cool feature to share your work with others. Click on the **Share Theme Link** button at the top of the tool to get the link that you can share with others. Anyone with this link can directly access, use, or work on a copy of your theme.

# 11
# HTML5 and jQuery Mobile

In this chapter, we will cover the following recipes:

- ▶ Using the new HTML5 semantics
- ▶ Improving speed and taking your application offline
- ▶ Using Web Workers for intensive tasks
- ▶ Using local and session storage
- ▶ 2D drawing with Canvas
- ▶ Applying Gaussian blur on a SVG image
- ▶ Tracking your location with the Geolocation API
- ▶ Playing music with the `<audio>` element
- ▶ Viewing videos with the `<video>` element

## Introduction

HTML5 introduces new semantics and many new cool features, such as Application Cache, 2D Canvas, Geolocation, Local and Session Storage, Web Workers, and support for audio and video. The jQuery Mobile framework is built on HTML5 and CSS3, and provides excellent support for these new semantics and new features. This chapter introduces some of these features that you can use in your jQuery Mobile apps.

 There are many resources on the web for learning HTML5. To mention a few, you can read more at HTML5 Rocks (`http://www.html5rocks.com/en`), HTML5 Demos (`http://www.html5demos.com`), and the Mozilla Developer Network (`https://developer.mozilla.org/en-US/docs/HTML/HTML5`).

The support for HTML5 elements and features on various browsers and platforms is varied. You will have to take care while using a particular feature and ensure that it works on your target platforms. This level of support continues to improve with every passing day.

>  `http://www.caniuse.com` has a good reference on the updated status of platform support available for the various HTML5 features.

# Using the new HTML5 semantics

HTML5 defines new semantics to better organize an HTML document into more logical sections. This recipe shows you how to use the new HTML5 semantics to define your jQuery Mobile app. The following HTML5 elements are covered in this recipe:

- `section`: This defines the section in a document. Headers, footers, and the page content are all sections.
- `header`: This defines the document header.
- `footer`: This defines the document footer.
- `aside`: This defines the additional content related to the main content of the document, usually placed as a sidebar.
- `article`: This defines the content related to the document, but it can also stand alone and can be independently distributed.
- `nav`: This is a section providing navigation links and can contain one or more anchor links.

## Getting ready

Copy the full code of this recipe from the `code/11/semantics` folder. You can launch this code using the URL: `http://localhost:8080/11/semantics/main.html`.

## How to do it...

The steps to be followed are as follows:

1. Create `main.html` that uses the new HTML5 semantics for the page; do not use the `<div>` tag here:

```
<section id='main' data-role='page' data-theme='a'>
  <header data-role='header' data-theme='b'>
    <h1>New HTML5 Tags</h1>
  </header>
  <section data-role='content'>
```

```
      Main content goes here
      <aside style='border: 2px; border-style: solid;
        border-color: #666'>
        <h3>Aside</h3>
        Standalone content but related to main
      </aside>
      <section>
        <h3>Articles</h3>
        <article>
          <h4>Item 1</h4>
          Item 1 description here
        </article>
        <article>
          <h4>Item 2</h4>
          Item 2 description here
        </article>
      </section>
    </section>
    <footer data-role='footer' data-theme='b'>
      <nav class='ui-bar' data-theme='d'>
        <a href='#' data-role='button'>Link 1</a>
        <a href='#' data-role='button' class='ui-btn-
          right'>Link 2</a>
      </nav>
    </footer>
  </section>
```

## How it works...

Create main.html, and add the #main page to it using a <section> tag with the
data-role='page' attribute. Add the <header> tag with data-role='header'
to create the page header. Next, add a <section> tag with data-role='content'
to create the page content section. Finally, add the footer with the <footer> tag with
the data-role='footer' attribute. You now have the page with a header, content,
and footer ready. You will note that <div> has not been used so far.

Add the `<aside>` and `<article>` elements to the page content, as shown in the code. Since there are multiple articles, you can group them in a `<section>` element. Finally, add a `<nav>` element with two button links to the page footer. Add the `ui-btn-right` class to move the second button to the right side of the screen. Now, when you launch the app, the following screen will be displayed:

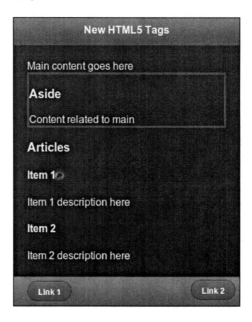

## There's more...

HTML5 supports many more new elements, such as:

- `figure`: This is used to contain images, photos, diagrams, illustrations, and so on.
- `figcaption`: This defines the caption for `<figure>`.
- `hgroup`: This is used to group a set of header elements (`<h1>`,`<h2>`, and so on).
- `mark`: This is used to highlight the text.
- `meter`: This is used to specify a numeric value within a min-max range. You can also specify a threshold value (low and high).
- `progress`: This is used to indicate progress.
- `time`: This is used to mark up a date/time value.

### About using <div>

Prior to HTML5, `<div>` was used as the container to group elements. But this was not very descriptive. The HTML5 document structure is much more descriptive and meaningful with header, footer, and so on.

When using HTML5, use `<div>` to group elements that do not fit the description of any of the new HTML5 elements, such as `<section>`.

### Using <section> with jQuery Mobile

Support for HTML5 semantics is varied and improving in the numerous platforms available on the market today. As of v1.1.1, the jQuery Mobile framework recommends using the `<div>` element with the `data-role` attribute to specify the various page components, such as header and footer. This is to ensure compatibility with the older versions of browsers, such as IE8, and also to support the maximum number of devices and platforms. This would definitely change in a near future version of jQuery Mobile, when support for the older browsers is dropped. Till then, use the new HTML5 elements, keeping your target users in mind.

## Improving speed and taking your application offline

HTML5 introduced a new feature called **Application Cache** that allows your web app to cache network resources locally. You can also control and configure this cache much better than the earlier browser caching techniques. With Application Cache, your mobile app can work better, even in situations where there is slow or no network coverage. Your app is faster, as it can find many of the resources stored locally instead of fetching them from the server. This also helps the user with lower data transfer costs that would be charged by the service provider.

This recipe shows you how to use the Application Cache feature in your jQuery Mobile app. It also shows you how to use a locally stored jQuery Mobile library instead of fetching the library files from the CDN.

### Getting ready

Copy the full code of this recipe from the `code/11/appcache` folder. You will have to host this code on a web server to see how Application Cache works. The `sources` folder contains a `nodejs` web server that you can use to run this app. You can launch this code using the URL: `http://localhost:8080/11/appcache/main.html`.

### How to do it...

The steps to be followed are:

1.  Create `main.html`, and specify the manifest file in the `<html>` tag:

    ```
    <!DOCTYPE html>
    <html manifest="jqmcookbook.appcache">
    ```

2. Add the following three links to the page content in `main.html`:

```
<div data-role="content">
  <a href="cached.html" data-role="button">CACHE</a>
  <a href="online.html" data-role="button">FALLBACK</a>
  <a href="network.html" data-role="button">NETWORK</a>
</div>
```

3. Create the following `jqmcookbook.appcache` manifest file and specify the files that are to be cached:

**CACHE MANIFEST**
*# jQuery Mobile Cookbook Edition 1.0*

*# Cached resources (also caching jQuery Mobile files for* `offline access`*)*
**CACHE:**
```
main.html
cached.html
http://code.jquery.com/mobile/1.1.1/jquery.mobile-1.1.1.min.css
http://code.jquery.com/jquery-1.7.1.min.js
http://code.jquery.com/mobile/1.1.1/jquery.mobile-1.1.1.min.js
```

*# offline.html will be displayed as fall back*
**FALLBACK:**
```
online.html offline.html
```

*# Accessible only when online*
**NETWORK:**
```
network.html
```

4. Create the following `cached.html` file, which gets cached by the app, and is available for offline access:

```
<!-- Cached Page : Cached and works offline too -->
<div id="cached" data-role="page">
  <div data-role="content">
    <h1>
      This page is shown from cache and even works when
        offline
    </h1>
    <a href="#" data-role="button" data-rel="back"
        data-theme="b">Go Back</a>
  </div>
</div>
```

5.  Create the following `online.html` file, which does not get cached and is fetched from the network every time it is accessed:

```
<!-- Online Page : Shown only when Online -->
<div id="online" data-role="page">
  <div data-role="content">
    <h1>This page is shown only when online</h1>
    <a href="#" data-role="button" data-rel="back"
        data-theme="b">Go Back</a>
  </div>
</div>
```

6.  Create the following `offline.html` file that gets cached and is used as a fallback when the `online.html` page is not accessible over the network:

```
<!-- Offline Page : Shown as a fall back -->
<div id="offline" data-role="page">
  <div data-role="content">
    <h1>This is a fallback for online.html</h1>
    <a href="#" data-role="button" data-rel="back"
        data-theme="b">Go Back</a>
  </div>
</div>
```

7.  Finally, create the following `network.html` file that does not get cached, and is always fetched from the network; it does not use any fallback:

```
<!-- Network Page : Shown only when online -->
<div id="network" data-role="page">
  <div data-role="content">
    <h1>This is always fetched from the network</h1>
    <a href="#" data-role="button" data-rel="back"
        data-theme="b">Go Back</a>
  </div>
</div>
```

## How it works...

Create `main.html`, and specify `jqmcookbook.appcache` as the manifest file in its `<html>` tag. This indicates to the browser that the HTML file should be cached. It also indicates that the manifest file must be processed for finding all the resources that are to be cached locally. Add three links for the `cached.html`, `online.html`, and `network.html` pages, as shown. These will be used as the resources that will be cached in this recipe.

Create the jqmcookbook.appcache manifest file with the text CACHE MANIFEST specified in its first line. You can add comments to the manifest file, and they start with the # character. Now, add the resources to be cached by your app to the manifest file. Each filename must be on a separate line, and you can use relative or absolute paths. The Cache Manifest file has three sections identified by the CACHE, FALLBACK, and NETWORK headers.

Define the default CACHE section and list the files that should be cached locally. Add main. html and cached.html to this section. When you launch the app and click on the first button, it opens cached.html regardless of whether the device is online or offline.

 Images, icons, stylesheets, JavaScript, and other static files are the resources that you should cache locally.

Cached files are downloaded only at the first time. When the app tries to access any of these files, they are always fetched from the cache first or, only if not available, they are fetched from the server.

 It is good practice to cache the main HTML file (with the manifest defined in its <html> tag) in your app.

Next, define the FALLBACK section with two filenames in each line. Specify online.html as the first file, and then specify the fallback as offline.html. Now, when you click on the second button in the app, online.html is shown only if the device is online. If the device goes offline, then offline.html is automatically shown from the cache. Here, the first file is always fetched from the network and is never cached.

Finally, define the NETWORK section with network.html listed in it. Use this section to define the list of files that should never be cached in your app. These files are always fetched from the network. Now, when you click on the third button, network.html is shown only if the device is online, and an error is shown if the device is offline.

## There's more...

You can see the list of currently cached files in your browser using the developer/debugging tools that most browsers provide today. The following screenshot shows the Chrome Developer Tool's view of the resources that have been cached for the main.html file in this recipe. The files listed in the manifest are all seen in the **Application Cache** section.

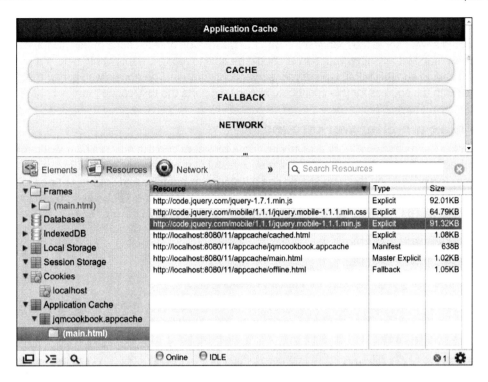

## Restriction on the cache size

There is a browser limitation on how much data you can store locally. Usually it is 5 to 10 MBs, and requires the user's permission to go over this limit. Some browsers, such as Chrome, allow you to set this value as unlimited. So, cache files with care and include the resources that you access often. Also include resources that you need to take your app offline.

## Refreshing the Application Cache

Each time the `main.html` file is accessed, the remote manifest file is fetched and is compared with the local manifest file. Only if the manifest has changed (this could be even just a comment), the new manifest file is fetched. Then the cache will be cleared and the entire set of cached files will be refreshed from the server. The flip side to this is that, just adding a single new file to the manifest file will trigger a full refresh, even if none of the other files have changed.

 Using a version number in the comment of the manifest file is a good way of keeping the cached files updated.

### The MIME type of the manifest file

You should always serve the manifest file with the **MIME** type of text/cache-manifest. You can name this manifest anything. Your server should be able to recognize this MIME type. If it does not, you should add this MIME type to your server configuration. The nodejs web server that is shipped with the sources for this cookbook, already supports the text/cache-manifest MIME type.

### The Ajax pre-filter workaround

Application Cache does not work properly on some browsers and the Ajax pre-filter workaround is required in this case. In these browsers, a successful Ajax call returns a 0 HTTP status on success. To work around this, you should use a jQuery Ajax pre-filter and set the isLocal attribute to true. The detailed github discussion thread on using the isLocal workaround is available at https://github.com/jquery/jquery-mobile/issues/1579.

## See also

- ▶ The *Using Web Workers for intensive tasks* recipe
- ▶ Chapter 2, *Pages and Dialogs*, The *Prefetching pages for faster navigation* and The *Using the DOM cache to improve performance* recipes

# Using Web Workers for intensive tasks

When you run a script that does some complex or lengthy activity, the browser thread freezes and does not respond till the task is complete. This can be overcome by using a Web Worker—a background independent thread that is used to run JavaScript. The browser thread is not blocked, and thus can continue to respond to user actions. This recipe shows you how to use Web Workers.

## Getting ready

Copy the full code of this recipe from the code/11/webworkers folder. You can launch this code using the URL: http://localhost:8080/11/webworkers/main.html.

## How to do it...

The steps to be performed are as follows:

1. Create main.html with a checkbox and a slider as its page content:

```
<div data-role='content'>
  <div id='msgdiv'></div>
  <div data-role='fieldcontain'>
    <input type="range" name="myslider" id="myslider"
      value='0' min="0" max="100" />
```

```
    <label for="myslider">Slide me:</label>
  </div>
  <div data-role='fieldcontain'>
    <input type="checkbox" name="countchk" id="countchk" />
    <label for="countchk">Count with Webworkers</label>
  </div>
</div>
```

2. Add the following script to trigger a long running loop when the checkbox is clicked. When checked, the loop is run in a Web worker and there is no UI freeze, and you can continue to use the page. When the checkbox is unchecked, immediately everything freezes till the loop is done.

```
$('#main').live('pageinit', function(event) {
  $('#countchk').bind('change', function(event, ui) {
    if($('#countchk').prop("checked")) {
      $('#msgdiv').html('Worker is counting ...');
      var myworker = new Worker('webworker.js');
      myworker.onmessage = function(event) {
      $('#msgdiv').html(event.data);
    }
    myworker.postMessage('start');
    } else {
      $('#msgdiv').html('Started Counting ...');

      var count = 0;
      for (var i=1; i<=10000000000; i++)
        count++;
        $('#msgdiv').html('Loops : ' + count);


    }
  });
});
```

3. Finally, add the `webworker.js` JavaScript file to handle the loop:

```
self.onmessage = function(event) {
  var count = 0;
  for (var i=1; i<10000000000; i++)
    count++;
  self.postMessage('Worker Loops : ' + count);
};
```

## How it works...

Create `main.html`, and add a slider and a checkbox with `id='countchk'` to the content of #main. Also, add an empty #msgdiv attribute to display the messages. Bind the `change` event of the checkbox to an event handler in the `pageinit` callback.

When the checkbox is selected, trigger the loop in a Web Worker. Initiate the Web Worker by calling `new Worker()`, and pass it the name of the JavaScript `webworker.js` file. Define the `onmessage` event handler to handle messages received by the worker. You can display this message in #msgdiv. Finally, invoke the worker by posting a `start` message to it. This message can be anything, and the code must be written in the worker to handle it. In the file `webworker.js`, define the `onmessage` callback to handle the incoming message from the browser thread. Run the loop and return an appropriate message to the main thread.

When you launch the page and select the checkbox, the loop is initiated in a Web Worker. You can use the slider and see the messages being updated in the page even though the loop is still running:

When the checkbox is not selected, the loop runs in the main browser thread itself. Now, the entire UI freezes even before the checkbox can reflect your click, and the UI responds only after the loop is completed:

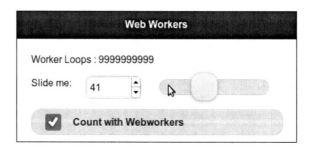

## There's more...

Support for Web Workers might not be available in all browsers. You can check for the Web Worker support in your app by calling the following code, which checks for the presence of the `Worker` property of the `window` object. If undefined, the feature is not available.

```
if (!!window.Worker)
  // Web workers are supported
else
  // Web workers are not supported
```

### Using Modernizr to check for Web Worker support

**Modernizr** (available at `http://www.modernizr.com`) is a very popular and handy library that can be used to detect the support for Web Workers and other HTML5 and CSS3 features in your browser. It provides **polyfills** or **fallbacks** in case a particular property is not supported in a browser. It comes with an **MIT license**, and can be freely used. The `Modernizr.webworkers` property would be defined and available if your browser supports Web Workers.

## See also

- ▶ The *Improving speed and taking your application offline* recipe

# Using local and session storage

**Cookies** was the mechanism used to store client-side information earlier. But a cookie can only store up to 4 KB of data, which is sent to the server with every single request. **Web Storage** is the client-side storage standard introduced with HTML5. It has two types: **Local Storage** and **Session Storage**. Data stored in Session Storage is available till the user's session is active, and is lost once the session ends. Local Storage data is persisted across sessions. This recipe shows you how to use Local Storage and Session Storage.

## Getting ready

Copy the full code of this recipe from the `code/11/storage` folder. You can launch this code using the URL: `http://localhost:8080/11/storage/main.html`.

## How to do it...

The steps to be followed are:

1. Create `main.html` with its page content having three text fields and a **Save** button:

```
<div data-role='content'>
  <div data-role='fieldcontain'>
    <label for='nostore'>No Storage</label>
    <input type="text" id="nostore" name="nostore"
      autofocus placeholder="Enter text" value="" />
  </div>
  <div data-role='fieldcontain'>
    <label for='sessionstore'>Session Storage</label>
    <input type="text" id="sessionstore"
      name="sessionstore" placeholder="Enter text"
      value="" />
  </div>
  <div data-role='fieldcontain'>
    <label for='localstore'>Local Storage</label>
    <input type="text" id="localstore" name="localstore"
      placeholder="Enter text" value="" />
  </div>
  <button id='savebtn'>Save</button>
</div>
```

2. Add the following script to persist the text field contents by clicking on the **Save** button:

```
$('#main').live('pageinit', function(event) {
  $('#savebtn').bind('click', function(event, ui) {
    window.localStorage.setItem('localval', $('#localstore').
val());
    window.sessionStorage.setItem('sessionval',
$('#sessionstore').val());
  });
});
```

3. Finally, restore the persisted values when the page is shown:

```
$('#main').live('pageshow', function(event, data) {
  $('#localstore').val(window.localStorage.getItem('localval'));
  $('#sessionstore').val(window.sessionStorage.
getItem('sessionval'));
});
```

4. Refresh the page, and later close and reopen the page to see how these persisted values behave over a single session and across multiple sessions.

## How it works...

Add three texts with IDs: `nostore`, `sessionstore`, and `localstore`. Add a button with `id='savebtn'`, and bind its `click` event to a callback in the `pageinit` event handler. In the callback, persist the text fields by calling the `setItem()` method with unique keys (`localval` and `sessionval`) on the `window.sessionStorage` and `window.localStorage` objects respectively.

To restore these persisted values when the page reloads or refreshes, add an event handler to the `pageshow` event. Pass the `localval` key to the `window.localStorage.getItem()` function to read from local storage. Pass the `sessionval` key to `window.sessionStorage.getItem()` to read from session storage. Set these values to the respective text fields.

When the app loads, enter the text values and click on the **Save** button to persist them.

Next, refresh the browser to reload the page. The session is still alive, and you will see the local and session storage values get restored. The first field is cleared as it was not persisted, as shown in the following screenshot:

Finally, close the app and reopen it. This time, the session is terminated. You will see that only the **Local Storage** data is shown and the other two text fields are cleared:

## There's more...

Support for Web Storage might not be available in all browsers. You can check if the `window` object has a valid `localstorage` or `sessionStorage` property to verify if you can use the feature by running the following code:

```
If (('localStorage' in window) && window['localStorage'] !== null)
    // Local storage is supported
If (('sessionStorage' in window) && window['sessionStorage'] !== null)
    // Session storage is supported
```

You can also use the free `Modernizr` library to test for Web Storage support by checking if the `Modernizr.localstorage` and the `Modernizr.sessionstorage` properties are valid.

### Inspecting the Web Storage

You can open the developer tools in your browser and inspect the current set of key-values stored in your browser for the Local and Session Storage. The following screenshot shows the Local Storage key-value that was saved in this recipe:

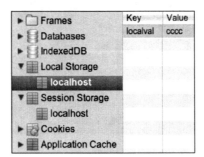

The following screenshot shows the key-value stored using **Session Storage**:

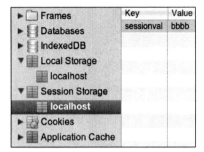

## WebSQL Storage

WebSQL Storage is another feature that was defined in HTML5 to store client-side data. It uses SQLite queries to perform the data operations. Both IE and Firefox do not support this feature. This specification is no longer being maintained and might be dropped going forward.

## IndexedDB Storage

The **IndexedDB Storage** is another form of client-side storage using indexed data queries. Only Firefox and Chrome browsers support this feature well at the time of writing this recipe. Older IE versions, Safari, and Opera do not support this feature.

# 2D drawing with Canvas

**Canvas** is a rectangular region in your web page where you can draw 2D shapes using JavaScript, and also render bitmap images. It is used for graphs, animations, images, photo compositions, real-time video processing, and games. This recipe shows you how to use the Canvas in your jQuery Mobile app.

## Getting ready

Copy the full code of this recipe from the `code/11/canvas` folder. You can launch this code using the URL: `http://localhost:8080/11/canvas/main.html`.

## How to do it...

The steps to be followed are:

1. Create `main.html` with its page content having a `canvas` element:

```
<div data-role='content'>
  <canvas id="myCanvas" width="500" height="500">
    Canvas is not supported on your browser
  </canvas>
</div>
```

2. Add the following script to get the 2D context, and then draw two rectangles:

```
$('#main').live('pageinit', function(event) {
  var cxt = $('#myCanvas')[0].getContext("2d");
  cxt.fillStyle = '#5f98c5';
  cxt.fillRect(20,20, 100, 100);
  cxt.strokeRect(10,10,120, 120);
});
```

## How it works...

Create `main.html`, and add a `<canvas>` element with `id='mycanvas'` to the #main page with `width` and `height` of 500 pixels. The text **Canvas is not supported on your browser** is shown if the browser does not support the Canvas feature. Next, add a script to the `pageinit` callback function to get the 2D context (`cxt`) of the `mycanvas` element. Define the `fillStyle` of cxt with a grey shade #5f98c5. Now, draw a filled rectangle using `fillRect()`, passing the origin, length, and breadth as parameters. Next, use `strokeRect()` to draw a rectangle outline without any fill. The screen is now displayed, as shown in the following screenshot:

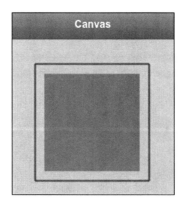

## There's more...

This recipe just gives a basic introduction to the Canvas element, and shows you how to use it in your jQuery Mobile app. The Canvas is a very powerful element and supports a wide array of APIs. You can set colors, styles, gradients, patterns, fonts, and text alignment. You can draw geometric shapes, such as lines, rectangles, paths, arcs, and bezier curves. The canvas supports transformation APIs, such as scale, rotate, translate, and transform. You can draw images and also manipulate them at a pixel level. Canvas helps in photo composition. You can also save the drawing state of the canvas in a stack, and restore any previous saved drawing state from the stack.

> The elements drawn on a canvas take in absolute coordinates. So, take care while using these values, keeping in mind the actual screen size of your target devices.

## See also

▸ The *Applying Gaussian blur on a SVG image* recipe

# Applying Gaussian blur on a SVG image

**Scalable Vector Graphics** (**SVG**) is a family of specifications for 2D Scalable Vector Graphics. They are XML-based and can be static or dynamic (animated or interactive). This recipe shows you how to use a SVG image in your app, and apply a Gaussian filter when you click on it.

## Getting ready

Copy the full code of this recipe from the `code/11/svg` folder. The SVG image is available in the `code/resources/images` folder. You can launch this code using the URL: `http://localhost:8080/11/svg/main.html`.

## How to do it...

The steps to be followed are:

1. Create `main.html` with a SVG element in its page content. Draw a SVG rectangle and display the SVG image within the rectangle:

```
<div data-role='content'>
  <svg xmlns="http://www.w3.org/2000/svg" version="1.1">
    <defs>
      <filter id="gausfilter" x="0" y="0">
        <feGaussianBlur in="SourceGraphic"
```

```
                     stdDeviation="5" />
        </filter>
      </defs>
      <rect width="180px" height="220px" x='10' y='10'
        style="fill:none;stroke-
        width:2;stroke:rgb(0,0,0)"/>
        <image id='svgimg' width='160px' height='200px'
          x='20' y='20'
          xlink:href='../../resources/images
          /Chrisdesign_green_comic_egg.svg'>
        </image>
    </svg>
  </div>
```

2. Apply the Guassian filter to the SVG image when the image is clicked:

```
$('#main').live('pageinit', function(event) {
  $('#svgimg').bind('click', function(event, ui) {
    $(this).attr('filter',
      'url(#gausfilter)').trigger('refresh');
  });
});
```

## How it works...

Create `main.html`, and add a `<svg>` element to its page content. Specify the SVG namespace and version, as shown in the code. Create a rectangle using the `<rect>` element, and specify its attributes, such as the width, height, and x and y positions, and also set its `stroke` style. Next, add an `<image>` element with `id='svgimg'` pointing to the SVG image, and specify the image's location, position, and size to be used. When you load the page, the following screenshot will be shown:

Now, define the Gaussian filter by adding a `<filter>` element with `id='gausfilter'` inside a `<defs>` element. Add the `<feGaussianBlur>` element inside `<filter>`, and set a standard deviation of `5`. Finally, bind the `click` event on the `#svgimg` image to an event handler in the `pageinit` callback function. Here, add the `filter='gausfilter'` attribute to the `<image>` tag using the jQuery `attr()` call. Now, when you click on the SVG image, the Gaussian blur gets applied, as shown in the following screenshot:

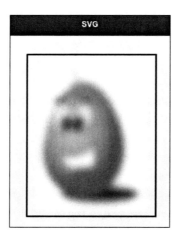

## There's more...

SVG supports vector graphics, raster graphics, and text elements. It allows you to transform, clip paths, apply alpha masks, and filter effects on the SVG images. The SVG image used in this recipe was designed and contributed to the *Open Clipart* website at `http://openclipart.org`, by ChrisDesign (`http://chrisdesign.wordpress.com`). The Open Clipart website also has thousands of free SVG images available in the public domain.

### SVG Tiny specification

The SVG specification has a mobile version, and it is called the **SVG Tiny** (**SVGT**) specification. Currently, SVGT v1.2 is the W3C recommendation. It has good support on most of the mobile devices and platforms, and support for it continues to improve by the day.

## See also

▸ The *2D drawing with Canvas* recipe

# Tracking your location with the Geolocation API

The **Geolocation API** is a separate specification and is part of the HTML5 stack. You can use JavaScript and locate the client device location using various techniques, such as IP address, Wi-Fi, GSM/CDMA cell IDs, or device Global Positioning System (GPS). This recipe shows you how to find the current location using the Geolocation API in your app.

## Getting ready

Copy the full code of this recipe from the `code/11/geolocation` folder. You can launch this code using the URL: `http://localhost:8080/11/geolocation/main.html`.

## How to do it...

The steps to be followed are:

1.  Create `main.html` with an empty `div` tag to display the geolocation information.

    ```
    <div data-role='content'>
      <p>You current Position is ...</p>
      <div id='geopos'></div>
    </div>
    ```

2.  Invoke the `getCurrentPosition()` method to obtain the current location using a `show_pos()` callback function.

    ```
    $('#main').live('pageinit', function(event) {
      if (navigator.geolocation)
        navigator.geolocation.getCurrentPosition(show_pos);
      else
        $('#geopos').html('Error: Unable to get your position!');
    });
    ```

3.  Finally, display the current location in the `show_pos()` callback function:

    ```
    function show_pos(pos) {
      var geostr = '<p>Latitude (deg): '
        + pos.coords.latitude
        + '</p><p>Longitude (deg): ' + pos.coords.longitude
        + '</p><p>Altitude (m): ' + pos.coords.altitude
        + '</p><p>Accuracy (m): ' + pos.coords.accuracy
        + '</p><p>AltitudeAccuracy (m): '
        + pos.coords.altitudeAccuracy
        + '</p><p>Heading (deg): ' + pos.coords.heading
        + '</p><p>Speed (m/s): ' + pos.coords.speed
    ```

```
      + '</p><p>Timestamp: '+ pos.timestamp;
    $('#geopos').html(geostr);
}
```

## How it works...

Create `main.html`, and add an empty `div` tag with `id='geopos'` to the `#main` page to display the location information. Use the `pageinit` event handler to first check if the `navigator.geolocation` object is available. If available, invoke the `getCurrentPosition()` method with a callback function, `show_pos()`, to get the location information. The `show_pos()` callback function can access the position (`pos`) object, which has the various properties of the current location. Access `pos.coords` to obtain information, such as the latitude, longitude, altitude, and accuracy. The `pos` object also has an associated timestamp for the current location reading. Now, display the location details in the `#geopos` attribute of `div`.

When you launch the app, the browser first asks your permission to access the location information. Once you agree, the following location details are shown on the screen:

 The Geolocation API specification mandates that the user location information is confidential, and that the browser should warn and obtain the user's permission before accessing or sharing this information.

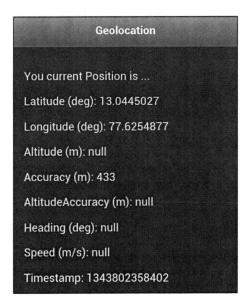

## There's more...

In this recipe, the `getCurrentPosition()` call pings for the user location only once, and displays the information using the `show_pos()` callback function. But, if you wish to track a moving device, you can access continuous location readings using the `watchCurrentPosition()` call. The syntax remains the same, but this method continuously and periodically keeps pinging for the device location and invokes the `show_pos()` callback every time. This method also populates the `pos.coords.speed` and `pos.coords.heading` attributes to give feedback on the speed and direction of the moving device. The user is prompted for permission to share the location details only on the first call.

```
if (navigator.geolocation)
    navigator.geolocation.watchCurrentPosition(show_pos);
```

### Google Gears

Prior to the Geolocation API specification, the Google Gears JavaScript library was very popular for fetching location information. Google Gears subsequently contributed quite a bit to the development of the Geolocation API and is now deprecated.

### Geolocation on desktop browsers

The location information obtained on desktop browsers is based on the IP and MAC address details obtained from the ISP servers. So, this information has a wide accuracy margin, sometimes in the range of a few kilometers, whereas mobile devices rely on the network towers and on GPS devices (if enabled) for positioning. Thus mobile devices can very accurately pinpoint the position, altitude, speed, and heading information within a range of a few meters.

# Playing music with the <audio> element

HTML5 introduced a new `<audio>` element that can be used to play audio files directly in the browser. Prior to this, browsers had to use plugins, such as Flash Player, Real Player, or Quick Time to play audio files. The `<audio>` element provides a lightweight alternative, and this recipe shows you how to use it in your app to play audio files.

## Getting ready

Copy the full code of this recipe from the `code/11/audio` folder. The audio snips are available in the `code/resources/audio` folder. You can launch this code using the URL: `http://localhost:8080/11/audio/main.html`.

## How to do it...

The steps to be followed are:

1.  Create `main.html` with the `<audio>` element in its page content:

```
<div data-role='content'>
  <audio controls autoplay preload='auto'>
    <source src='../../resources/audio/song.mp3'
      type='audio/mpeg' />
    <source src='../../resources/audio/song.oga'
      type='audio/ogg' />
    <source src='../../resources/audio/song.webma'
      type='audio/webm' />
    <p>Browser does not support audio tag</p>
  </audio>
</div>
```

## How it works...

Add the `<audio>` element to the #main page with the `controls`, `autoplay`, and `preload` attributes. The `controls` attribute displays the play button, volume slider, and other controls. The `preload='auto'` option indicates that the browser can start streaming the audio file in the background as soon as the page is ready. The `autoplay` attribute tells the browser that it can directly start playing the audio file when downloaded and ready.

 The `<audio>` element also supports a `loop` attribute, which keeps the audio playing in a continuous loop.

Different browsers support different audio formats, and the first supported audio format is picked and played. So, add URL links to the audio file in the `.mp3`, `.oga`, and `.webma` formats using the `<source>` element, as shown in the code. One of these three audio formats will be recognized by most browsers. Finally, add an error message, `Browser does not support audio tag`, at the end. This message is displayed if the browser does not support the `audio` element. Now, when you load the page, the screenshot similar to the following is seen, and the audio file starts to play:

## There's more...

Older browsers, such as IE8, do not support the `<audio>` element. You will have to use a flash fallback mechanism in this case.

For a note on audio formats and codecs, using the flash fallback and HTML5 media players, refer to the next recipe on the `<video>` element.

## See also

▶ The *Viewing videos with the <video> element* recipe

# Viewing videos with the <video> element

HTML5 introduced a new `<video>` element to play video files directly in the browser. Prior to this, browsers had to use plugins, such as Flash Player, Real Player, or Quick Time to play video files. The `<video>` element is a lightweight alternative, and this recipe shows you how to use it in your app to view videos.

## Getting ready

Copy the full code of this recipe from the `code/11/video` folder. The video snips are available in the `code/resources/video` folder. You can launch this code using the URL: `http://localhost:8080/11/video/main.html`.

## How to do it...

The steps to be followed are:

1. Create `main.html` with the `<video>` element in its page content:

```
<div data-role='content'>
  <video controls autoplay preload='auto' width='300'
    height='300'>
    <source src='../../resources/video/spiral.mp4'
      type='video/mpeg' />
    <source src='../../resources/video/spiral.ogv'
      type='video/ogg' />
    <source src='../../resources/video/spiral.webmv'
      type='video/webm' />
    <p>Browser does not support video tag</p>
  </video>
</div>
```

## How it works...

Add the `<video>` element to the `#main` page with the `controls`, `autoplay`, and `preload` attributes. The `controls` attribute displays the play button, volume slider, full screen button, and other controls. The `preload='auto'` option indicates that the browser can start streaming the video file in the background as soon as the page is ready. The `autoplay` attribute tells the browser that it can directly play the video when ready. Also, add the `width` and `height` attributes to size the video in pixels.

Different browsers support different video formats, and the first supported video format is picked and played. So, add URL links to the video files in the `.mp4`, `.ogv`, and .webmv formats using the `<source>` element, as shown in the code. One of these three video formats will be recognized by most browsers. Finally, add an error message, `Browser does not support video tag`, at the end. This message is displayed if the browser does not support the video element. Now, when you load the page, a screenshot similar to the following is shown, and the video file starts to play:

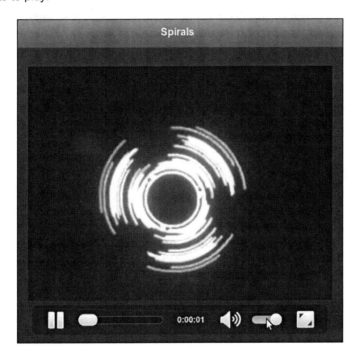

## There's more...

The `<video>` tag also supports a few additional attributes, such as `loop` (to play the video in a continuous loop), `muted` (to turn off the audio), and `poster` (the URL of the image to be displayed at the beginning as a poster, before the video begins to play).

Set preload to auto to automatically download the media file, as some browsers do not support preload due to security reasons.

## The flash fallback

Older browsers, such as IE8, do not support the <video> and <audio> elements. You can still play HTML5 audio and video in unsupported browsers by using a flash player as the fallback mechanism. You have to embed the player using the <object> tag at the end of the <video> or <audio> element. The browser in this case does not recognize the new HTML5 tags, and falls through to play the audio/video using the flash fallback.

## The Codecs

There are multiple audio/video formats that are popular on the web today. The support is varied in different browsers, which support only specific audio/video codecs. You have to ensure that your app works on maximum platforms, by including different formats of the same audio/video files, if necessary, as shown in this recipe. Detailed information on this matter, including tables showing the support matrix, is available at http://diveintohtml5. info/video.html.

## The Audio and Video API

**Audio API** and **Video API** are now available for you to directly control the <audio> and <video> elements using JavaScript. They allow you to trigger actions (play, pause, and so on) and listen to events (playing, ended, and so on).

## HTML5 media players

The HTML5 tags by themselves give you very plain looking UI and controls. You can enhance the look and feel and add additional features using the Audio and Video API. Instead, with minimal effort, you can also use any of the popular libraries that are available, such as **jPlayer** (http://jplayer.org), **MediaElement.js** (http://mediaelementjs.com), **JW Player** (http://longtailvideo.com), **Video.js** (http://videojs.com), and **Audio.js** (http://kolber.github.com/audiojs/).

## See also

▶   The *Playing music with the <audio> element* recipe

# Index

# D

**data**
  fetching, GET used 130-132
**data-attribute**
  used, for configuring list divider theme 159
  used, for configuring list search filters 159
**data- attributes**
  about 79
  data-corners 79
  data-icon 79
  data-iconpos 79
  data-iconshadow 79
  data-inline 79
  data-shadow 79
  data-theme 79
**data.deferred.reject() method 200**
**data.deferred.resolve() method 201**
**data-dom-cache attribute 29**
**data-inset attribute 139**
**data() method 222**
**data-placeholder attribute 122**
**data-prefetch attribute 25**
**data-role='none' attribute 108**
**data-theme attribute 92**
**data-url attribute**
  used, for handling login page
        navigation 44-47
  using, as href link 48
**default icon sprite**
  replacing 86, 88
**default namespace**
  configuring 176, 177
**default transitions**
  configuring 170, 171
**deferred.resolve() function 43**
**desktop voice readers 136**
**Dialog**
  about 17
  building, with custom styled header 32
  custom styling 32-35
**directory component 231**
**disppath() function 232**
**dispPath() method 229**
**domain component 231**

**DOM cache**
  limitations 32
  using 29, 30
  working 31
**durationThreshold**
  about 189
  configuring 189
**dynamically added button**
  scripting 78, 79

# E

**each() method 141**
**errMsg() error handler 132**
**errordialog.html 49**
**error messages**
  configuring 174, 175
**event.clientX parameter 188**
**event.clientY parameter 188**
**event.pageX attribute 193**
**event.pageY attribute 193**
**event.preventDefault() method 200, 201, 230, 233**
**event.stopPropagation() method 230, 233**
**event.target.innerHTML property 211**
**existing swatch**
  overriding 252, 253

# F

**fade transition 36, 170**
**fallbacks 273**
**filename component 231**
**filtertext attribute 158**
**fixedtoolbar plugin 59**
**fixed toolbars**
  about 55
  fixed CSS property 59
  fullscreen mode 55
  position 59
  using 55-58
**fixed toolbar visibility**
  toggling 59
  toggling, JavaScript used 59
**flash fallback 288**

# I

# J

**Thank you for buying**
# jQuery Mobile Cookbook

## About Packt Publishing

Packt, pronounced 'packed', published its first book "*Mastering phpMyAdmin for Effective MySQL Management*" in April 2004 and subsequently continued to specialize in publishing highly focused books on specific technologies and solutions.

Our books and publications share the experiences of your fellow IT professionals in adapting and customizing today's systems, applications, and frameworks. Our solution based books give you the knowledge and power to customize the software and technologies you're using to get the job done. Packt books are more specific and less general than the IT books you have seen in the past. Our unique business model allows us to bring you more focused information, giving you more of what you need to know, and less of what you don't.

Packt is a modern, yet unique publishing company, which focuses on producing quality, cutting-edge books for communities of developers, administrators, and newbies alike. For more information, please visit our website: www.packtpub.com.

## About Packt Open Source

In 2010, Packt launched two new brands, Packt Open Source and Packt Enterprise, in order to continue its focus on specialization. This book is part of the Packt Open Source brand, home to books published on software built around Open Source licences, and offering information to anybody from advanced developers to budding web designers. The Open Source brand also runs Packt's Open Source Royalty Scheme, by which Packt gives a royalty to each Open Source project about whose software a book is sold.

## Writing for Packt

We welcome all inquiries from people who are interested in authoring. Book proposals should be sent to author@packtpub.com. If your book idea is still at an early stage and you would like to discuss it first before writing a formal book proposal, contact us; one of our commissioning editors will get in touch with you.

We're not just looking for published authors; if you have strong technical skills but no writing experience, our experienced editors can help you develop a writing career, or simply get some additional reward for your expertise.

PhoneGap Mobile Application
Development Cookbook

Over 50 recipes to create mobile applications using
the PhoneGap API with examples and clear instructions

Matt Gifford                    [PACKT] open source

# PhoneGap Mobile Application Development Cookbook

ISBN: 978-1-84951-858-1          Paperback: 316 pages

Over 50 recipes to create mobile applications using the
PhoneGap API with examples and clear instructions

1. Use the PhoneGap API to create native mobile
   applications that work on a wide range of mobile
   devices

2. Discover the native device features and
   functions you can access and include within your
   applications

3. Packed with clear and concise examples to show
   you how to easily build native mobile applications

jQuery for Designers

An approachable introduction to web design in
jQuery for non-programmers

Beginner's Guide

Natalie MacLees            [      ] open source

# jQuery for Designers: Beginner's Guide

ISBN: 978-1-84951-670-9          Paperback: 332 pages

An approachable introduction to web design in jQuery for
non-programmers

1. Enhance the user experience of your site by
   adding useful jQuery features

2. Learn the basics of adding impressive jQuery
   effects and animations even if you've never
   written a line of JavaScript

3. Easy step-by-step approach shows you everything
   you need to know to get started improving your
   website with jQuery

Please check **www.PacktPub.com** for information on our titles

Lightning Source UK Ltd.
Milton Keynes UK
UKOW020709020613

211618UK00004B/48/P

9 781849 517225